I'VE SEEN WORSE

Glimpses of
IAN M FRASER

shared with
IAN CRANSTON

Published by Ian Cranston

10 Aitchison Drive

Larbert FK5 4PB

07581551432

iancranston@talktalk.net

from whom further details may be obtained.

ISBN: 978-0-9570989-0-9

Photo of Ian Fraser (Front Cover) © John McLaren

Photo of Ian M Fraser (Back Cover) © Mitchell Bunting

Ian Cranston and Ian M Fraser gratefully acknowledge the support of the Baker Trust
and a personal legacy in producing this book. They also acknowledge the significance
of the publishing opportunities afforded to Ian M Fraser in the pages of *Coracle,* the
journal of the Iona Community and in *Open House.*

A catalogue record for this book is available from the British Library.

Printed by Riley Dunn and Wilson Ltd

Huddersfield, West Yorkshire

Ian and Margaret Fraser

Margaret

I love, my dear
You, combing out your hair.
Quick, light step in a windswayed frock,
Quick needle shining in shirt or sock,
washing, gay on a dancing line,
dance of your eyes as they meet mine!

Wife, witch, lover
my joy and crown.

Eyes whose sympathy soothes so much,
voice which, at the dusting, sings
delicate hands, whose craftsman touch
twines love around the commonest things.

Ian M Fraser

Dedicated to
MARGARET
and
CATHERINE

A Conversation

In my dream, dad was prigging God for a word of approval on me. 'Ian?' said God. 'I've naithin' against him; he's daein' a' right, by and large.'

Dad stubbornly looked for more.

'Weel,' said God with a kind of exasperation tempered with tenderness. 'He'll dae, he'll dae. But weel he micht, Alex, weel he micht. I gien him Mergrit.'

Dad persisted.

'Ian?' said God, 'O aye, Ian . . . *I'VE SEEN WORSE!*'

An Apology for making no Apology

Those who have their lives written up usually have the decency to die before the work is published.

The fact that I am still breathing may indicate the want of even that most elementary decency.

Ian M Fraser, March 2010

CONTENTS

LIST OF PHOTOGRAPHS

Front Cover – Ian M Fraser (copyright John McLaren)

Frontispiece – Ian and Margaret Fraser

1. Alex (A.B.) and Annie Fraser, parents of Alex, Ian and Margaret
2. Ian, Margaret and Alex Fraser
3. The family business then . . .
4. . . . now. (Ian on a recent visit to Forres)
5. Margaret Stewart (Fraser), head girl, Dumfries Academy 1937-38 (seated next to Rector Lodge
6. Edinburgh University Association Football Club 1940–41 Winners of Lothian Amateur League; Ian Fraser 2nd left, front row
7. Ian M Fraser Graduation
8. Margaret Stewart (Fraser) Graduation
9. Alex (RAF); Margaret (ARP) Ian (Home Guard) in Forres during wartime
10. Ian M Fraser (Industrial Chaplain) with the 1943 Permanent Staff on Iona: Ian M Fraser, Lex Miller, George MacLeod, Robin Martin, Bill Amos, George Wilkie and upstage John McMillan (Copyright unknown – printed in The Coracle February 1944)
11. Wedding of Ian M Fraser and Margaret D.D. Stewart
12. Ian M Fraser during a recent visit to Tullis Russell paper mill, Markinch/Glenrothes
13. Ian and Margaret Fraser, Rosyth

ACKNOWLEDGEMENTS

The encouragement, help and support of the following folk are readily recognised.

Louise, Miriam and Tracey; Ann, Keith and Ian and the extended Fraser family; Ron Ferguson, Norman Shanks, John Bell; members and associates of the Central Scotland family Group including the late Maxwell Craig, Janet Craig, Billy and Betty Milne; other members and associates of the Iona Community including David Coleman, Mitchell Bunting, Ishbel Maclellan, Ruth Goodheir, Ruth Burgess, Brian Crosby, Neil Paynter present editor of Coracle.

Pam McNamee and David Erdal, Tullis Russell; members of the Rosyth Parish Church; staff and friends of Scottish Churches House; Alastair Hulbert, Elizabeth Templeton; Douglas Gay, theologian and Scottish church historian; members of churches in the world church in the 95 countries visited by IMF; staff and students of the Selly Oak Colleges particularly Bishop John Davies; fellow strugglers in the Poll Tax campaigns.

Catherine Hepburn, formerly parish minister in Gargunnock with others in the congregation and village who made local community with Ian and Margaret, specifically Eric Abell and John McLaren; Tim Duffy of Open House; Jim O'Halloran from Ireland.

As the years have passed and the contributions of others multiplied it became clear that 'faults and failings' in this work were to be mine alone. Readers will benefit from the skill and patience of our project manager, Hazel Goodes: the greater her expertise the more invisible she remains. Finally my thanks to Catherine who with others took on editorial duties including the removal of detailed thanks to her for allowing 'I've Seen Worse' to see the light of day.

Ian Cranston

PREFACE

Ian Fraser was one of the most significant Scottish churchmen of the 20th century. Yet to describe him as a 'churchman' is to put him into a too-narrow category, considering the range of his activity and interests. Not only that, to place him simply in a 20th century frame is also too restrictive, given his influence, through action and writing, in the early part of the 21st century. As I write this preface in June, 2011, he is still very much alive and kicking against injustice, at the age of 93.

Ian Fraser is a hero of mine. I first came across him when I was a young journalist in Edinburgh in the early 1960s. I was surprised to receive a letter from him inviting me to take part in a symposium about the ethics of journalism at a place called Scottish Churches House in Dunblane. I remember being impressed by the letter. Here was a minister of the Kirk recognising the dilemmas and possibilities of the world of journalism, and seeking to facilitate a discussion amongst people working at the journalistic 'coal face'.

Over the years, I got to know Ian much better. He became a good friend and wise counsellor to me when I was a minister in Easterhouse, and later when I became leader of the Iona Community. Right from the early days when he was a kind of worker priest in the Tullis Russell paper mill in Fife, he was a pioneering spirit. In his parish ministry in Rosyth, his ground-breaking wardenship of Scottish Churches House, and his imaginative work with the World Council of Churches and Selly Oak Colleges, Ian's gritty realism, grounded theology and committed faith made him an inspirational figure. And all, of course, in collaboration with his dear wife Margaret, the love of his life.

I was delighted when I heard that Ian Cranston was going to write a biography of Dr Fraser. It is so good that the life of this pioneer, pastor and poet is now on the record. Ian Cranston's well-researched book deserves to be read widely.

Even those who knew Ian intimately will learn new things. Only Ian could have addressed a funeral congregation with these words: 'You know, as I know, that the deceased man was a real bastard.' After detailing some of the deceased's well known faults, Ian went on: 'God sees the whole of his life and sees it from beginning to end. God can judge as we cannot; and in him is abundant mercy. So this is what we are going to do. We are going to entrust this life to the Creator who gave it, the Saviour who redeemed it, the Spirit who searches to the depths of everyone's being in confidence that there it will be truly judged and mercifully dealt with.'

This lack of sentimentality and refusal to judge is the hallmark of the man. We are indebted to Ian Cranston for this affectionate, well-grounded and measured tribute to one of the great Scots of our time.

Ron Ferguson

INTRODUCTION

'You are taking us to Iona for the October school holiday week!'

It was the first morning of the 1988 autumn term in Grangemouth High School. I had other things on my mind. I should have known better. What the girls, who had taken to organising my life, did not know was that they were not the only ones to have been on Iona that summer. They had been at the Iona Community's Youth Festival. They were evidently keen to return as soon as they could. Soon after their visit I had commuted to Iona for three or four days from Fionnphort on Mull. That year the earliest and latest ferries did not allow my friend Jim and I to attend morning or evening worship. Prayers for Justice and Peace in the middle of the day were possible.

We became aware that a pilgrimage round the island visiting sacred sites was organised on Wednesdays and was open to visitors. We joined the pilgrims for the day. Later it became clear that it had been Ron Ferguson's last pilgrimage as leader. The mantle of leader passed to John Harvey the following day. All I knew at the time was that the inspiring 'Chasing the Wild Goose' that I had read before getting to Iona was enhanced by walking in the author's footsteps that glorious summer day. With some trepidation I mentioned to

Ron as the group began to disperse how much I had appreciated both book and pilgrimage.

So Catherine and I found ourselves in the recently opened MacLeod Centre on Iona with eight senior pupils contributing to a work week that October. During our week in 'The Mac', which had been opened that summer on the Jubilee of the Iona Community, Billy and Betty Milne acted as house parents to our Grangemouth group and to a group of teenagers from the Motherwell area. Under supervision we were encouraged to continue with some interior finishing; building bunk beds, painting anything that did not move! First work morning Catherine was presented with a five litre tin of white glass paint and invited to paint the skirting boards along the downstairs corridor. She was given a paint brush from a child's paint box. It lasted till morning coffee then she purchased her own brush in one of the village shops!

At the end of the October work week we made preparations to return home. Billy and Betty Milne encouraged me to join the associates group of the Iona Community who met once a month in the Central Scotland area. Another Milne, John by name, also an associate of the Community and one of the leaders of the Motherwell group was anxious that I should understand one thing: 'Remember,' he said, 'Iona the place is important – but nowhere near as important as the folk you meet there!'

Soon after returning to the work-a-day world it was arranged that I should go with Billy and Betty to an Associates' meeting being held in the Stirling home of one of the local group. It was explained that among the group of associates I was likely to meet an Ian Fraser – a longstanding member of the Iona Community who by his presence sought to encourage local associates.

I remember nothing of the discussion that evening. Yet I sensed that the folk gathered including Ian were committed to listening as much as speaking. The evening concluded with a simple communion that Ian led. I did not know that eighteen months earlier he had lost his beloved wife, Margaret. What I did realise was that her presence with us in that home was an immediate reality for him. I come from a church tradition that celebrates communion every week. But I was aware that as Ian led us he wove together our remembrance of Jesus with the cares and concerns that we had shared earlier in the evening. It had been different. I came away with a sense of a real privilege from having been present.

In 1990 when I sought membership of the Iona Community it seemed appropriate to ask Ian if he would be my 'walking partner' as I tested my conviction that the Iona Community was to be part of my continuing pilgrimage. Over the years I have valued his company and the space he gave me to do my own thing within the Community. On the occasions when I have questioned my continuing in the Community he was one that I have turned to more than once.

The day came in the new millennium when I approached Ron Ferguson and asked him to consider writing a biography of Ian Fraser. His celebrated life of George MacLeod, founder of the Iona Community convinced me that he would respond positively for all that I knew him to be a busy man. Imagine my surprise when he immediately declined my invitation. Imagine my horror when he suggested I get on and do it myself.

In 2004 when I had been offered and accepted early retirement I spoke to Ian. I acknowledged that in the 20 or so books he had written there was much of a biographical nature. I argued that a more systematic autobiography would be helpful not least to those who were forever finding his writing an inspiration. He declined without hesitation. In some despair I confessed that I had spoken with Ron Ferguson. 'Well,' said Ian, 'I think you might be the person to undertake the task. I will certainly do what I can to help you to get the story written if you are minded to get it done.'

The Ayrshire bard was right when he noted that 'there is many a slip between cup and lip.' The appropriate time to produce a biography of Ian seemed to be the occasion of his ninetieth birthday at the end of 2007. Ian generously spent time in lengthy recorded conversations and made available to me much of what he had written and published over half a century. 15th December 2007, Ian's 90th birthday, passed with the manuscript far from complete. Other matters further pushed back the completion date even when we agreed that Volume 1 would have his 90th birthday as a cut-off date. Volume 2 will need to be the work of another and he/she will surely struggle to keep up with the pace of his continuing busy life. And so to the beginning of this remarkable life.

Ian Cranston, November 2011

CHAPTER ONE

EARLY DAYS

TWO BOYS CREPT down the still dark stair. No one else in the house stirred. Alex and Ian had been persuaded to go back to bed when they woke at five in the morning. At last it seemed that the parents had relented and they could come downstairs. There in the living room were the Christmas stockings.

Ian, the younger of the brothers, was either two or three that morning. He still remembers a terrible sense of disappointment. Peeping out of the top of his stocking he saw a pair of braces. 'Surely,' he reasoned, 'I could get a pair of braces without them being made into a Christmas present!' His parents were never short of love for their children. They just seemed to lack some imaginative understanding of children's minds. Christmas stockings tended to be filled with useful rather than exciting gifts.

The Forres Gazette of Wednesday 19th December 1917 carried the following notice on page 3:
> 'Fraser at Leys Cottage on 15th Inst. To Mr. and Mrs. A.B. Fraser, a son'

Thus was the yet unnamed child announced to the world.

That copy of the Forres Gazette gives some useful insight into the world of those far off days. As was the practice then, advertisers took pride of place on the first page of the newspaper. That edition carried these notices

- 'Scientific Correction of every foot ailment – Dr. Scholes Foot Appliances'. Ian, as will become obvious, would in time submit to this correction. He would have cause to question the science that was so applied.

- J. Morrison advertised 'special teas' which may have been purchased by the Fraser household. Ian certainly developed a taste for a strong 'cuppa' over the years. The paper also advises that margarine, 'the equal of butter,' was selling for one shilling (5p) for 1½ pounds (0.75 kilo).

- In 1917 a train left London Euston daily at 1.30 p.m. and arrived the following morning at 6 a.m. in Forres before continuing its northern passage.

- A Calendar printed under the Forres Gazette banner for 1918 could be purchased for 6d. The 2008 calendar from the same source costs considerably more but sadly failed to inspire – surprising given Forres' new found fame as a 'Britain in Bloom' winner in recent years.

- Alex Fraser, a chemist not a butcher, and no relation, included stationery in his advert as well as the expected medicines. There is something notable in this modern world of 'buy one, get one free' and 'health with everything' when we read that they were selling Lambert and Butler's Waverley Cigarettes at 10 for 4½d and 20 for 9d! No great incentive there to damage your health by increasing your consumption of the weed! At least if you developed a cough you would be able to get something without leaving the shop!

One might wonder if the editor and his staff had an eye for the slightly absurd. The first page carried an encouraging advert commending Ontario, Canada, to 'farmhands and domestic servants'. A promise is given of an assisted passage. A later page takes time to detail a local court case. A certain farmhand had taken up the offer of a new life in Ontario. The grass failing to prove greener across the Atlantic the bold boy returned to Forres and expected to take up with his previously abandoned wife. In the absence of postal or telegraphic communications in the intervening years the neglected wife was seeking help from the courts to reject his now unwanted advances.

And of course there was a war on. Evidence of this comes in the record given of a speech made by the premier Mr. Lloyd George. He is at pains to counter the suggestion from some quarters that an accommodation should be sought with Germany. Lloyd George is quick to affirm that 'There is no half-way house to peace.' There follows news that 'the peace of Jerusalem has been achieved: the Allies had recently captured it.'

The edition of the Gazette, which carried the news of the new arrival in the Fraser household, also reported that there had been a sharp spell of winter weather. Disruption of normal routines had been widespread. It also noted 'a magnificent display of the aurora borealis being seen in the north of Scotland when the whole heavens were enveloped in a flood of light, the streaks of which darted with lightning speed from every point of the compass converging in the zenith.' Signs in the heavens surely to mark the new arrival!

Ian Masson Fraser arrived into a world not just at war but also into a world that was changing locally as well as internationally. A revealing poem 'A Deserted Country Smiddy' in that December newspaper is worth quoting in part:

> 'The smiddy is deserted noo,
> The smith has gane awa',
> Nae mair we'll hear the study (sic) ring
> Nor hear the bellows bla'.
> The sheen (horseshoes) are doon frae aft the wa's
> The hearth is caul an' bare,
> The ploos (ploughs) an' harrows roon the door
> We'll never see them mair.'

In an uncertain world the child and his parents had not far to look for 'Words of Wisdom' and 'Things worth Knowing' for they also grace their weekly paper. Readers will make their own judgements as to the extent they reflect the life begun these ninety and more years ago. A selection must suffice:

- Life's best balm is forgiveness.
- Who best can suffer, best can do. (Milton)
- It is a great mistake to try to live tomorrow, or even yesterday, today.
- The more you pour out the more you can take in;
  The higher you think, the wider the vision;
  The greater the struggle, the stronger the muscle;
  To the man or woman who takes it seriously,
  all life is a continuous demand.
- All life is a gamble.
- The fate of nations in the last resort depends on individual character.

- Ideas are often poor ghosts . . . but sometimes they are made flesh. Then their presence is as power, they shake us like a passion and we are drawn after them with gentle compliance as flame is drawn to flame.
- Learn to think and act for yourself.
- Do all the good you can in the world and make as little noise about it.

While the good book is quite clear in its preference for spiritual rather than earthly wisdom it may be true that the spirit can, when given free rein, inspire the minds of mere mortals. Loving with heart and soul and mind and spirit has been well commended more than once. While we must avoid confusing cost and value it can be noted that for many years the Forres Gazette was sold for the princely sum of 1d.

His brother Alex had been born sixteen months before Ian. The way their schooling took place the apparent difference became two years. When Ian was four a sister, Margaret arrived to complete the family of Alexander and Anne Fraser.

Early memories can be revealing. Ian recalls the occasion of Margaret's baptism in the parlour of the Fraser's home. The location may have been chosen to accommodate her dad, Alex, who had just lost his sight. The home was crowded with friends and family. It is almost certain that Mr. Campbell, the minister of Castlehill Church officiated. During the baptism Ian slipped round behind the minister without him noticing. There the lad mimed the motion of winding him up, as he had often seen done with the family gramophone.

Mother, as mothers do, got hold of Ian and shepherded him from the room. She was beside herself. She could not yell at her wayward son: her wrath would have been only too clearly heard in the room adding to the disruption already caused. She could not even skelp her boy. The sound of slapping would have been heard. No more seems to have been said or done on this occasion as far as Ian can remember. To him it had been merely a humorous interlude. The 'congregation' by and large seemed to have appreciated it.

Ian's dad, Alex though often called A.B. (Alexander Bell) to distinguish him from his father, was born in 1885 into a well-known Forres family. The first son, he was a handsome lad in his youth sporting as he did a wee moustache. He was a bit of a comic. At weddings he would have folk helpless with laughter often just by the expression on his face. Sadly these days were behind him by the earliest days Ian can remember. Blindness was robbing him of more that just the cash in the shop.

By the time Ian was four his dad was blind. He had a bungled operation in Aberdeen. Moreover, he did not help himself. He was told not to read but continued to do so until the paper was almost touching his nose. He was very independent. He insisted on going to Aberdeen on his own. On one occasion, visiting the eye specialist there, he got out of the train on the wrong side and fell on to the track. Eventually he was left being only able to tell the difference between night and day. When Ian was about fifteen his dad was offered an operation, which might have restored some sight. He decided not to go ahead with this; perhaps the loss of sight had been so traumatic but something he had come to live with – he just could not face the possibility of everything changing again.

Ian's dad was, for a while, chairman of the YMCA in Forres. He used to give a talk there each year. Because he would not learn Braille he kept losing touch with his thoughts. It meant that what he eventually shared was more superficial than his original thinking.

Ian's mum, Annie Masson (pronounced Mason in the Forres area) did not have an easy life. Her parents had died by the time she was thirteen. She came from near the village of Dallas, high in the hills, seven miles south of Forres. The contrast with the land round Forres was considerable. The author, H.V. Morton in his 'In search of Scotland' said of the Forres area that the climate was so mild that you could comfortably drop it in Devon for appearance and climate and you would not notice any difference. Harvest began in the lowland around Forres in the first week in August and that was before the modern grains, which have been modified to suit local conditions. It might be October before the harvest could be brought in around Dallas.[1]

Ian remembers one of his uncles getting a beery face for all that he was teetotal. It was one December. The sun was shining. There was snow on the ground. With his scythe he was winning the very last of the harvest. He was sweating in the sun and rubbing his face with his hands. He massaged part of the grain into his face and produced what for all the world looked like a toper's complexion.

In the hungry thirties grain sold at less than its cost of production. The Depression cut deep into the life of rural Scotland. It would not be the last time the Scottish farming community knew real hardship.

Ian's mum had a three-mile walk to school when she was a lass. When drifting snow came, she used to walk to school on the top of dry-stone dykes. It must have been very dangerous. We should not assume that this was necessarily a very frequent occurrence. What she lived with on a daily basis was a longing to be free of heavy boots. She was forced to wear them at all times; the same pair would do around the farm, at school and for church on Sunday. She got hold of an old pair of boots and cut the uppers down to produce shoes. She hid them under a tree and from time to time she would steal away and put them on. Ian imagined her singing, 'When I get to heaven I'm gonna put on my shoes and dance all over God's heaven.'

When she was older Ian's mum went to Atholl Crescent Training College in Edinburgh to study domestic science. Later another in the family would follow in her footsteps to further his education in Scotland's capital. At one point Annie became a housekeeper to her brother John. He was a wee man who fell off a loaded cart he should never have been on in the first place. He did not tell his father and the damaged bones caused him to develop as a hunchback. He married Nellie. She was a great auntie to Ian. She had worked as a chauffeuse.

During Ian's childhood his dad worked as superintendent of the Sunday school with another local man. This meant that Ian was able to be at a Sunday school soiree before he had earned attendance in his own right. He could only have been about four. He remembers standing in a circle facing his mother. Someone asked if anyone could do a turn. Ian was volunteered. His mother was horrified when she heard his name mentioned. She could not think what he might sing. She was afraid he might give them some awful ditty:

'I'm 92 this morning, I'm 92 today, and I'm getting old and grey. But my 'hairt' is young and I'm full of fun, and I'm very proud to say, I'm getting married on Monday, though I'm not as young as I used to be, I'm 92 today!'[2]

Ian watched his mother circling towards him. He moved off in the opposite direction keeping as much distance from her as he could. She was clearly intent on getting hold of him. The look on her face was a picture when Ian launched into 'Little lamb who made thee . . .'[3] Ian has always had the gift of remembering things very easily. She clearly did not know he knew these words. He was happy to shock her, when he could, not least in a pleasant way.

At about this time Ian was told he had an awful temper and that it would destroy him and other people if he did not get rid of it. He finds it hard to be sure to what extent this was true. Parents lie by exaggeration to get children to behave. At any rate he tried to get the better of his temper. He found that he could not. He recalls a particular example of this.

In those early days Ian was a keen collector of cigarette cards. These were picture cards printed in series and used to give substance to packets of cigarettes. Boys cadged these cards as and when they could. They tried to complete each set in turn. Ian remembers playing with his brother in the front porch of their home and then going in to his mother complaining bitterly that brother Al was destroying his 'Wonders of Nature' and 'Struggles for Existence'.[4] The unfeeling woman just stood and laughed! Ian stomped out in a temper.

Then he said to God, 'We could manage this temper thing together, might we not?' They did. Ian's parents were believers, real believers. The reality of God did not seem to be something to be grasped or to need to be supported by persuasive words. God was there. He was tested in circumstances like these.

Ian values another childhood memory. He was playing with Alex around their front door. His face was grubby as is the way with little boys. Dr. James Black, who was the minister of Castlehill for three years and was such an influence on dad's life while he was there, came visiting. He lifted Ian up and kissed his dirty face. In such small kindnesses does a child learn that he/she is valued.

In Margaret's early years Ian was taken out for family walks. Mother pushed the pram; Dad held on to the handle and walked alongside. Ian has memories of always wanting to sit on the end of the pram. Usually he was refused. His dad held to the opinion that walking was good for you. It promoted good health. Everyone needed exercise and fresh air. It was some years before anyone took notice of Ian's complaints of sore feet. He was taken to a local doctor, David Beaton. He examined his feet and said he had 'fallen arches.' So now the boy was forced to wear 'horrible metal Scholes' insoles. They hurt his feet all the time. But they had to be worn. They were going to be good for him. It was not until Ian was in his twenties that the problem with his feet was properly diagnosed and useful remedial action taken.

Some strange memories remain from Ian's earliest days. On one occasion when the Fraser's half-wild cat had kittens, mother did not know how to get rid of them. Uncle Bob, who was passing, heard of the problem. He picked up a spade and hammered them all into the ground. Ian remembers being quite unaffected by this for all that it has remained in his memory. Mother was horrified. Ian reasoned that she had wanted rid of the kittens after all. Uncle Bob had seen plenty blood shed while he was in the army.

In his early years the family sometimes called Ian 'the dreamer'. It seems to have begun with his school days. For Ian primary school was a great . . . let down. It had been built up as a significant new stage in life. Sadly when he went to school he found it totally uninteresting. The lessons were not on anything that mattered. Too often Scottish education, which has a name for being world class, has failed to capture the imagination of those it is designed to serve. Ian sat in the classroom and daydreamed. His thoughts escaped through the classroom windows. He allowed his mind to roam.

The only excitement at school was playtime. There was a log fire in the school corridor. Ian got twigs, lit them, and then used them to chase the girls. He was somewhat taken aback when his teacher threatened to report him to the headmaster. What a spoilsport!

When Mum and Dad asked about progress at school in these early days Ian was able to assure them that he was an excellent pupil – at least an 'x' was regularly appended to his school work. It later transpired that what he had read as a mark of approval was in fact a badly written 'F'. It stood for 'fair' the lowest grade awarded at that time. He could not be bothered with what was being presented to him. It appears that even in these early years Ian had discovered that learning needs to be engaged with. As another has said, 'Education is about lighting a fire, not just filling a pail'.[5]

Ian recalls one occasion when he was about eight. It confirmed in his mind that teachers had not grasped anything of significance. In Miss Crowe's class he was given five colouring crayons and asked to draw something. He drew a cowboy. He had a crayon that was beige in colour. He used that for his hero's face. Teacher came round and said, 'Cowboys are white people. Everyone knows that. You have a white crayon. Why are you not using it?' So Ian spent some time producing a grotesque death mask for his cowboy. On this occasion he said nothing. Perhaps nothing needed to be said.

As a youngster Ian was left very little time for hanging round with pals. The family business made constant demands. Even at school in the early years he seems to have led a fairly solitary existence. He recalls one occasion taking a skipping rope to school. He used to skip at playtime. One of the male teachers saw this and took him aside. 'Skipping ropes are all right for girls and women but for men it is only softies that use skipping ropes.' 'You mean like boxers!' Ian quipped. The teacher suddenly discovered that he had something else to do. He probably was not the first shallow thinker that Ian had seen through. He certainly would not be the last. It brings a smile to Ian's face even after eighty years. It might also be fair to see even then in this youngster, an independence of character which would so mark his later years.

Ian had only one playground fight that he can remember. Ginger Milne had attacked Alex. It was the prerogative of brothers to hammer one another. Outsiders had no place in this. Ian tore into Ginger until the authorities arrived to separate them. Honour was served. The younger brother had established his exclusive rights in this matter. Sadly Ian has some memories of fairly frequent playground bullying. Boys ganged up and victimised the weak. In those days it was treated as part of life. You just had to put up with it.

John Budge and Ian contended for the top of the class later in primary school. One day they were talking in the playground about parents. Ian mentioned that his mother regularly cast John up as a role model. 'Just look how neat and well dressed he is,' she would say. 'Why can't you be like that?'

'Well,' said John, 'it is just the opposite for me. You are the one held up by my mother as an example of how I should look.' After that these boys had the parents taped!

Miss Morrison was keen on verse speaking. In the final year of primary school she entered her class for the Elgin Schools' festival. She required of her pupils, 'good English' and threatened to, and then did remove Ian from the group. He refused to say, 'Along the gowlden road to Semerkand' when the book said, 'Along the golden road to Samarkand.' He felt justified when he was awarded a prize – his memory suggests it may have been for sight-reading an unseen text.

It is important that there is no misunderstanding about Ian's early irritation with primary school. This was, thankfully, not his last word on the matter. By his final year in Forres Primary School he had decided to play the education game. He was dux medallist at the end of his primary years.

With a blind father Ian had a very busy childhood. Ian's grandfather, also Alexander, had founded a butcher's business that was to play a large part in their family life. Ian's dad decided his sons should start work each day in the family butcher's back shop in North Street at quarter to six in the morning. This began when Ian was seven. Alex his older brother was nine by this time. Dad became dependent on his brother Robert who had come through the First World War. He wanted to be a farmer but Ian's dad was being robbed left, right and centre in the shop. Robert decided to take over the front shop, cutting and selling. Ian's dad worked in the back shop on the manufacturing side. He produced white puddings, black puddings, sausages, mince, cooked hams and steak pies, finished by Cant the local baker.

The family shop was originally in Tolbooth Street just off the High Street in Forres. It was next to the Red Lion. His daughter-in-law labelled Grandpa Fraser a boozer. It is difficult to be sure: it may just be that he nipped next door on occasion for a beer. Today the establishment is more domesticated. It is called the 'Red Beastie' and is just the place for a warming soup in the middle of the day. It was accepted in the family that Grandma Fraser was the one who really established the shop. She put in the hard work. She was like that.

When she was dying in Ian's middle teenage years he was given the responsibility of sitting with her. Looking back on these days long ago it may seem strange to have chosen a young lad to do this. Maybe not so strange when we consider the man the young lad became.

Ian's mother was very tearful when it became clear that her mother was not to be long for this world. The grandmother spoke up. This was the woman, who hardly ever said anything; who was seldom known to say anything religious. 'What ails you, woman. It is tae oor

Father we're goin' – and whaur could you get a better welcome?' Recalling this Ian said, 'That was deep. What was seldom spoken of had a reality that should not be missed or underestimated. That was Grandma.'

A few days later the Fraser home was very quiet and still, as if the smallest sound could be heard for miles. Ian's mother was sitting on the couch; her eyes were bloodshot from all the crying she had done. Her face was tear-stained. Ian felt it was like looking into a mirror. They both had faces scarred with sadness and loss. Grandma had died the day before.

Ian had never experienced so much sadness, helplessness and loneliness. He was afraid to say anything to his mother thinking that he would start crying again. His mother looked as if she had aged twenty years over night, and it pained him to look at her. Speechless, he left the room. Later there were words.

'The kitchen was filled with roses and food that people had sent as gestures of condolence. Ian remembered the rose garden his grandmother had kept. It had been so beautiful. He used to play there for hours with Grandma. She had never been too busy to spend a little time with him. Ian leaned over to smell the roses a neighbour had sent them. The sweet smell caused his eye to sting and produced a single tear that landed on a petal. The sadness of thinking that he would now only sit alone in the rose garden without Grandma was too much to bear. He felt a hand on his shoulder. He turned and saw his mother. She tried to smile but her face crumpled and eased into the gentle sobbing they had become so familiar with. Not knowing what else to do or say her son just held her. Between sighs and shudders his mother whispered to him, 'Life isn't always as sweet as a rose.' Ian just nodded and with tears running down his face, he told his mother that he loved her.

'For days the house seemed imprisoned in grey. Everybody was trying to be strong for each other, but no one was really succeeding. They were all experiencing the same loss, but seemed to be going through it alone.

'About three days after his grandmother's death, Ian got a letter in the mail. It had no return address; it was written in shaky handwriting. When he opened it he found an old picture of his grandmother and himself sitting in the rose garden. In the envelope were the dried petals of a small rose. They still had their soft scent. He realized his grandmother had sent him this a few days before she died.

'Ian turned the picture over and on the back she had written in shaky, but graceful handwriting, 'Life is like a rose. It begins in the spring as a small bud, but when it blooms it shows the world how beautiful and magnificent it is. And in the winter it begins to fade and finally sleep, but is not forgotten. Remember me with happiness and love, not with tears and sadness, for that is how I will always remember you. I love you, Grandma.'

'For the first time in what seemed like forever, he smiled and thought, 'I love you too, Grandma.'[6]

Life must go on, or as someone once said, 'I don't know that it must, but it certainly does.' Business was clearly good in Fraser's the butchers. The second shop was round the corner in the High Street. The third and last shop was just further along the High Street in a building vacated by a bank. The business also needed the use of two vans. Fraser Brothers was going places in more ways than one.

Later, when Ian was in Rosyth, he was required to visit a parishioner in his place of work, a butcher's shop. Ian asked for the man. 'He's in the back shop,' was the reply. Ian went through and found him making sausages. He washed his hands and began to plait the sausages as they were being made. It was a wonder. News travelled fast round the town, 'We have a minister who knows how to plait sausages.' Clearly this was just unbelievable. But why so? Lessons learned in childhood are never forgotten.

For all that, Ian is adamant that one of the worst things you can give a seven-year old before school on a frosty morning is a pail of half-congealed pigs' blood and then require him to make black puddings. He was well into his twenties before he was able to eat these 'bloody awful things.' White puddings were a totally different matter. The special Fraser recipe of oatmeal, fat and rusk and good quality dripping in just the right proportions – Ian could do fine with one even now. 'Black puddings you can keep them!'

Ian may not have been at his best in the morning in his earliest days. He remembers being sent to the dairy in the High Street. He presented the tin for filling with fresh milk. When asked for payment he had shamefacedly to admit that the money was at the bottom of the tin! Errands of all kinds kept the brothers busy. There was always sawdust to collect from the local sawmill. The same place provided wood shavings for use in the smoking shed at Leys Cottage, which Ian was given charge of from the age of thirteen.

Ian and his brother were keen to help make a living possible, lending a hand in the shop. Alex went on to work there. In all the family business lasted one hundred and ten years, a commitment to continuing service in the community. The family opened a fish shop on the High Street. It never prospered in the way the 'fleshers'' business did. Hired hands were employed and they seem to lack pride in the quality of the produce that so marked the meat trade. Alex, Ian's brother had an arrangement with a local farmer to produce quality beef for Frasers'. Some of this beef was so highly regarded that roasts found their way to the Savoy Hotel in London.

Ian had to all intents and purpose served his apprenticeship in the butcher's business. He took pride in the fact that his mother preferred him ahead of his older brother when it came to carving a roast. Just do not offer him an electric carving knife. As he says, 'As much use as an electric toothbrush! Can folks no just use the hands God gave them?'

The family home, just off South Street, was just a few hundred yards from the first shop in Tolbooth Street. Dad used to set out in the half-light of the early morning. With his limited sight he was forever falling over ash-cans left out in the street. On one occasion he had just removed the metal grill from the doorway of the shop. It let the cool night air into the shop and kept the meat fresh. Dad became aware of a mass behind him. Unseeing he reached out only to find he was touching an elephant, just off Forres High Street! The circus was in town. The keeper had taken the elephant for an early morning walk then left it while he went up a close to fill a pail with water to give the beast a drink.

When Ian considered this incident, his mind turned to the Highland Clearances. As a boy he did not know about the Clearances but he was somehow aware that something had gone wrong in Scottish society. More than this, the church or at least the clergy had reacted badly, blaming the people for the troubles rather than the landowners. Ian had read 'The Silver Darlings', about the shoals of herring long gone due to over-fishing. He began to understand how people came to be living along the Moray coast, forced to fish without the necessary knowledge. No wonder lives were lost. Others were forced on to land to improve it. As soon as they had done this, the landowners demanded unreasonably high rents so that folk could be turned off the land they had worked. The shadow of a great injustice fell over the land. Ian sensed a strange foreboding just as Dad had sensed the strange visitor just beyond sight at the shop door.

Another childhood memory has remained with Ian. He remembers seeing boys who worked in the shop hanging out at street corners while the respectable middle-class folk made their way to church on a Sunday. Clearly this was not something open to folk like them. This class distinction left its mark on young Ian's mind. He would spend much of his later life seeking to right this wrong. Ian thought of his family as lower middle-class; with a trade, 'a bit like Jesus'. There was a family business and you were expected to get involved in it.

Sunday was a dreary day for Ian as a child. You attended church and then read 'an improving book'. Brother Al was not one normally to step out of line. Ian persuaded him to go up to Nelson's Tower, a local landmark high above the town, and join with a few others in a game of 'kick the can'. Someone was 'it'. That person had to close his eyes and count up to twenty while the rest of those playing hid. Then if you were seen by the person who was 'it', your name was called and you became 'it'. The thrill of the game was to try to kick the can before your name was called. It was a good game. But when Mum and Dad somehow got to hear of it, they squashed it. It is easy to see why Ian did not grow up to be a strict sabbatarian.

There were three churches in Forres. Dr James Black was minister in Castlehill Kirk before he went to Edinburgh. When Ian's grandfather who had been in the High Kirk heard Dr. Black preach he shifted his lines to Castlehill. It was preaching that mattered in those days. The other parts of the service, the prayers and readings, were even called preliminaries. So Ian grew up in Castlehill Kirk. His experience there did not seem to have offered him much though it was almost certainly more important than he realised at the time.

Ian's mother had a regular habit of going upstairs after lunch. She went to pray. No one told Ian this. He just knew it to be true. More than that, he was convinced that he was the one singled out in her prayers. He felt like Samuel of old. Just as Hannah lent Samuel to the Lord, his mother was intent on loaning him to God. When he went to university he said to his mother, 'I think you have been praying me into the ministry. That's the last thing I would ever do.' It is interesting that the Margaret who would become his wife was busy about the same time telling her mother that the last person she would marry would be an ordained minister. Ian's mother had some kind of psychological problem about attending church. Whether it was fear of large spaces or the crowd of people no one seems to know. By the time Ian was seven she had stopped attending church. He went with his father and brother.

But her faith mattered to her. When Ian was serving on Dunfermline Town Council he supported publicly the opening of halls for dances on a Sunday. This was anathema to his mother. While he respected her point of view Ian was concerned for young people for whom Sunday was a day of inactivity. He was concerned that they should find something to do rather than causing trouble to others and themselves. Mum had been brought up in the 'Wee Free' tradition. Dancing was more or less of the devil. She said, 'God only asks one day of us.' 'Not so,' Ian retorted 'Seven!'

Ian's mother took her responsibility as a parent seriously. When they were very small she tried to find ways of amusing her family. On one occasion she put a sheet over some poles and made a tent for the children to play in. Interest in this novelty lasted all of five minutes. On a summer's day a picnic would be arranged. Usually the matches were forgotten or the sticks for the fire were damp.

A beach hut was hired for the summer on Findhorn back shore. Mother sat and knitted and enjoyed the sea breezes. She occasionally took Dallas relatives down there for a blether. When Ian went there, once he had had a swim there was nothing much to do, that would interest a teenager. One exception was when Mrs. Duncan, a Forres neighbour, showed him how to recognise unblemished stones, which could be polished to be used as the centrepiece of costume jewellery. Ian took to spending hours wandering along the beach looking for stones that were just right for such a purpose. He also learned to catch crabs from the piers in Findhorn Bay. Brass curtain rings were enough to attract attention. Crabs could be relied on to hold on to their shiny prize even when they were lifted out of their natural habitat in the shade of the piers.

Parties were also arranged; so-called children's parties. 'Mothers' parties they were in reality; an opportunity to show off your children. Boys dressed in velvet trousers and silk shirts with girls in their finery, the children were expected to show that they were well cared for. Daft games are remembered; horror of horrors some required the boys to kiss the girls.

When Ian was growing up there was a certain loneliness. He looked for space to live. Ian's dad was tone deaf; Alex not much better. Music was not wanted in the home. If there was music on the radio when dad came back from work he would say, 'Put off that rubbish!' There was nothing more to be said. Ian longed to learn to play strings. He wanted to learn the violin. The problem was that the local violin teacher was not a customer in the shop. Dad felt he was under obligation to his brother Bob and the shop. Ian was put under the same obligation. So Ian was sent to learn the piano. The piano teacher was a customer; that made it all right. In addition to teaching piano she sold coal and gravestones. She seemed to do more selling than anything else when her piano pupils were with her. Ian had no time for learning from someone, with neither talent for teaching, or the time to do it properly. His musical talent would have to wait. He would find other ways to use his creativity.

Alex had a different hobby. He was an enthusiastic amateur photographer who would spend no end of time on the latest project.

In his later years he took photographs for the Forres entry for the Britain in Bloom competition. He thought nothing of waiting for hours, even as a youngster, taking a shot of a bird returning to its nest until the action and the light were just to his liking. Ian's part was to stand on his hands on a chair to produce something a little different for the photographer. He had no time for all the fuss. He remembers that his most expensive camera by contrast was one bought for a dollar in the USA.

On the whole, Uncle Bob and Dad got on quite well. In Ian's early days the shop was kept open on Christmas Day. To close would have been 'Catholic' (anything you did not like or that your granny did not favour was 'Catholic'). Later the shop closed half-day for Christmas and later still was open only till church time. Ian loathed this last arrangement for after the Christmas church service Uncle Bob and Dad always had a verbal confrontation. It was usually about something to do with the shop. The beneficial effect of a Christmas service seemed to last less than an hour.

Ian's Aunt Meg, Uncle Bob's wife, chose not to do the washing at home but sent it to Taylor's laundry. Ian would be dispatched to their house on occasion to help out. Ian had his bike and Aunt Meg would give him a huge bundle of washing to walk down to the laundry. On one occasion Uncle Bob turned up unexpectedly. He was appalled. He asked how much Aunt Meg was paying him. When he heard that it was a penny he immediately produced a sixpence and went on to give his wife the rough edge of his tongue.

On occasion Bob took Alex's children to the Nairn Highland Games. He provided money for some of the shows. Ian remembers a sideshow with a wall of balloons half-inflated so that they were difficult to burst. For sixpence you got 3 kicks at a football and for each balloon you burst you won a sixpence. At the first attempt, Ian burst two so doubling his money. He took another shot and won a further shilling. He had his sights set on continuing to double his money. The showman was minded otherwise. He insisted that Ian should move on and share his talents round!

When Aunt Meg needed a holiday she might go to Nairn. Ian was sent for a couple of days and was required to take Cousin Margaret as a baby out for walks in her pram. This task the 11-year old boy undertook reluctantly. She seems to have survived his ministrations and has developed an independence of thought not unlike her carer!

Uncle Bob and Aunt Meg had known sadness in their early-married life. Their first child, a girl, was stillborn. The next, a boy, Robert, died at three months. Uncle Bob was deeply affected by this early death. He was heard to say on occasion that he heard the brush of angels' wings taking the boy to heaven. Ian thought a lot about death in his early years. The questioning was neither morbid nor fearful. It was more a thoughtful consideration of the mystery of it all.

Bob comes across the years to us as a man of integrity. He was certainly a shrewd businessman who would expect to profit in deals he made in business. That said he had a softer side. He knew his customers and their circumstances. It was not unusual for him to order that an outstanding account be marked paid. As he would say, 'They can't afford to meet the debt. They need to eat.' Of an evening Bob spent time with the financial columns of his newspaper. He had a good broker in London and made money in stocks and shares. He reckoned this to be a form of gambling and so refused requests to become an elder in the kirk. Others might have been even more insistent had they known the extent of his generosity, but he had his own standards and these could not be ignored.

Ian went on to secondary school. He took the dux medal at the end of his third year only to miss out on the senior dux medal at the end of his fifth year. He lost out to his main opponent for honours, Tony Crowley: there was never much between them all through school years. Ian concluded that perhaps justice had been served.

Ian has a memory of a mock election in the school literary society when he was in his third year. He is rather embarrassed looking back on this. His election address promised the construction of a tunnel from the Academy along the High Street to the door of the Picture House. Ian was elected as 'provost'! How easily some votes can be bought!

At the Academy Ian encountered 'Tommy', a teacher of English. He was a Mr. Thomson who was hated by many of his pupils. He was immensely sarcastic, forever putting pupils down. This man regularly picked on Margaret, Ian's younger sister.

Margaret took scarlet fever when she was a young girl. She was in hospital for about six weeks. When she came out she immediately caught a second dose and had to return to the fever hospital. She was left with deafness, which was not diagnosed. This led to her being treated as a bit stupid. Dad was especially hard on her. Ian can still picture Margaret standing outside the window while mother read her report card to Dad. In this way Margaret could estimate how long she would have to keep clear until the storm subsided.

The situation was at its worst when Margaret had to take Dad from the shop at the end of the day when she had received her report. The whole of Forres heard his condemnation. Dad did not ease off even when his own report card was found. It revealed that he had made a pretty poor showing himself at school. Margaret was always grateful for the headmaster of the secondary school. Mr. Simpson was kind and understanding. His wife was also deaf.

Yet it was through Tommy that Ian developed a feel for words. He encouraged Ian in the habit of hunting for their root meanings. He was later to discover in Kittel's Greek Dictionary there are about 20 pages on 'soteria' the Greek word for salvation. Ian discovered that the heart of the word is neither about evangelism nor conversion. The word is in fact about 'spaces – giving people space to live'. It was this space that Ian had yet to discover.

In his last year in the Academy a former pupils group put up a prize for an essay. No subject was specified. Ian chose to write on the life of a Japanese worker-saint, Kagawa. Tommy said to Ian, 'If I had been correcting the essays I would not have given you the prize.' Ian assured him, 'If you had been correcting the essays, I would have written a different one.' Clearly Ian had already reached the conclusion that a writer should have his readers in mind before he began any given task.

There was a prevailing assumption that life in the shop was real work: schoolwork was not. It never seemed to occur to Dad that children needed space to do things. Most of his school life, Ian had to do his homework in the sitting room where Dad would have the radio on; Alex and Margaret would be doing whatever. It certainly taught Ian to concentrate. Only when Ian was in fifth year in secondary school and facing the Leaving Certificate examinations (he achieved 'A' passes in all five subjects) did his mother put on a fire in the kitchen so that he could work in peace. He was expected to do well at school. But the thought that any concession should be made to that was absent.

Scotland was divided in two for the correction of the Leaving Certificate examinations and Ian learned that there was a great buzz in the staffroom when they were told that he had come first in English in the half of Scotland into which Forres fell.

'Tommy' entered Ian for the Edinburgh University bursary examination. He came nowhere in that competition. When the young student went up to university he was for a while in awe of someone who had achieved, say, fortieth place in the bursary examination. In time it became clear that, for the glory of their schools, some pupils had undergone 'hothouse' preparation to bring them forward artificially for the bursary examination. They could not cope so well with the rigour of university courses. Ian was pleased to have been allowed to mature properly in due time.

Tommy started something that has lasted a lifetime. No teacher could ask more. He helped Ian to see the difference between something which was true, and something that would bring easy and superficial approval from others.

From the age of fifteen in addition to everything else Ian had to read to Dad. Al was excused this for he was doing real work in the shop. During these reading sessions Ian tried to develop a monotonous voice. He hoped this would encourage Dad to sleep. A 'Rover' or 'Wizard' comic was ready beneath the book if he did indeed doze off. But in some strange way, even if Dad was snoring, and Ian stopped, the listener woke and was able to quote back the last words read as proof that he was actually still listening.

In his final years at secondary school, Ian, on occasion, took over the house for a couple of weeks at a time to let his mother have a break. On one occasion she took Auntie Nellie with her to Edinburgh. They stayed in a Princes Street hotel. The first morning Auntie Nellie looked out of the window on crowded pavements. She was amazed. 'All these folk, Annie! Hae they nae work to go to?'

Back home Ian had rump steak to fry for the midday meal. He had been told to cook it slowly on a low gas for twenty minutes. He followed his instructions only to be told that the meat was tough. The following week it was to be steak again. The stand-in chef had not been keeping an eye on the clock. He suddenly realised that Dad and Al would be in for lunch in three minutes. Ian got out the big frying pan, put two gases on full and served it at the normal time. The verdict was that it was just right. Ian kept his own counsel.

When he was left in charge of housework he was up at 6 a.m. to clean out the porch and scrub its surrounds. The early start made sure that the boy who delivered the morning rolls did not see him doing 'woman's work'. Such was the culture of those days.

Ian loved his football. Along with the goalkeeper, John Tulloch, Ian was chosen to represent Moray schools against Banff schools. The game took place at Mosset Park in Forres. It is still the home of Forres Mechanics who play in the Highland League. What should have been a memorable occasion turned out to be a disappointment to Ian in three ways. He was selected as a centre forward from the start. He preferred to begin at least in midfield to get the feel of the game. Then the Elgin boys soaked the ball before the match. This did no kindness to Ian's light-boned ankles. And they spoiled the game by limiting themselves too much to passes to boys from their own school, rather than working for the good of the whole team. The memory of that match is saved only by its last action. Ian's team were losing four-three late in the match. A ball landed between Ian and the Banff goalie. Ian got to the ball first and taking it round him he walked it into the net. The match was squared. The day was saved.

It might have been the Scottish Daily Express that sent a football-scout journalist to assess the status of schools' football across the north of Scotland. He wrote that Ian could make his mark in the Highland League. Sadly he was never asked to play for his home team. The journalist clearly believed that he was headed for further study in Aberdeen. There is no record of an Edinburgh student ever playing for Forres Mechanics during his student days. The capital was beyond the sphere of influence of Forres. In any case students could hardly make regular commitments. This meant it was difficult for them to establish a regular place in a team.

Ian was also the school cricket captain. He opened the batting with John Macdonald. His partner normally faced the first over. As a matter of policy he blocked each ball. Ian's strategy was somewhat different. He carefully received his first two balls and then went down the pitch to the opening fast bowler. They could not settle in to a convincing length. Ian was quick on his feet and had an ability to cut the ball. This led to quick scoring. It was not uncommon for Ian to reach twenty, while John had scored only a single. The school's philosophy was simple. You made runs. You got out. Sixty or seventy was a good team score. In short school matches twenty or thirty would have been considered an acceptable personal contribution. Batting was what cricket was really about. Ian also bowled. He returned best figures of 8 for 16 against Grantown. This is remembered but hardly recalled with the relish of a ball speeding to a distant boundary.

Golf was almost forgotten as Ian looked back to Forres' days. Under the age of 18 you got the freedom of the golf course for 10/- a year. Al and Ian played together some evenings. Al was a bit muscle-bound with all the heavy lifting in the shop. It impaired his swing. The local professional commented on Ian's easy natural swing. He was of the opinion that with sufficient practice Ian could make the grade as a golfer. No way! Golf, for Ian, was a leisure activity. In the two school golf tournaments he entered in his fifth and sixth year he came second in both. In one the prize was a fountain pen. In the other it was a golf club. In time he would find much more use for the former. When Ian arrived at university cricket and golf tended to take a back seat. Football was the winter activity and tennis occupied much of the summer.

In his last year at school Ian returned to school after lunch one day to find that most of his class had gone on strike. It had started on a whim, had no purpose and protested against nothing of substance. Ian did not join in.

On the other hand, in that year he and other classmates sometimes just failed to turn up for class. The local bowling green was opposite the headmaster's window but there was a hedge round it. You could play unobserved. Ian and his friends got quite proficient at bowls. Sixth year was in any case treated as an extra and rather relaxed year. Entry requirements for university had been more than achieved the previous session.

Forres in the twenties and thirties was a town of characters. Folk knew and were known by nicknames. Uncle Bob when he was a message boy was sent with a delivery to 'Carpet Billy'. He was only ever known as 'Carpet Billy'. He never wore shoes just carpet slippers. Bob went to his house. He asked for 'Carpet Billy', and then was chased for his life. The cheek of him!

There was Willy Hen, who as could be imagined, walked like a hen. He was nearly always late for his work. On one occasion someone shouted to him, 'Aye, Willie, slept in again?' Willie responded with a glint in his eye. 'Yes, it's a wee bit cold to sleep out!' If Willy was very late for his work, he used to carry his porridge in his jacket pocket. He would eat it as he went to his work. It is not to be supposed for a minute that it was a waterproof jacket or a waterproof pocket. It was surely the kind of porridge that needed to be eaten with a knife and fork.

Melodeon Nell as her name suggests went round the town playing for pennies. Then there was Davy Dottle – a dottle kind of family – not quite all there. He married a woman of the same ilk. They were well matched. Not to forget Troddler. He was a wee chap who walked like a seaman. He rolled along the street. The local wags coined this new word, 'troddler' for the man who toddled and rolled round the town. Surely that is language development at its very best!

A particular day came in the 1930s. Forres was caught up in a national celebration. A crowd had gathered. Someone had a new toy – a roving microphone. The owner of the new toy was going round the crowd asking them to say a few words. Many had their say. The microphone was placed in front of the oldest inhabitant, Willie Green. 'Well what are you making of today, Willy?' 'Och,' he replied, 'My backside is sore with all this sitting aboot!' Words of wisdom for all to share. Forres has produced a number of folk who valued plain speaking.

Happy memories. Ian remembers a football competition held as part of some civic celebration. He scored a goal in the first round to take the school team through. He scored again in the second round. The other team scored two, so Ian's side were out of the competition. Great days of long ago still fresh in the memory.

Market Day in Forres centred on a fish market. Fisher-wives used to take their creels and sell the herrings in the centre of town. The herrings were tasty fish. Ian assures us that herrings and new tatties – nothing to beat them.

Ian's dad never learned to say no to another new tattie. It was always just one more . . . and another one. And how his digestion suffered for it!

The Gala Day in Forres was marked by a procession of vehicles through the town to the Grant Park. A queen and her attendants held court for a day. On one occasion Ian thought to put something on the front of one of the shop vans, which was in the parade. He thought he would put one over the Cooperative, their competitors. He wrote, 'Fraser's give dividends in quality and service.' This did not meet with Uncle Bob's approval. It did not last long.

In the early war years Ian again tried his hand at advertising this time in the shop window. The advert went something along these lines:

> What's wrong with Mussolini?
> – It's an interesting question
> And Hitler seems to think the world's his fief –
> One never can be sure
> We think it's indigestion
> For they never tasted Frasers' famous beef.
> You try it! It makes people
> Feel content and at peace with the world!

To this day Ian finds it difficult to give a considered opinion of his childhood. To some extent he felt robbed. He had to spend long hours working. He did two hours every morning before school and worked from six on a Saturday morning till noon delivering orders as a message boy. At the age of thirteen he was given charge of the smoking shed where sides of pork were smoked for bacon and later, also fish. All this was decided over his head. It was just the way things were done in those days.

The first smoking shed was made of wood. It caught fire and burnt to the ground. The insurance money paid for a more substantial replacement. It also paid for a bike as more than one had been destroyed in the fire. A bike was replaced for Ian but it had to be a lady's bike, just in case his mother ever needed to ride it! She never did. Ian was left with the ridicule of his peers: a boy using a woman's bike. Lack of consideration, of course, is not confined to days long ago or even to the young. And childhood does not last forever.

In Forres Ian would not join the church. Everything there was second hand, passed on to him by his parents. He neither wanted to conform to their lives or to rebel against them. He just needed space to be his own man and develop his personal commitment to Christ. Like Mary who 'kept these things in her heart and mulled over them' Ian found that in a blind man's home it is very hard even for faith not to be second-hand. So it was when the question arose of where to go to university Ian rejected Aberdeen. It was too close to home.

Endnotes

[1] This is the place which gave its name to Dallas, Texas.

[2] A Scottish traditional song.

[3] William Blake.

[4] Two popular series of cigarette cards at that time.

[5] William Butler Yeats.

[6] Eighty years after these events, Ian confesses to finding it difficult to distinguish between the actual events and the thoughts and feelings they inspired.

CHAPTER TWO

PREPARATION

IAN DECIDED TO go to Edinburgh University not Aberdeen as it was too near home. He needed some space. So much time had been spent in the family shop; a blind man can try to get not only a map of his surroundings but a map of a young man's mind. Ian longed for space to do his own thinking in company with other young people. He needed to explore life's meaning.

Ian recalls what appears to be a trivial matter that was symptomatic of his early days. Dad had defined constipation as afflicting anyone who was unable to go first thing every morning. Medication was the order of many days. In his first year in Edinburgh Ian bought a medical book in Grant's the bookseller. It said if someone is supposed to be constipated leave him or her a week to see if it is in fact true. This relaxed Ian. Things took their natural course from then on!

Ian only knew two people in Edinburgh at that time; one was Dr. Black of St. George's West and the other was the Rev. Ian Mackenzie in Cairns Memorial Church. The latter had been good enough to take Ian's dad out for walks and their conversation had helped him towards the ordained ministry.

Ian went up to university in Edinburgh in 1936. He was eighteen. He had no intention of getting involved with theology; he didn't even know what theology was! 'Tommy' filled in Ian's application for university without consulting him. The teacher was keen on history so his pupil was entered for that subject. Sadly that lecturer did little to enthuse his students. He had a practice of taking groups of students out for afternoon tea. On the occasion when Ian was with him he had a stand-up confrontation with his wife in front of the student group. Hysterical rather than historical!

Ian had to take a science subject. He chose mathematics. It seemed the least scientific of the options available. He tried to get through the class doing little or no work in it. Ian failed in Mathematics. He went in to the examination casually and made a mess of it. He had to take the resit. While awaiting the second result he was playing for a university cricket XI in St. Andrews. A spectator after the match commented on his distinctive style of fielding then enquired further as to whether he was the Ian Fraser who had recently taken a resit paper in Mathematics. The stranger introduced himself as professor of Mathematics at St. Andrews University. He had been correcting resit papers for Edinburgh University. 'I've never known anybody before,' he said, 'who got over 90% in a resit!' For Ian this simply demonstrated that with diligence progress was possible even in areas where initial interest was very limited.

On one occasion Ian captained the first team at football for Edinburgh University. On another occasion Tommy Walker of Hearts and Scotland was in the opposition. During the game Ian trapped the ball awkwardly. Only when he returned home 6 months later did an osteopath near Nairn sort the problem. Men and their football!

Ian's main interest was the study of English. The first year class comprised some one hundred and twenty students. This reduced in the second year to about sixty. Ian's results placed him second in the class until one particular essay was set. It was deemed to fall below his normal standard. He dropped to about sixth in the class. His vivid memory of this suggests it mattered to him.

About this time the professor of classics encouraged Ian to do honours in Latin and Greek. Ian had a good ear but knew himself he lacked depth in the fundamentals of these languages. Further study there would have been unsuccessful. In due course Ian was awarded a general M.A. degree.

For Ian more important than his academic studies in these undergraduate years was his meeting up with folk in the Student Christian Movement. It is difficult to appreciate the significance of the SCM in the 1930s with its significantly lower profile at the beginning of the 21st century. In 1935 of 72,000 university students in the United Kingdom, 11,500 were signed up members of SCM. There you were not invited, as was the case, Ian believed, in the Christian Union, to come and sit and learn at the feet of others. Rather you were encouraged to embark on a voyage of discovery and to share this experience with others. In his second year Ian became convinced of the truth of the Christian faith and was converted. It was an exceptional experience. He lost interest in food for a time. 'I had meat to eat that you know not of' (John 4:32).

The space to work things out had borne fruit. Ian Mackenzie felt he had to rein Ian in: he seemed in danger of overwhelming others in his enthusiasm for his new-found faith. Ian held this friend in high regard. He remembers him as the best preacher he ever heard. This was not because he had a reputation for preaching. He continually drew lessons from his own life and the lives of people he met. Dr. Black, by contrast, was the great orator.

On one occasion when the electricity failed in the church during a service, Ian Mackenzie began from the prevailing circumstances and explored how Christians should face up to trials. The sermon was developed as he spoke. People were able to follow him. He was speaking to their daily lives. That approach also marks Ian. Now when he leads communion at the end of the day amongst his friends he draws on the preceding discussion as the group has wrestled with matters of life and faith. He begins where the folk are and brings them to the table to remember the Lord Christ. The Spirit leads as life is informed by faith. Ian has developed a habit of listening. He is ready to learn from others and to take on their insights, old and new.

In the SCM Ian got the chance to work things through. It was this that moved him in the direction of New College and divinity. Ian had looked at some ministers, and had concluded – not for me. Now he felt 'landed on'. Ian's understanding of election has been worked out personally. It might involve something you are naturally attracted to. Equally it might not. It is a privilege – if it is hard at times to give it such a name. It was important to find out what was meant for you. Ian moved from being convinced that church ministry was not for him to discovering that it was in fact the way he was being led.

By the time Ian got to New College he was taking a larger role in the life of the student body. In 1940 when the Challenge of Faith week took place, he was the student leader. This was a Christian mission to the university. George MacLeod, Mervyn Stockwood an Anglican and Mrs. Isobel Forrester led it. She said that Ian had been instrumental in her 'coming out' in matters of faith by his encouragement to her to be the woman missioner. In time Isobel did a lot for Margaret. She had been head girl in her sixth year at Dumfries Academy. In that same year a science teacher who was promoting either agnosticism or atheism disturbed Margaret. She thought it was a matter of integrity to resist any chance of falling in love with a minister!

Ian first set eyes on Margaret in Edinburgh. The circumstances are instructive. He decided to return to a reading room he had used as an undergraduate in the Old Quad of the university. He chose not to spend his time in the company of theologues. With Margaret it was interest if not love at first sight. Ian saw where she was sitting and waited until the student sitting next to her left. He wandered over, sat down and introductions were made. She was, as he would later discover, Margaret Davidson Dow Stewart, born 24th May 1920, the eldest of four children. Her father was a butcher's assistant! The family lived in Thornhill, Dumfriesshire.

At this time Ian was working in the Pleasance Settlement in his spare time. This initiative sought to do something alongside people in a run-down area of the city. It was an attempt to bring town and gown together. In 1905 a dozen or so Edinburgh University Students moved into the city slums with the purpose of helping people less fortunate than themselves. They worked among an impoverished, mainly Irish, immigrant community who lived in the Cowgate,

Southside and in the Pleasance – hence the project name. Founding members of this group included Joseph Bell, the city doctor, famous as the real-life inspiration for Sherlock Holmes. The main mover in the early days was a history professor, Sir Richard Lodge. In exchange for cheaper rents the students did a variety of community work. While the original houses have long since gone the work continues particularly in the form of art therapy classes.

Ian spent time visiting families in their homes and helping with services. He was principally involved in bringing some colour and light into the lives of people for whom existence was rather drab. Concerts were arranged. First tickets were sold. Then a programme had to be arranged. 'Turns' were sought. Margaret was a member of a quartet that was willing to sing at such a concert. Their paths kept crossing.

Margaret and Ian had to overcome some obstacles. Ian fell for her before she developed a similar affection for him. Then there was the matter of the Christian faith. She was fearful of simply adopting his faith second-hand. Ian told here often enough that he would happily marry her as the most convinced atheist in Scotland rather than marry anyone else.

Isobel Forrester helped Margaret to discover that what she in fact believed had its roots in just this faith. Isobel had such integrity and humility that Margaret found her to be someone who by life commended the Christian Faith. Isobel was married to Willie Forrester, the professor of ethics at St. Andrews University. Ian, 'in mischief-making mode', reckoned that she would have made a better professor then her husband. Her son Duncan Forrester was later to become Principal of New College. Many members of that family have made their mark on Scottish life.

In New College Ian discovered that theology mirrored the way he normally thought. It encouraged him to get beyond the superficial, and probe deeply into matters. His background in SCM prepared him for this further study. John Baillie was like an uncle to him not just his professor. Baillie lectured in divinity. He was surely the leading Scottish theologian and teacher of his generation.

John Baillie, a Scot, had returned to Edinburgh from Canada in 1934. He was a major contributor to the Oxford Conference of 1937 which was led by the leading ecumenical thinker of the day, Joe Oldham. The Church of Scotland in the early 1930s seemed more interested in maintaining its distance from the Roman Catholic Church in Scotland than in confronting the rise of totalitarianism in Europe. John Baillie was to play a significant part in changing this and promoting ecumenism.

In his 'What is Christian Civilisation? (1937) Baillie wrote:
'Christians today who defend the Church's slowness to concern itself with social reform by standing fast on the distinction between 'religion and politics' and 'religion and economics' too often find themselves in the same camp as men of the world whose opposition to projected reforms proceed only from the defence of their own vested interests in the existing order.'

From 1934 onwards Baillie was involved in various peace movements. He was visited in Edinburgh in 1935 by Dietrich

Bonhoeffer. Baillie also increasingly involved himself in the stuff of economics and the right response of the church in this area.

It is hardly surprising that during Ian Fraser's time at New College his professor John Baillie was called in May 1940 to head up a Commission to reflect on the place of the Church of Scotland in wartime and post-war Scotland. John Baillie was apparently keen that Ian be involved in the write-up of one of the reports of the Commission. Other members refused to countenance the participation of anyone not within their number.

The Commission saw their deliberations as having two main themes; the crisis they faced in wartime and the issues that would face the life and work of the Church in the post war world. The 1941 report gives support to the notion of the 'just war' they had entered into. In the May 1943 report great emphasis is placed on the significance of the Church. This was at the beginning of the year when John Baillie was the Moderator of the Church of Scotland. While the reports deal with matters within the institutional life of the church e.g. baptism and inter-church relations, they make important observations on social and economic matters e.g. marriage and education. Some have seen the orderly transition to post war-society in the United Kingdom as having significant roots in the work of the Baillie Commission. We can understand why Ian believed that he could hardly have had a better mentor in his time as a B.D. student at New College.

John Burleigh lectured to Ian in New College on church history. He read his whole lecture from notes. There was a day when he included a quotation in a lecture. Then he looked up and said, 'The words are those of a subversive third-century monk. The voice is the voice of Ian Fraser.' Then he put his head down and read on.

William Tindal was a great encouragement to Ian. He and Archie Craig both applied for the post of lecturer in Practical Theology. Tindal was chosen. It was too easy for folk to believe the fact that he had been Montgomery's chaplain had swayed the decision. Not so. He was in charge of the settlement in the Pleasance and encouraged Ian and his other students to develop their own understanding in theology. He set students free to grow as the Spirit led. Particularly he encouraged a search for justice in society. About Archie Craig we shall have more to say presently.

George MacLeod came to New College every year, fishing for members for the Iona Community. There was a rapport between Ian and George from the first. George was committed to finding men to go into church extension parishes. He had started off paying scant attention to the church authorities. Professor White opposed George and his Iona Community at the General Assembly. He argued that this new venture was the formation of an unattached, voluntary society. Ian recognised in George, however, a great constitutionalist. He understood every effort George made to link the Iona Community into the life of the Church of Scotland. He did this without compromising the ecumenical nature of the Community.

George spoke to Ian when he visited New College in Ian's last year, 1942. He encouraged him to choose between membership of the Iona Community and industrial mission. Ian responded that he could see no good reason why he could not do both. This made George think. He came to the conclusion that membership need not be limited to those who went into church extension parishes. In this way the conditions for membership of the Iona Community were freed up almost as soon as it began although women and lay members would only be admitted in adequate numbers when George had taken his hand off the tiller.

George and Ian developed a good relationship. Ian recognised that not too many members joining the community had taken academic prizes. Ian went first to Iona probably in 1939, in the earliest days of the Iona Community. At this time, as a student for the ministry, he was labouring in holiday time on the abbey-rebuilding programme. He remembers having the opportunity of leading worship in the abbey church. Mr. Campbell, who had been a minister in Ian's younger days in Forres, happened to be present. He is reported to have said to George after the service, 'That was one baptism that took!'

Ian met a group of Eastern Orthodox pilgrims visiting Iona in these early days. They were seen to sniff the incense in the air in the church. They were puzzled. 'Here we are in the West and we feel at home.' The influence of Orthodox liturgies and practice on George MacLeod has been noted in other places. These were important days as they gave a breadth to Ian's understanding of the Christian Church.

The practical work that Ian undertook on Iona left its mark. In days that followed when he visited small Christian Communities he was known to pick up an axe and to start chopping firewood. It did not go unnoticed that the visiting clergyman was not afraid to get his hands dirty. Wherever Ian went he discovered that by sharing manual work you could get alongside people.

Later when Scottish Churches House was being developed Ian chose to do the work that required him to be at the top of their tallest ladder. No one else was allowed to clear the ivy. If a Japanese volunteer had fallen off there would have been trouble. They were not adequately covered by insurance. If Ian fell off, well, there was always the NHS.

George saw the need in the fledgling Iona Community to have a Rule. This was hammered out in the 1940s. Ralph Morton saw the need to have smaller groups where people might have confidence in contributing. Then in time insights might be shared in larger groups. Moreover, Ralph saw the need to curb George when he was manipulating plenaries of the Community for his own ends!

On one occasion Ian managed to get on the agenda the need for a broader community, which included women and a greater representation of lay people. In plenaries the nuclear issue was always to the fore. George highlighted it. Roger Gray always supported George in this. A long discussion meant that Ian's item was conveniently not reached. George could be unscrupulous. If anyone managed to confront him then he would listen. It often fell to Ian to act as the loyal opposition. It was decided that the Community should have a peace commitment. George pressed this on the Community and Roger backed him. Ian said that peace made no sense without justice. George said that true peace always included justice. But argued Ian, if that is so, there is much that is taken for peace that lacks justice. At that point George got his way; the

Community adopted the Peace Commitment. Peace with Justice would have to wait.

Ian worked on the principle that if the Community adopted something he would take it on board. If on the other hand George acted unilaterally Ian felt free to decide the matter for himself. George decided that the Community should on formal occasions wear blue serge suits. He would pay for them. He based this on what he thought was proper formal dress for fishermen. Ian never wore a blue suit in his life. It was not a Community decision.

At one point George concluded that more discipline was needed. He decided that those staying in the Youth Hut on Iona should close their doors by 10.00 p.m., after the evening service. During the week that seemed sensible. On a Friday however, there was a dance in the village hall. Ian organised that the door should be closed by ten, and encouraged the men to leave by a window. They danced till the last dance at four in the morning. A boat had been sent out to fish. The new members moved on to a house in the village. It had a large room. A ceilidh followed. The fish were cooked and shared. At seven in the morning the men dived off the pier and then went back into their hut through the windows. They were ready at 7.30 a.m. for the new day with its worship and work. George never knew.

There are many instances in the gospels when Jesus encourages his friends to 'Keep your eyes skinned. Watch. Keep alert!' Ian brought this to George's attention. He dismissed it as 'hardly the heart of the gospel!' Ian begged to differ. George and Ian clearly had different understandings of matters theologically. This is perhaps never better seen than on the occasion when Ian announced to George: 'You can be a Christian. You can be a pacifist. You cannot be a Christian pacifist.' We can imagine the sparks that flew that day. We need to understand that only where mutual respect was complete could such convictions be shared.

Ian's uncles and aunts were mainly small farmers. They had three unstated understandings of law. There was the law of the land. Anything that flew over or ran over the land belonged to the laird. There was the law of God, which meant that anything that flew over or ran over the land belonged to the people who worked it. Then there was the law of expediency, which said that you did not need to fight every battle. One harvest time when he was young Ian was out with a gun. He shot a grouse. On his way home he saw the gamekeeper's bike against the wall of his aunt's house. He went down to a harvested field and put the gun in a stook. He then took the middle out of a sheaf and put the bird in it. He walked back with the sheaf and its contents under his arm. No questions were asked. Auntie Nellie was delighted to have the main item for an unexpected meal! George MacLeod was the leader of the Iona Community: infallibility belonged elsewhere!

George never suggested Ian for any of the prominent committees in the Community. He knew that Ian would be liable to ask awkward questions. The leader was on one occasion preaching a sermon on the scripture text, 'You shall not see me unless your brother is with you.' (Genesis 44:23) George applied 'the brother' to the poor. Ian challenged him on this. It really referred to Benjamin, Israel's beloved youngest, putting him in danger. George did not want to know. Why spoil a good sermon for the sake of faithfulness to the text!

The work of the Spirit in the life of George in bringing the Community into being was easily recognised. The irony was that he was such a great individualist. He knew that what was needed was a community that was truer church than they had then. He was committed to community and driven by his vision, which often saw so much more than others. On occasion it was limited and limiting due in part to his own life experience. His war experience left its mark. It coloured to a considerable degree what he believed about the fellowship of men. The community fed off him but on occasion needed to stand up to him. Ralph Morton brought some balance into situations. Ian saw him as a brilliant foil to George.

Ian has some very clear and cherished memories of the folk he met on Iona. He shares a picture of a member, a wee man who terrorised his much larger wife. Better perhaps even at this distance that he remains anonymous for everyone's sake.

Bill Amos arrived on Iona out of the blue when a skilled mason was a godsend at that period of the rebuilding. Bill believed in what was being done. On one occasion Ian was distressed to hear two craftsmen discussing communion. The one asked the other, 'Are you going in for a wee snifter?' It seemed to be all that it meant to them. Bill was different. He recognised purpose in the rebuilding and was entirely committed to it.

Lex Miller brought in the economic discipline. He hailed from New Zealand. He had been in an economic discipline group elsewhere. Ian remembers hearing him comment that the person in the Community who committed most thoroughly to the Iona economic discipline was

George himself. It could not have been commonly known at the time. Perhaps no one should be surprised. George had much to say about the importance of money in the Kingdom. In the privacy of his own life he practised what he preached. Those who have shared in an Iona family group with Ian know that he has faithfully and enthusiastically followed the lead George gave in this matter.

We need to remember that during the later years when Ian was in Edinburgh there was a war on. Church ministry was a reserved occupation. Many pacifists changed their views in the circumstances then prevailing. On behalf of his class, Ian was encouraged to ask Colonel Campbell, the university gym tutor whether they should volunteer for active service, during their New College days. The colonel had come to faith in Canada; he was in awe of the mountains he saw there. The military advice Ian got was that they should continue with their studies with a view to service that would be required in a post-war world.

Ian served on fire watch in Edinburgh in his student days. While on duty one night and mindful of his commitment to the common good Ian went and gave blood. He was then unsteady on his feet. It was suggested that he should not repeat this type of donation. That night was one of the nights of the Clydebank blitz.[7] Had Ian been required to be part of a rooftop watch he fears with hindsight that he might have gone over the edge. Fortunately fire-watching for him that night was at street level.

Later Ian was in the Home Guard. In Edinburgh he was handed a long dark cloak to wear. He was on watch on George IV Bridge in Edinburgh; those who passed by were unsure what they should make of him. One soldier saluted him. When Ian was issued with a weapon he returned it and someone else took the responsibility for cleaning it. He had never handled such a gun in his life. No training was given. The boots he was supplied with, he was assured, were his size. He was sent out on a long route march. When he got back to Edinburgh his boots were filled with blood. His feet were blistered.

On a visit home to Forres the Home Guard was called out. Paratroopers were reported to have landed in the area. There were not enough guns to go round. Ian was told to follow a lad who had a gun. 'When he gets shot, you pick up the gun,' was the helpful instruction given to him. In fact some fabric had been shot off a plane. It was this that had floated to the ground. Ian was based in a school later that night. He found a map of the world, wrapped himself in it and had a good sleep. In later days he would get to know his world map even better.

Ian decided in the last year of his B.D. to clear the decks. He wanted to apply himself even more carefully to his studies. He resigned from 13 committees. These related to a whole range of interests from devotional groups to others focused on political action. He recognised that he had two main gifts. He was good at chairing meetings and could write a good minute of what had been said and what had been decided. Later in his World Council of Churches days when others could relax in the evening Ian was busy writing up reports that were needed for the following day. Some gifts are to be regretted.

For his final papers in theology Ian gained his BD with distinction and was awarded the Cunningham Fellowship and Gunning Prize.

Professor Baillie wanted Ian to apply for a teaching post in a university. When Ian explained that he intended to work alongside men in a paper mill the professor changed his mind. Ian's intention seems to have fitted well with the direction being taken by the Baillie Commission. Baillie encouraged his student to follow his inclination; it was recognised as a genuine calling. Later Ian was invited to share something of his experience of risk-taking, with Donald Baillie's students at St Mary's College, St Andrews. He encouraged them to think beyond the safe haven of academia.

There is a part of Ian that is pure student. Research attracts him. He wants always to balance this with action. He understands theology as the faith basis for living and far too important to be left to academics.

In his decision to go to the paper mill Ian was fully supported by Margaret. She married him while he was still on labourer's wages. Many people remember her gracious manner. Ian knew that with this there was toughness, a determination to face difficult situations. She often seemed to sense the way ahead before he did. She had a great sense of what was being asked of them. It was never to do with money or prestige.

Endnote

---

7 13th – 14th March 1941.

CHAPTER THREE

THE FORTIES

'ONE OTHER PROVISION which Sir David made for his employees must be mentioned, for it was characteristic of his outlook. In 1943 (sic), during the Second World War, he appointed a full-time Mill Chaplain, an ordained Presbyterian Minister, the Rev. Ian Fraser, B.D., . . . who was to visit the sick, comfort the distressed, conduct short Sunday services, talk over day-to-day problems on a man-to-man basis, and perform the other usual services of a padre . . . but at the same time he was required to do manual work in the Mills alongside the regular workers that he might win their confidence, learn their needs, and by daily contact convey something of the life of the Spirit. It was an experiment, one closely analogous to the Worker-Priest movement in the French Catholic Church; and in the one case as in the other it proved a disappointment to its originators, and has been abandoned.[8]'

When the history of Tullis Russell came to be written in the 1960s this was the record of and conclusion reached about the next stage in Ian's life and work. Some light needs to be shed on the two years from 1942 to 1944 that Ian spent in the paper mills. They were operated by the firm which had developed first under the leadership of the Tullis family and by the time Ian arrived was led by David (later Sir David) Russell. The works, the Rothes and Auchmuty mills, were located near the village of Woodside in central Fife some miles west of Markinch. The site today is within the boundaries of the new town of Glenrothes. It still operates under the Tullis Russell name and remains one of Scotland's foremost paper-making companies.

The interests and character of David Russell are best understood from the Forewords that he wrote for each edition of the company magazine. The Rothmill Quarterly as it was called in the early years was first published in 1929 and continues in publication down to the present time.

In the Foreword for the Easter edition of the Rothmill Quarterly in 1930 David Russell wrote,

> 'The great problem for the organiser and for the worker is how to create the conditions under which work will become interesting, how to give zest to its fulfilment. It is an all-important problem, for it is just as necessary that we should live our lives to the full during working hours as in the times of so-called leisure.[9]'

In the 1920s the New York Chamber of Commerce was encouraged to support the rebuilding of the living quarters of Iona Abbey. Even earlier David Russell spent many happy holidays on Iona. In the 1920s he had initiated retreats for theological students from Scottish universities. David was friendly with George MacLeod. In 1930 George was one of the lecturers at the Iona Retreat.

In 1931 David commissioned plans for the restoration of the Iona Abbey ruins. In 1933 he bought a house on Iona for his family for summer holidays. Friendship between David and George grew. When George was given permission in 1938 to rebuild the abbey living quarters, the plans drawn up earlier by David became the basis for the work under Ian Lindsay the architect. David Russell took a keen interest in what was happening on Iona. In his company magazine, the Rothmill Quarterly in October 1938 he wrote of George MacLeod and the emerging Iona Community:

> 'At Iona there is growing up just now a Community of workers inspired by the faith of one man who has a vision for the future, which by the sheer force of his character and the loyal support of those working with him, is being made real – not as a criticism of the Church, but as a new realisation of the needs not only of the Church but of the Nation.'

What David Russell does not say, although it is believed to be true, is that he provided considerable sums of money to support the rebuilding programme on Iona. As an interesting aside, the cross which stands on the centre of the communion table on Iona was seen by Ian in the British Empire Exhibition of 1938, held in Bellahouston Park in Glasgow. George MacLeod had also seen it there or elsewhere. He was entranced by it. He tried to buy it for Iona only to be told that it was sold. He was later to discover that Dr. David Russell had bought it for the Iona Abbey communion table.

In the summer of 1941 Ian went to a conference on Iona. The work in his father's shop was very much on his mind. He wondered how he could turn the lessons he had learned to good use in his ministry.

During his stay on Iona he met Dr. Russell and heard about his paper mill. Ian discussed the possibility of working alongside the men as a labourer-pastor in the mill. David Russell was sympathetic to Ian's ideas and seemed ready to give him an opportunity to put them to the test.

For years Ian had read reports of committees deciding that, as people would not go to church, the church must go to the people. Yet nothing seemed to happen apart from a note in the minutes of such meetings. By the time Ian had completed his studies he was sick of theories. When God's call came to him he was ready to go wherever he was sent. Ian had always seen his faith as that of a pioneer, willing to take risks. He was willing to tackle the impossible as part of his daily routine.

So it was that in 1942 with the blessing of George MacLeod and through his contacts with David Russell, Ian Fraser committed himself to the post of labourer-chaplain in the Tullis Russell paper mills near Markinch. The omens were good for this new venture given the ethos of the company. Less helpful was the fact that, while the principle was clear – an Iona man was to make a contribution to the Russell family firm – the details had not really been worked out.

Ian had not forgotten the young workers from the shop back in Forres who were unchurched. He was convinced that there were many like them in the Scotland of that day. An echo is surely to be heard here of George in Govan in the thirties. MacLeod had been responsible for a vibrant church but he knew that beyond the boundary wall of the church daily life had gone sour, untouched as it was by the gospel.

Ian was given board and lodging in a house in the middle of the paper mill grounds. The mother of one of the managers, Mrs. Thomson, looked after him for the first year. A paper mill turned out to be ideal for the experiment. In every department labourers were required. The mill operated a three shift system. Ian could work as part of two shifts on any one day, working over the end of one shift and the beginning of the next. In the course of two weeks in a department those who had been on night shift changed to day shift. In time Ian had contact with everyone in each section and as a result worked alongside most of the 1200 men employed at the mill.

Ian recalls arriving at the paper mill, both terrified and determined. He had realised little of what he was committed to. No one had voted for his arrival, and him, a minister. He took his legs, one after another, and made them walk into that alien territory!

In the mill Ian laboured among the men. They seemed impressed that he sought no favours. He had been blessed with good strong shoulders. There was evidence in some of the workers of the damage the work could cause if good technique was replaced by brute force. In the vats it was necessary to fork the paper pulp to get it to the next stage. Ian had learned the technique for lifting weights in the university gym.

In the midst of this costly experiment one thing made it a little easier. Men destined for management in later years were made to do basic work in the various sections to learn about the whole industrial process. In the early days Ian was viewed as one of this group. He found it hard to know how he should introduce himself. If he announced from the beginning that he was a minister it might have looked as if he expected to be treated differently. If he said nothing and the truth emerged later he might be thought to be spying on the men. He prayed about this matter and tried to let his situation and his relationships develop naturally.

When his status became known some men at once apologised for their bad language. As time passed their speech remained colourful but the worst of the cursing was suppressed. In time as Ian moved from one section to another, word went ahead. 'The minister will be with you next week, but he's alright.' That assurance was a theological statement. Some time after Ian had settled in to the mill the company magazine made reference to his arrival.

'The experiment in factory chaplaincy now going on in our mills is part of a general movement of the church towards industry. It is an experiment which, whether it succeeds or fails, will have much to say regarding the attitude of the Church and the worker towards one another in our generation . . . The Tullis Russell experiment differs from (other chaplaincies) in being a full-time job and involving manual work with the men as part of the minister's approach. The length of its duration will depend on the value it proves to have for all concerned. 'The chaplain attached to the Mills is the Revd Ian M Fraser BD who can be found either in the Mills or in his office near the main entrance of the Canteen[10].'

The mill was continuous process, as it was steam powered. A head of steam had to be kept up from Monday to Saturday. On Sunday maintenance people were on site. That day Ian led three short services in different parts of the mill. They were in demand even from people with no connection with the Kirk. The services lasted about twenty minutes. They were held during smoking and tea breaks. Ian had to learn the language that had meaning for the participants. If that had not been done the message would simply have gone over the heads of those for whom the services were designed.

Story telling played a significant role. Jesus' theology was to be found in his day in lived and spoken stories. Stories flow. They both are aided by memory and are aids to memory. When Ian preached sermons in later days when he was at Selly Oak, he included a children's message. The children of one family used to work on these stories until they were word perfect. Years later they would retell the stories and correct one another if mistakes were made. In such a way oral tradition and oral history lives. They can be more accurate than the written word for the very tone of voice can be remembered.[11]

In his use of stories Ian did not neglect scholarship. The traditional understanding of Jesus as meek and mild when he called children to him jarred with Ian. He examined the text and discovered that in fact the main thing to be understood was that Jesus in his reaction exhibits absolute annoyance[12] and frustration, not with the children but with those who should have known better.

Ian went into the paper mill to live the gospel. Opportunities to live the Kingdom arose naturally. These sat alongside the informal worship times. The experiment was always for him to be about more than recruiting new or lapsed members for the local church.

The company magazine carried reports of some highlights of the work Ian was doing in his ministry. In December 1942 this was mentioned:

'A workers' Christmas Service was conducted by the Reverend Ian Fraser, B.D., at Auchmuty Mill. The Service was largely attended and much appreciated.' In the early months of the following year we find: 'The Rothes WRI held their Scottish night on 12 January 1943. The Rev. Ian Fraser, B.D. read some Robert Burns' poems, told some amusing stories and sang a solo.'

As early as January 1943 Ian made known his findings in light of his experience in the paper mills. He sent these conclusions to John Baillie in the Divinity Faculty in New College. He contended that the six-year period of academic training could too easily detach students from the real world. This detachment can lead to a desire for a life of comfort and security. Ian admits to being saddened by men who began their study for the ministry with fresh ideas and enthusiasm who by the end of their course were willing to accept things as they had always been.

Ian concludes that no words will adequately convey the lessons he learned in the paper mills. He suggests that academic training for the ministry be limited to five years. The sixth and final year should be spent in work in the area intended for ministry. The student who intends to minister in an agricultural area should work for a year as a farm labourer: another who intends to work in an industrial area should spend a year in some industrial establishment. With this suggestion he includes his support for participation in 'evangelistic campaigns' such as those run by D.P. Thomson. While he saw no benefit of such campaigns within the workplace he believed they had a part to play in church life as a means of quickening the spirit of congregations. The question of evangelistic campaigns would later be raised when Ian was in Rosyth some ten years after his time in the Mills.

During Ian's first year in the mill, Margaret was teaching in Lockerbie. The company magazine carried this notice of marriage in the summer of 1943:

> 'FRASER – STEWART. At Greyfriars Church, Edinburgh, on 27th July 1943, by the Revd James Black B.D. Edinburgh assisted by the Revd Ian A Mackenzie, M.A. Edinburgh. Revd Ian M. Fraser B.D. (of Forres, Morrayshire [sic]), to Margaret D.D. Stewart M.A. Thornhill, Dumfriesshire. Mr. Fraser is Industrial Chaplain at the Mills.'

Ian has remained grateful that Margaret should have agreed to marry him while he was working on a labourer's wage. The couple were allocated a 3-roomed company cottage in the nearby village of Woodside. There was a very large garden. It had become a wilderness. The neighbours complained. Ian cleared the place of weeds and scattered a few seeds. He was sure nothing would grow. He was no gardener. Much to his surprise plants grew even for him!

Margaret told Ian she would be happy to share in his work. He thought she meant to work among the dozen or so women who worked in the mill shovelling shavings or sorting rags. In fact she intended to use their new home as a place where people from the mill and their families would be welcome.

In the second year Ian had a small office in the mill. He was doing more pastoral work. It could not always be done as the men worked. He was one week in the office, one week labouring. It allowed him to revisit all the departments. His pastoral work involved a wide range of family circumstances and problems. In that second year not only did the pastoral work increase but Ian took time to think through what the experience was teaching.

The company magazine continues to make reference to Ian's work:
> 'Services were held in Auchmuty and Rothes Mills on Christmas Day (1943) and were conducted by the Rev. Ian Fraser B.D. A good representation of workers attended though not all found it possible to leave their jobs. Mr. Charles Thomson, painter, led the praise.'

Ian was clearly intent on involving workers in his ministry where he could.

There is an extremely interesting reference to Ian's work in a farewell discourse from R. Kinnes, an employee in the mill who was retiring in 1943 after 44 years of service to Tullis Russell. He gives details of the various paper making machines he had worked on and gives details of the Markinch Institute with its various provisions for the workforce. He concludes his review of his time in the mill thus:
> 'We have a Padre amongst us now, . . . (he) has literally been through the mill, working his way from the rag-cutting department to the finishing house, and has therefore come in contact with most of the workers. His presence is bound to have an influence on the workers which will show through course of time. His duties consist in visiting the sick and going

amongst the workers in general. He also gives a short service or two on Sundays for those working unavoidable overtime. Ten minutes are allowed for this purpose. The service is followed by man-to-man talk, which is very helpful. The Firm has built a small 'shack' for the padre, where he can be consulted at any time by those who are in trouble of any kind, or by any who would like advice on any matter.'

Ian recalls the friendship of Andy Grant. He was wicketkeeper for the Freuchie Cricket Team. As Ian worked alongside him he was encouraged to re-connect with the church. He took a much larger part in it in the years which followed. Robert Davidson, Professor of Old Testament in Glasgow, later a moderator of the Church of Scotland, said in a speech to the General Assembly that part of his formation in the Christian faith could be traced back to the time when his father worked alongside Ian in the paper mill. At that time Ian had not even known his father. Contacts were made in these days that could not have been established in any other way.

Over time Ian discovered practices, which he believed to be unfair to the workers. He took these matters to the management. This was happening in the years before worker-priests in France found themselves in a similar position. The mill Ian was in did not recognise trade unions. A previous attempt to introduce a union led to the proposer being thrown down a flight of stairs. The management argued from its paternalistic position: 'we are a kindly firm so there can be no need of unions here.'

There was a government requirement that there should be a work's council. Ian encouraged men to put themselves forward to represent the interests of the workers in terms of pay and conditions. They responded, 'All they will allow on the agenda is whether we need a few more hooks to hang our coats on.' In this the workers knew better than Ian what would happen. Management kept discussion to the trivial, the insignificant. Nothing of substance was allowed in that forum. Ian wrote to the management to highlight the injustice of the situation.

Another matter arose. A new canteen was to be provided. Ian got a hold of some of the management people and said, 'This is a chance to break down some of the divisions in the workforce.' Dr. Russell told him that the only division was to be between those with dirty overalls and those with clean clothes. It seemed a reasonable division. The reality of the new canteen meant an even greater degree of division into 'them' and 'us'. Ian wrote to the management and told them that they had missed a chance to build community in the workplace. His letter was very much resented by the company secretary, Mr. Black, who in other establishments would have been known as the General Manager.

After two years an assessment was made on Ian's time in the mill. He indicated that given one more year he believed he would be able to leave behind a core group of twelve who could continue a caring remit for their fellow-workers. Only one of the twelve was a churchman. The number twelve was coincidental; it had nothing to do with the twelve disciples. Ian hoped to move after that year to another mill or industrial concern. Ian was asked for his opinion but no one consulted the workers. Nor was Dr. Russell asked to comment. Ian did ask that the workers have their say. He was convinced that he had the backing of the workforce, including the Communists. His request went unheeded.

The management announced that they did not want the experiment to continue. It was to be ended forthwith. It was reported that their decision was unanimous. The reason given was that Ian had interfered with management decisions. Ian had dealt with the management only by letter. There was no opportunity to meet with them even though Dr. Russell said he thought of Ian as management.

While what Dr. Russell initiated then hardly seems out of the ordinary at the beginning of the 21st century in terms of worker participation and chaplaincy, it was clearly ground breaking in the 1940s. Dr. Russell was disappointed that the experiment was deemed a failure. He took the disappointment personally. He blamed Ian for not seeing the project through. George MacLeod took a different line. He concluded that if there had not been 'failure' it would have suggested that not enough had been risked. He said that if there had been no problems that would itself have been a problem – suggesting too cosy a relationship on all sides.

Some fifty years later, Mr. Smail, the engineering manager in the 1940s phoned Ian. 'There is something you should know. You should have been told this, years ago. The management team wanted the experiment to continue. The General Manager, Mr. Black, had told the management group, 'You will vote unanimously against any continuation of this experiment, or else . . . We caved in!'

Dr. Russell, the proprietor of the mill, trusted his staff. Some of them were worthy of his trust, some not. That said, Dr. Russell was a kind man. During the worst of the Depression in the thirties he had kept on workers and employed them in painting and re-painting rooms; cleaning and re-cleaning machinery. This was just to give the men work. He failed, however, to see how ruthless people in power could be in an industrial situation.

It appears that the company magazine makes no direct reference to the ending of the chaplaincy experiment directly. In the autumn of 1944 David Russell writes:

> 'If it could be said that a business organisation could have a vocation, our Firm's vocation would not be just to make paper . . . The purpose behind it all, the vocation, would be something else, something based upon responsibility to the community – its health, its happiness; the encouragement and development of craftsmanship and all that is best in life . . . Something easy to imagine, but difficult to realise.'

Mr. John Black, who had been so keen to be rid of Ian, lived only months after Ian's departure. The autumn 1944 edition of the Rothmill Quarterly Magazine includes a fulsome appreciation. Given the Scottish tradition of never speaking ill of the dead it is to be expected that an in-house publication will major on praise and tend to gloss over shortcomings. That said there seems to be a genuine affection for the man in his obituary.

John Black died on 7th October 1944. He was sixty-eight years of age and passed away after a short illness. He rose from the position of cashier when he joined the company at the age of thirty to become Company Secretary before he was fifty. He became a Director in the family firm in 1942. That was the year Ian arrived at the instigation of David Russell. The newcomer was just a third of John Black's age. It is possible that this difference goes some way to explain the distance between them in the two years they shared at the mill.

The record in the company magazine gives insight into John Black's interests. These included motorcycling, rifle shooting and golf; he was twice club captain at Markinch Golf Club. In his later years he took a particular interest in solving chess problems. He had a deep love of Scotland and was never short of a story when he spoke, often with good humour. A mathematician of note, Mr. Black was interested in technical developments which could profitably be adopted by the Firm. While negative evidence must always be treated with great care nothing is said of his involvement in church life. In another obituary for a long-serving member of staff the religious commitment of the deceased is given at some length. It is an open question as to whether he failed to value the contribution of a churchman in 'his' mill or whether he preferred the church to know its place beyond the boundary fence.

What can be stated with greater assurance is that Mr. Black took a particular personal interest in the welfare of the Firm's employees. He developed an Employees' Savings Association. One of his pet projects had been the development of a new work's canteen. He felt he was principally involved for its smooth running. It was this venture that Ian had dared to criticise. Moreover the writer of Black's obituary notes that 'any employee seeking advice or assistance could always approach Mr. Black confident that he would have a sympathetic listener whose help would not be withheld.' Is it not probable therefore that John Black saw Ian Fraser as either unwelcome or unnecessary competition? Did he resent an industrial chaplain foisted on him by an owner who had failed to realise his contribution to the life and welfare of 'his' workforce. We might also ask whether in his close involvement with the workforce Ian failed to build the best of relationships with management.

As Ian's story was shared some folk said admiringly, 'You are really identified with working-class people!' Ian replied 'I am not! The people in the mill are tied to their jobs. I have escape routes. I have two degrees. All I am doing is identifying as far as possible with people in a situation strange to us. We can get alongside, bearing the consequences. That's all. Jesus consorting with publicans and sinners, his having nowhere to lay his head, his being excluded and dishonoured, are signs for us.'

Ian's considered view of the time in the paper mill was given most extensively in July 1943. Dr. Joe Oldham[13] from the Christian Frontier Council invited Ian to report on his time at the paper mill. His response was published as a supplement to The Christian Newsletter under the title 'Masks and Men'.

This makes interesting reading sixty years after it was written. The military analogies are clear. One example will suffice – describing the way clergymen (sic) and laymen view one another Ian writes 'We smile at one another across no-man's land . . . A frontier lies between'. It reminds us that Ian's time at the mill fell during war time. This was a difficult time because many of the experienced mill workers were away to the war but it also meant that Ian's time at the mill was in some ways facilitated for there were many men undertaking unfamiliar work. Oldham noted that Ian saw his new venture as crossing a frontier. He was clear that this was not a 'revolt against academic training but the completion of that training.' In fact Ian had spelled out where he stood with care. The edited version printed lacked the force of what he had in fact written. 'The move into industry was not a rejection of ministry but a search for authentic ministry, not a rejection of theology but a search for relevant theology, not a rejection of scholarship but its completion.' A threefold cord should have remained unbroken.

Ian explains the nature of his labouring work and the other duties he undertook as a chaplain. In time the men came to see he wanted them to be nothing but their real selves. His time in the mill brought him to believe that normally, 'As ministers we go about daily, shaking hands with masks. We rarely know people as they are, but only the face they put on towards us. We see them in their leisure hours, their tempers curbed, under conscious restraint. Working with men in the mill ripped these masks aside. Character cannot be hid because hitches are unavoidable.' Ian went on to discover that church visitation can similarly be very superficial. When he visited men he really knew in their own homes, something more worthwhile became possible.

Other changes followed. The language of all of his sermons became earthed. Prayer which so easily can become monotony, in the mill was 'agonising entreaty to God for courage to face another day of open tension and opportunity.' Ian found it healthy to be reminded that one can be a teacher in one field and a learner in others and that leads to healthy relationships for human beings. In an echo of the great early days on Iona Ian discovered that spending time working on a common task deepens real bonds of fellowship. He is convinced that spending time with people produces the best opportunities to share the faith. If there is some truth that George MacLeod on Iona spoke more about 'nothing building community so well as the shared common task' as a theory, we can be sure that Ian put it into practice in the mill. With a twinkle in his eye, Ian recalls one incident when he actually caught George doing manual work!

Clearly the rough and tumble of the mill with swearing and profanities challenged Ian but he refused to allow such matters to hinder the task he had set his hand to. He concludes, 'We must first affirm what is in men before setting them right and not be put off with trifles which are external.' Beyond industrial chaplaincy Ian saw that the Christian church must never stand aside from sport, social items such as dancing or rambles or it will give credence to the idea that Christianity is not to do with the whole of life – whereas in fact it brings true pleasures and true perspectives to it.

It is interesting to see the characteristics that Ian lists as requirements for any person who undertakes the work such as he gave himself to in the paper mills. Those who know Ian best will recognise many of his own qualities. Those listed are
- Not easily embarrassed, and ready with a witty retort in answer to attempts to embarrass.
- Not easily shocked by morals and manners different form one's own
- Willing to work faithfully and hard
- Ready to take part in ordinary conversation without forcing it into religious channels
- Wakeful to opportunities for teaching
- Not demanding special respect to begin with, but willing to work for a good reputation

- Prepared to be continuously afraid, and yet go out to face another day, and another and another, not flinging the whole thing up when sparks begin to fly
- Willing to be overwhelmed by complexities and rely only on prayer.

The conclusion reached in this overview of the time at the mill is not that such qualities will be difficult to find, but that 'the Christian gospel is able to meet the desperate needs of the day.'

Ian's disappointment at the premature end, in his eyes, of the paper mill experiment was very real. But he continued involvement with the church's industrial mission. Within the Iona Community he worked with Penry Jones; with the Church of Scotland he collaborated with a recently appointed chaplaincy organiser, George Wilkie – a fellow enthusiast who was both Iona Community and Church of Scotland. Further afield Ian debated with Ted Wickham who belonged to Sheffield Industrial Mission. Ted, an Anglican, believed in dog-collared men going into industry to talk with the work force during 'smoke-times' and lunch breaks. Ian considered that approach intrusive, lacking solidarity with people. In time the Church of Scotland developed their industrial mission which followed neither the Fraser nor the Wickham approach. Ordained ministers were attached to industries and left to make their way by informal contacts. Cameron Wallace, also an Iona man, in the shipyards on Clydeside was a notable example.

Ian took heart in all this. He was content that he had established by his time at the mill that ordained ministers could move beyond the traditional role they had in parishes. He also recognised that talk of industrial mission was becoming more acceptable within churches generally.

In June 1944 the company magazine had carried the following announcement:

'Fraser – At Elsie Inglis Hospital Edinburgh on 1st June 1944 to Rev Ian and Mrs Fraser, a daughter (Anne). Rev. Ian Fraser is Chaplain at the Mills.'

So at the end of his second year, Ian found himself unemployed with a wife and a daughter to support.

Ian had no alternative plan in view for the year that lay ahead. Vacancies in the ministry normally take time to fill. The minister in Hopemount Church, Arbroath, had gone to be a chaplain in the wartime army. Ian was offered the opportunity to stand in for him for a month or two. It gave Ian his first involvement in parish life. As he had been committed to work in The Pleasance in Edinburgh he had not been required to undertake parish attachments during his time at New College. The time at Arbroath was not easy particularly because it was a time of uncertainty. The war was on.

Then in 1945 Ian was appointed as Scottish General Secretary for the Student Christian Movement. He was responsible for the SCM in Edinburgh and St. Andrews Universities while an American Dale Brown looked after Glasgow and Aberdeen. Structurally Ian had responsibility for the matters affecting the whole of Scotland and was the link person to the United Kingdom SCM bodies.

In the SCM Ian prepared material for 24 study groups during his first year as Scottish Secretary for SCM in consultation with the local committee. He took a firm approach with group leaders and assistant leaders. A preparation weekend was held before term started. If a group leader missed this weekend without good reason the assistant leader was promoted to do the job.

Ian remembers a weekend spent on a school campsite doing such preparation. The studies for the weekend were based on Colossians. David Reid, minister in Greenbank Parish Church in Edinburgh and an ex-prisoner of war, was asked to lead the weekend. Ian was of the opinion that if a person speaks first and time is then left for questions, the discussion is limited. He asked David to prepare material for each session then to keep it in his back pocket. The participants were put into groups of five or six. They were asked to spend half an hour or more working on the text to discover what it said to them in their own lives. The groups then shared their findings in plenary session. David listened to this and then made his contribution. Rich insights were made available to all.

An opportunity arose for Ian to contribute to a series of twelve SCM discussion leaflets. Ian produced the last of these on the subject of prayer. It had the provocative title: *I Don't Pray – It Rains; I Pray Hard – It Still Rains.*

In his introduction he exposes flawed understandings of prayer. By way of contrast he goes on, 'Christian prayer begins, not with man and what he wants but with God and what He is and how He acts. God is love. His purpose in making man is that he should learn freely to choose to live as a son of God.' Ian then tackled some practical matters relating to this subject of prayer which was clearly already close to his heart.

A quadrennial SCM conference in London was arranged for just after the war. One hundred places were reserved for students from Scottish universities. Ian was appalled. The places would never be filled! To supplement the numbers, he wrote to a wide range of university societies offering each one a place at the conference, if it were booked by the given deadline. If more than one place was required requests would be placed in a queue. This highlighted the importance of the event. Names of 133 delegates in all were put forward. Buses were hired. Finance was found. Assumed scarcity can generate a market!

The SCM group as a whole met weekly in Edinburgh. The study groups also met on a weekly basis. They would be working away on different topics: the arms trade, nuclear weapons relating prayer and politics. Each study group might have input into one main meeting in an academic session. About 70 people met in the general meeting. SCM speakers were encouraged to generate debate and discussion.

Ian was Scottish General Secretary of SCM for three years. The post involved administration and pastoral care of student members. Opportunities were given to be involved more widely. He was invited to participate in a mission to Edinburgh along with David Reid, JKS (Jacko) Reid, the father of David Steel (first presiding officer of the Holyrood Parliament) and David Easton, who had come to the fore in wartime. As someone in touch with student life such calls came to Ian.

The SCM group in St. Andrews were mature folk. They needed only minimal input from Ian. Most of Ian's work was undertaken in Edinburgh. Ian had found real benefit from his contact with SCM in his own student days. This was surely part of the basis for the work he was now undertaking. As surely, the time he had spent in the mill informed his leadership among the students he now served.

When Ian and Margaret moved to Edinburgh from Arbroath they rented a 'flat'. It was three stairs up in the Meadows area. The furniture arrived from Arbroath with two men, one of whom had a medical certificate to say that he was not lift anything heavy! That let lasted a week. An eccentric owner was intruding on their space. Unreasonable rules were increasingly applied. Margaret and the baby were temporarily sent to Margaret's mother. A sheriff officer helped Ian rescue their furniture from this first flat. He knew the woman. When he arrived at her door he opened the letterbox and shouted 'Post!' He then stood aside out of sight. The woman opened the door. He put his foot in it to keep it open. The furniture was re-possessed. Margaret returned to Edinburgh and family life went on.

A share in a house appeared in Mayfield Terrace: the share was two rooms and access to a communal kitchen and bathroom. Six other family groups lived in what had been at one time a single residence. When Keith was born it was explained that children were very welcome as long as they made no noise during the night! The parents had almost to smother the weans.

At one point Margaret got the shock of her life. One of their rooms was upstairs. She suddenly realised that her daughter had disappeared. Anne, who must have been about two at the time, found a window which had been left open to air the room and had climbed out on to the window ledge. She was standing there with a drop of about 40 feet below her. Margaret had to discipline herself to cross that room as naturally as possible, without alarming Anne, till she could grab her safely. Afterwards Margaret was all shook up inside. Little wonder!

The time arrived for the Fraser family to move on. After just three years in the capital they answered a call and returned to the Kingdom of Fife.

Endnotes

8 Tullis Russell 1809–1959 CDM Ketelbey 1967 p240 Ian remembers the events differently as will be seen later.

9 Foreword Sir David Russell RMQ Easter 1930.

10 Ian is certain that he was not provided with an office until his second year at the mill. Perhaps it had always been the intention of management to provide an office – it just took time to construct it.

11 An example of one such children's sermon is included as Appendix A.

12 The Greek here suggests that 'Jesus got his birse up and bawled out the disciples' IMF.

13 Joe Oldham had been secretary to the influential Edinburgh Conference in 1910.

CHAPTER FOUR

ROSYTH

IN 1948 JOHN (Ben) Johnston, the minister in Inverkeithing, in the shadow of the Forth Rail Bridge, asked Ian if he would be interested in the vacancy in the parish of Rosyth. This parish lay to the west of his own and Ben was interim moderator. Rosyth Parish was at that time dominated by the Naval Dockyard on the north shore of the Forth Estuary.

The parish seemed to have everything going for it! The situation was one of complete meltdown. During the period of the church vacancy a short leet of possible appointees had been drawn up. They were less than impressed when they discovered that the congregation had largely deserted and a breakaway group had started meeting in the local Co-operative Hall. The members of the short leet said a polite 'no thank you' and left. A second short leet was drawn up. The result was the same. It was at that point Johnston contacted Ian Fraser. With Margaret's complete agreement Ian accepted the call. At his induction, the charge was given by his teacher and mentor, the Very Rev. Professor John Baillie.

Writing at the end of his time in Rosyth, Ian recalls spending time, taking in the prospect of Rosyth Parish. To the north lay Dunfermline with its Abbey. At Ian's feet was Rosyth, Dunfermline's residential satellite, with too few shops and too few amenities for its thousands of inhabitants. The planners, however, had attempted to encourage neighbourliness with curving streets and short cul-de-sacs which opened on to grassy communal squares. To the south lay the naval dockyard: bread and butter for most of Rosyth's inhabitants, though in post war years, employment there was sometimes less certain than it had been.

The Parish Church stood in the centre of the community; railings long gone for the war effort, the church hall a wooden construction surely erected to meet a temporary need some thirty years earlier. Like an adopted child making his way in the new family, Ian began the process of getting to know the place and the people. He was minister to the whole parish.

It is surely no accident that the published record[14] of the time in Rosyth is dedicated by Ian to his wife, Margaret. She was active in their early days in Rosyth helping to heal the breach in the congregation. The Women's Fellowship was too fundamentalist in its approach to the Bible. The Women's Guild used it too little. Margaret sorted them both out. She helped the Fellowship to see that there was no value in being biblically concerned if that had no relation to the way you lived in the world. She helped the Guild to see that life in the world needed to be nourished and guided by biblical insights. She helped both sides to see that the church would be stronger if they worked together side by side. Beyond anything else Ian thought it was Margaret's capacity to relate with understanding to all kinds of people which meant the rift between the women's groups was healed.

People drew strength from her. To spend time in her company enabled people to leave refreshed.

One of the first tasks Ian undertook with the men of the church was the building of a wall round the church to replace the railings. An Irish woman turned up while the work was going on. 'What does your minister think of all this?' she asked the workers in general. 'Well if you go down there, that is him with the cement barrow!' Ian was never slow at rolling up his sleeves and getting on with the work.

Once the Frasers got settled in to Rosyth and looked around it became clear that the work really required them to have a car. In the parish itself there were 12,000 people. Hospitals and nursing homes were scattered around, some miles away. The problem was money. A friend of Ian's had a baby Austin which he fancied. But it was to cost £80 and he only had £30 to spare. On hearing the position his father stepped in and provided the balance so that he was able to get the car.[15]

It was 23 years old when they bought it. Ian said *they* bought it but Margaret would never have allowed him to go ahead with the purchase if she had been there at the time. The bodywork was good. The engine was good. The inside was a wreck. However, once Margaret was faced with the situation, she just rolled up her sleeves and got going. The inside of the car was stripped out completely, apart from the bucket seats at the front which were still in reasonable order. Ian was fortunate in finding some green plastic material being sold off cheaply in a shop. He got plywood, cut out panelling for the sides, stuck on the plastic and fitted the panels. Down in the ship breaker's yard in Inverkeithing he found an armchair. It was the size of half the space for the back seat, so he cut the chair in half and fitted the two parts together on a wooden base. They had been given a mill felt when they left Markinch and Margaret dyed this green, covered the bucket seats and the new back seat. It completed a very neat internal transformation.

The wee green pea was a great wee car. They had it for seven years. If it ran out of water or oil, it would just stop like a pony which had lost its way and wait for fresh orders. When it was filled up it just toddled on happily. It was recognised everywhere in the area. People would look up from their shopping or from their conversation and wave to the wee green pea as it passed along the road.

There was no boot in the car. When the three children were occupying the back seat, there was very little storage space, mainly at their feet. The answer was a roof rack. Ian could not afford to buy one. So he made one. A discarded playpen was adapted. This 'roof rack' meant that the family were able to take baggage, tent and equipment not only to many parts of Britain but also to the continent. When Ian was asked to speak at a conference (he was fortunate to have this happening from the time he was in his thirties) he would ask whether he could take the air fare and find his own way there. He then took the car and the family with him. They would stay on a camp site while he did his stuff – but they could then often stay on for a holiday in the country where the conference was being held.

Otherwise the Frasers had to find cheap ways of holidaying. On one occasion they got the opportunity to lease for a week or two a building up at Glen Devon. It was more of a glorified hut than a house but it did have beds and basic kitchen equipment. As Ian remembers it, they had to carry their bedding, pots and pans and so on – all in the roof rack. When it came time to return, he wondered how the wee green pea would manage. They had found themselves in an area where wild raspberries were plentiful and could not resist the temptation. Somehow, somewhere they got enough jars and returned with thirty-six pounds of raspberry jam under the back seat with the children sitting on it.

Another time the family got a loan of a small marquee from the Boys' Brigade in Rosyth. They put it up in cousin John's field (John McLean) near Balfron, north of Glasgow. Cows are curious creatures and they came around, catching their legs in the guy ropes. So Ian built a hedge of thorns to keep them out. He was quite proud of himself. He found, however, that the cows treated the thorns as fodder specially provided for them, ate their way through, and when the family returned after a jaunt, had actually got inside the tent!

Ian realised that one of the gifts of parish breakdown is that people are desperate enough to try alternative ways of working. Once he had assessed the situation he considered that hope for the future lay in rooting the life of the congregation in the bible. He started with the kirk session. He raised the matter at one of his first meetings with his elders. He was rebuffed. The consensus seems to have been 'That's not session business!' After a month or two Ian tried again. It was grudgingly agreed to allow ten minutes of bible work at the start of each meeting. So half of the session turned up with apologies ten minutes late; with the others discussion was like getting blood out of a stone.

Ian persisted. At last God gave that precious gift of frustration. Mr. Taylor, a painter in the dockyard said, 'I am fed up with this. It is neither one thing nor the other. I move that for a year we have half an hour's bible study to start our meeting, that all of us turn up on time, and that if it doesn't work we kill it off at the end of the year.' This was unanimously agreed. In the months that followed the members of the session became so fascinated by the relevance of biblical texts to the issues they faced in the dockyard that they did not notice when the year was up. It was about 18 months before the painter rose again.

'I got this all wrong,' he said. 'At first when I told the wife that the minister wanted us to do bible study, she said, 'It's eleven o'clock at night before you come home as it is. If you do bible study as well it will be midnight!' It hasn't been like that at all. The bible itself has given us a better judgement on what matters. We now get rid in no time things which previously would have taken us an age. I move that from now on we have an hour's bible study at the start of every meeting.'

Ian remembers the following incident. The kirk session had spent an hour on Jesus' encounter with the epileptic boy when he came down from the Mount of Transfiguration. Ian observed that he felt they had got deep into that incident and had shared perceptive comments from their own experiences.

An elder disagreed. 'We dodged the difficult bit!'

Ian came back. The experiences of prayer which they had shared, he thought were fresh and full of insight.

'Aye, that was good,' the elder admitted. 'But it wasn't just prayer that was needed for the young lad to be cured. It was prayer and *fasting*. We did nothing about fasting.'

Ian took up the challenge. 'When copies of the bible were made by hand the copier might occasionally add something, which accorded well with his own conviction. For instance a monk who led a very austere life could have slipped in the words 'and fasting' even if the words were not in the original text.

'It says *and fasting*', was all that Ian got by way of reply.

He tried another tack. In the Middle East and in eastern countries there was a tradition of fasting which made it a far more natural part of life than it would ever be for us in this part of the world. Even if the words were original, they need not apply to every church everywhere.

'It says *and fasting*,' the elder insisted.

He would not budge. Ian had to agree that they would look into the matter at the next meeting. He would try to identify relevant passages of scripture. It was then that they discovered the marvellous reflection on fasting in Isaiah 58; that the reality of fasting is not in outward conformity or even in self-denial as such, but in self denial which promotes justice: a fairer sharing of food and other resources which God has supplied for the needs of the whole human family. In this way lessons were learned.

Those who occupied offices in the church also had to be sorted out. It became clear that as the situation had deteriorated, members who had appropriate skills had given up, and others, out of the kindness of their hearts, had occupied the abandoned posts. If the church was to serve the world effectively, steps had to be taken to replace these volunteers. One of the hardest jobs Ian has done in his life was to go to these people, affirm their concern for the church and urge them to see that their gifts lay elsewhere. He suggested that they demit their current responsibilities. They did so. Not one person left to go attend another church.

The minister worked with a team of elders to do God's work in the parish. There came a time when three new elders were needed. Ian talked with those who, the congregation thought, might have undertaken this work. He suggested that they come back to him when time had been taken to consider the matter. Some weeks later he asked if a time could be arranged to meet with them. They replied, 'It's alright. We've been meeting and praying. We've seen what is required. We'll all come forward.' That is clearly different from landing on someone in a fairly arbitrary way.[16]

On one occasion a neighbour said to Margaret, 'Ian terrifies me!' 'I am not surprised,' she replied, 'but in what way in particular?' 'Well, when new members join, he consults the person himself/herself and the designated elder about their gifts, interests, spare time and so on, and he/she is given a part to play in the light of these.' 'So?' 'Well, then he just leaves them to get on with it!' 'And would they get on with it if he fussed round them like a hen round chickens?' asked Margaret.

On a Sunday morning in Rosyth, Ian had a strong march of worship in the service. People knew where they were going and so could be involved. In the evening a much greater variety of church experience was the practice. After the Reformation, psalm singing and later hymn singing allowed the people to be involved in worship. Hymns can be used to carry faith through the generations. The poorest hymns will generally fall by the wayside. Individuals can associate themselves through the hymns with the communion of saints. The church is a community on the move. In time unnecessary baggage can be left behind. Too often, Ian heard baptism being related to cleansing by water. He responded by writing a hymn which restored the original understanding in baptism that of dying to self and rising to new life in Christ; losing your life and finding it again. Hymns were no mere space-fillers!

Ian was known in Rosyth as 'the man who will not baptise'. It was a half-truth. It should have been 'the man who will not baptise without sitting down with the parents to make sure they have understood what they were doing.' The truth was that in Rosyth Ian had baptisms galore. Baptisms were always held in front of the whole congregation. There was one occasion when he baptised a baby of a few weeks and a man of seventy at the same service. There was a folk myth in Rosyth, which had some basis in fact. When, at a baptismal service, Ian picked up a child exercising it lungs, silence descended. There is no record whether he had the same effect on his own youngsters in the family home.

Too often Ian felt that I Corinthians 14 was dismissed as significant only for the ecstatic fringe of the church. Ian noted that the passage starts with the Greek word '*hotan*' – 'every time' – every time you meet this is how worship should be. To the church in Corinth Paul gives two main guidelines. Whatever you offer in worship should help to build up the people and if someone else has something that needs saying, know when to shut up. For Ian the section which calls on women to be silent has all the marks of a later insertion. Take it out and the text flows. Ian was clear that variety in worship keeps it fresh and relevant. One of his Easter services included a dialogue presented by members of the congregation. It was entitled Easter Encounter:

'How goes your life?' said the pastor.

'My life is humble, sir' said the man, 'and full of monotony. Day follows night.'

'And what is your service of God?'

'I dung the ground and turn it. I plant and sow. I gain food for my family and food for my neighbour, the ironmonger, from whom I have my spade.'

'But what of your worship of God?'

The man held out his arms knotted and wiry. 'I am my offering,' he said.

Somewhat testily the pastor persisted. 'What is your work for the church?'

'Anyone who needs a fence or a gate mended comes to me,' was the reply. 'I am secretary of my trade union and sit on the Hall Committee. In my spare time, I make toys for the children of the village.'

'Have you no understanding of spiritual things?' asked the pastor.

Supposing him to be the gardener, he turned on his heels and went on his way. With a sigh, the man picked up his spade, spat on torn hands and resumed his work.

From the beginning Ian saw the Sunday evening service as an opportunity to try out different approaches. On occasion he would organise a communal sermon. Ian reckoned these were some of the biggest risks he ever took. Communal sermons could only take place when there was some concern which affected the whole Rosyth community. Their work was overwhelmingly in the dockyard. The concern might have related to one of the recurring threats to close the dockyard. Passages of the bible were given out beforehand focused on the importance of work. In the week leading up to the service, people would get hold of their neighbours. 'Come on, you have to help us understand how as Christians we should face the possible closure of the dockyard.' 'But I'm a Roman Catholic!' 'We need Roman Catholics' 'I'm an atheist!' 'Good, we are short of atheists!' About 140 people would gather for the service, saying under their breath, 'He's not going to get me to speak.' At the communion table Ian would have four people two on each side. They were there 'for starters', contributing two sentences each which had to lead from biblical insights to realities which had to be faced. Then Ian held his breath!

In every case a thoughtful experience resulted. Not only so, but members disciplined one another. If someone said something which interrupted the development, the next one might say, 'Look, we may get round to that point later on but first we have to do a better job on the matter we are dealing with.' Ian was convinced that no one man/one woman band, can compare with the richness of experience of different committed people seeking light for their communal path through prayer, bible study and the sharing of faith perceptions at the heart of worship.

In Bible, Congregation and Community Ian has much to say about the significance of prayer in the life of the individual and the church. He highlights what he learned of prayer through the prayer discipline of the Iona Community. 'Prayer is a continuing relationship between Christ and the Church.'

While visiting in the parish, Ian came across a woman with cancer. She had no church connection. In time she asked Ian to pray for her. She believed that Jesus could heal her in the moment and return her to health in this life. Equally she believed that she could go down into death with Jesus and be raised beyond the grave, healed of the cancer. Jesus said in a similar circumstance, 'I have not found such faith no, not in Israel.' (Matt 8:10)

He recalls another occasion when a young man in the congregation was involved in a serious accident. Ian shared the news in the Sunday morning service which followed and led the congregation in prayer for the lad, trusting God 'to do whatever is good for him, whatever the odds against him might be.' He records that after many months the lad was 'given back to us almost in full health and took his place once more in the life of the church.' The great mystery which is prayer encourages Ian to record another time when a little boy belonging to a church family fell ill with a brain tumour. They prayed for the boy morning and evening for 10 days. The boy died. Lessons went on being learned.

In all of this one of the other activities which built up the church and blessed the community was the prayers for healing which were held at the end of every evening service. About 40 people would wait for these. They learned to be alert to needs around their doors and in the wider world, and to call on the power of God who delights to restore and bless human life. Without such involvement prayer can too easily become a ritual deprived of reality.

One of the strength's of Ian's ministry in Rosyth was the programme of visitation in the parish. When someone arrived at the church, having perhaps moved into the area, that person was encouraged to fill in a card. Ian would make the first call and alert an elder to follow up his visit. A network of support meant that folk were less likely to fall through the net. The other side of this was that if folk chose to distance themselves from the church their names were removed from the roll. It was pruned regularly but never without being sure that folk knew where their rights and responsibilities lay.

In Rosyth it was always clear that there was a place for visits by the minister and visits by elders. No complaints were heard suggesting that a ministerial visit was lacking if elders had visited. Nor was there any sense that visitation was just done as part of a routine. The people in the church were also encouraged to be there for their neighbours.

There was the exception that proved the rule. A woman complained that she had been ill for a week and the minister had never looked near her. Ian went to visit.
'I understand you've been ill.'
'Aye, for a week and you never came near me!'
'You haven't got an elder?'
'Aye, Mr. So-and-so.'
'You haven't got a street contact?'
'Aye, Mrs. So-and-so.'

'You haven't any neighbours coming in?'
'Aye, the neighbours were in and out all week'
'So what kind of Christian are you. You are surrounded by those who care for you and all you do is lie back there and complain. So many people you could have asked to let me know. You should give up the membership of the Kirk!'
Before Ian left she was all apologies.
'I'm awfy sorry . . . I'll never be ill again without letting you know!'
Ian's had an unorthodox approach to visitation but always with a smile and a twinkle in the eye.

In Rosyth when an elder called at a home he was not to be kept at the door. If the folk in the house were busy at something else they were to open the door and explain that it was not convenient. Together a mutually suitable time was to be arranged; the elders were encouraged to get involved with the families they were appointed to care for. Much pastoral work was done.

On one occasion Ian realised that an elderly woman in the congregation was rather apprehensive. He asked what the matter was. She had ordered new linoleum. The delivery date had been set. She did not know how she was going to get it laid. Ian found out when the linoleum was due. He made a note so that he could go round and lay it. When he went to her house she said, 'It's OK, the elder's been.' It meant that the linoleum was already laid.

The resource, which is the congregation, needs to be used not just in worship but in pastoral care. Ian visited a family where a child had been killed in a road accident. The minister did what he could. He remembered a couple in the congregation who had gone through a similar experience. Ian brought the two families together. No minister in his own person has encountered the totality of human experience. Putting the right people in touch with one another may be all the minister should be doing.

When Ian later undertook his thesis the only real alteration to his parish work related to visitation. It sparked a positive development in the parish. Rather than visit families in their own homes, one family at a time, he made arrangements for a place where families from a few streets could get together with him as a group. This allowed him to keep in touch with his people.

Folk from three elders' districts at a time were brought together for a social evening. A wee card was given to be put on the mantelpiece to help folk remember date and time. Almost the whole congregation would attend over the months. Getting-to-know-you games were played. Folk caught up on personal news and news from the parish. In such a way a church community grows and knows it matters.

Early in his twelve year period in Rosyth Ian asked whether his ministry might extend to the naval dockyard. It was clear that his time in the paper mill had not dimmed his desire for industrial mission. He was ministering to the people in the community in their homes why not in their work place. Soon after making an enquiry about such work a visitor knocked at their door. He requested an interview.

The visitor's concern became clear in his questions. Ian was a known left-wing socialist. He was suspected of planning to penetrate the work force at the dockyard with left wing propaganda. The questions came thick and fast. 'Where did Ian really stand?' 'What were the real motives behind his request of access to the naval dockyard?'

In no time Ian turned the tables on their visitor. He asked him to produce his credentials. Defensively the reply was that he was not allowed to say what authority had sent him, but he assured Ian that he had a genuine mandate.

'Look,' Ian said, 'I have all kinds of people coming here with all kinds of stories. What do you mean coming here, probing into my life from a clearly biased political stance, without a shred of evidence that you have any valid authority to do so?' The poor man blustered. Ian went on to suggest that he might be a con man, in the pay of some right wing faction, looking for anything detrimental enough to make a headline in a newspaper. 'What is your game?' Ian pressed home his new found advantage. 'Did you think I could so easily be taken in?'

The man was completely taken aback. He was clearly accustomed to people being cowed by fear. He did not know how to handle the situation he now found himself in. He was glad to make good his escape at the earliest possible moment. Margaret showed him to the door and then collapsed, laughing into Ian's arms. How Ian wished he could have been party to the report taken back to the authorities. As it happened, a regulation, that went back to the time of Napoleon, meant he was unable to be involved as a civilian in chaplaincy work directly within the naval dockyard.

When Ian began his parish ministry he decided to keep a file of significant material that came his way. He learned to shape this material in his writing. On average about 5 hours a week were spent on gathering this material. When he undertook his PhD research the time set aside increased to about 8 hours on average. Ten years after leaving New College Ian felt it was time to do a disciplined piece of scholarship. He was pleased to be doing this in a parish context. It meant that it kept the research earthed and the parish work informed. He wrote to the PhD committee. When asked to suggest an area of research he offered 'The theological basis for wage and salary differentials'. This was rejected as he did not have a first class degree in economics. He then offered 'The theology of T.S. Elliott'. They said, 'You cannot do that he is still alive!' He wrote again and said that if they had something up their sleeves for him to do, they could forget it. He was not prepared to do three years' work on something inconsequential. Their interest it transpired was on social conditions in the last quarter of the nineteenth century. Keir Hardie had been taken by an American student. He had fallen down on it, but it had to lie for ten years in case he came back to it. They noted that no such work had been attempted on Cunninghame Graham.

It so happened that Cunninghame Graham's nephew, Admiral Sir Angus Graham was in charge of the Rosyth Naval Dockyard. When Lady Mountbatten visited Rosyth, the admiral showed her round the dockyard; Ian showed her round the civic community. Ian asked the admiral if he felt that an academic study of Cunninghame Graham was needed. He was of the opinion that it was.

Ian knew of Cunninghame Graham. When he had to read to Dad in his youth works by Cunninghame Graham were no hardship. In this they were unlike most of the rest of what he had been required to read! A month after the conversation with the admiral he came to visit Ian. His demeanour suggested that he wanted a favour. He said,

'We have just found seven notebooks and scrapbooks that belonged to my uncle. They were in an attic. We wondered if you would like to be the first person to see them.' What an offer!

This gave Ian a place to start. He had excellent tutors overseeing his research: including William Tindal. The British Council of Churches asked Ian to undertake a lecture tour in the United States in 1955. This allowed him to go to the library in New Hampshire where there was material on Cunninghame Graham collected by a previous biographer. Some papers were not available in the UK. All that was available in Britain had been researched.

In the States Ian was on the doorstep of the library when it opened and was last to be thrown out at the end of the day. Four days allowed Ian access to all that he required.

After a year Ian's tutors asked for a progress report. He indicated that Cunninghame Graham was a complex character. There were too many facets to report so early. The tutors accepted this. This exchange was repeated at the end of the second year. At the close of the third year Ian presented his thesis. It was well received. In time it was used as a guide for other students as a model of research, selection and presentation. Copies of the thesis were made. One was placed as is custom in the Scottish National Library.

Any précis of a PhD thesis needs to be treated with the utmost care. The nature of the study does however shed light both on the life studied and on Ian the researcher.

Robert Bontine Cunninghame Graham (known universally as R.B. Cunninghame Graham in this country or as Don Roberto in Latin America) was born in 1852 and as the eldest of a family of three was the claimant to the Earldom of Strathearn, Menteith and Airth.¹⁷ He developed Spanish connections through a grandmother and a love of South America from his mother. He married Gabrielle a gifted mystic. For a short time he was a Liberal MP for a Scottish Constituency. His wife died in 1906 and in 1928 R.B. Cunninghame Graham turned his full attention to the question of Home Rule for Scotland, becoming in that year the first president of the National Party of Scotland, and later in 1934 the honorary president of the Scottish National Party. Cunninghame Graham died in 1936 on a visit to the Argentine and his body was brought back for burial on the island of Inchmahome in the Lake of Menteith beside his wife.

R.B. Cunninghame Graham's writing divided into the period before 1895 when politics dominated what he produced and the years which followed when religion and philosophy were his main interests.

His early writing was enthusiastic about democracy which he believed required the judicious use of power, the liberation of people in terms of wages, conditions, leisure and education, a basis of social equality and of justice. In a world where too often the poor were encouraged to accept their God-given lot Cunninghame Graham was 'an outstanding figure who (changed the focus from) the relief of pauperism . . . to the protection of the workman in his employment. Graham had limited personal political ambitions and was convinced that leadership of the new Socialist movement would need to come from among the working class themselves. R.B.

Cunninghame Graham was among the principal midwives who brought the new (trade) unionism to birth, and he helped to preside over its early growth.

When the Scottish Parliamentary Labour Party was formed in 1888 he became its first chairman. Fraser considers the way in which Cunninghame Graham moved from his liberal roots towards the Labour Party. It can be argued it was others who moved more than he did. Fraser concludes that R.B. Cunninghame Graham's involvement in Scottish Nationalism after 1928 as his recognition that Home rule for Scotland was the priority for that time, as socialism had been at an earlier point. He was both socialist and nationalist.

Ian Fraser notes that R.B. Cunninghame Graham never speaks of politics except in disgust. 'Politics is a sorry business at heart.' The record shows that Graham was a conscientious constituency MP, but politics, for him, was a flawed instrument, a necessary evil. In his summary of R.B. Cunninghame Graham with regard to his social outlook a number of features are highlighted in the thesis.

- *His love of truth as he saw it.*
- *The unusual quality of detachment and involvement/commitment*
- *Like an Old Testament prophet his desire to rescue society from false gods*
- *His capacity as a socialist in the tradition of Robert Owen*
- *The status and dignity he afforded all human beings not least the deprived*
- *His personal contribution to society through a life of action embodying his thinking.*

Ian Fraser now turns to Cunninghame Graham's religious outlook. In a world where natural resources were seen as existing to be exploited, Graham notes 'Nature is sheer miracle.' His regard for animals that developed during his time on the Pampas in Argentina later encouraged him to address the care of pit ponies, cab-horses and the use of horse-power generally. 'Those who have blessed man with hell, allow no paradise to beasts.' R.B. Cunninghame Graham recognises the heights to which some human beings aspire and the depths of humankind at its worst. Humanity remained a mystery to him. Graham accepted the existence of God but concluded that he was unconnected to life as we live it. There is a residual respect for Christ 'who died upon the Cross to bring peace on earth' but who at the last leaves human beings to go it alone in the business of living.

Living as he did in a century of expansion of the church abroad and of a church on the defensive at home, Cunninghame Graham largely leaves the church out of his reckoning. For a sincere worshipper he retained respect but on occasion he characterised clergy as 'hard-working blind leaders of the blind.' For sectarianism he has nothing but contempt and in the churches in Scotland he found 'much faith and little charity'. In his judgement of the damage done in the name of missionary activity R.B. Cunninghame Graham stands vindicated by modern repentance for the excesses of these earlier days. He felt that the gospel should show the power to deliver at home before being launched abroad.

Biblical references and allusions run through Graham's speeches and writings but Ian Fraser concludes that it was as if he had 'already made up his mind about human life before he read (the

Bible) and so dismissed as incredible the saving work of the Cross and the reality of the Resurrection. R.B. Cunninghame Graham sees prayer as a human activity and he judges a 'staunch horse of more value than all the prayers of all the good men in the world'. Fraser concludes that Cunninghame Graham 'never really came to grips with the Christian conception of forgiveness . . . which sees the world's hope in a changed relationship, a reconciliation with all things which God offered through Christ.'

Ian Fraser's own assessment of R.B. Cunninghame Graham's religious outlook can be read as ambivalent. 'To Cunninghame Graham, the Father seemed too removed from life to be offered more than acknowledgement. Jesus Christ was the ideal of all life, a phenomenon. But he was in the end but a subject for meditation and longing. The Holy Spirit, whom dull human eyes, Cunninghame Graham once said, perceived only 'as a white dove', is scarcely mentioned. Yet to the Holy Spirit, teaching truth, unmasking sham, claiming an unqualified offering of life, he was alert and obedient. Fraser concludes that 'in grace, compassion and indignation of life Cunninghame Graham was a knight of the Holy Spirit.'

Yet this also is true of R.B. Cunninghame Graham. The sense he had of life's futility went deep and continually placed a question mark against his battle for the right. That his life was dedicated was not enough. He needed to know but failed to find the persistent love of the Father for His creation, the effective deliverance accomplished by the Son, and the flamboyant adventure of the Spirit.

A careful reading of all Ian Fraser wrote about R.B. Cunninghame Graham tends rather to the observation that Ian's genius is to recognise the complexity of his chosen subject. There remains scope for further study contrasting the political journey of Graham through three parties and Ian Fraser who has remained within the Labour Party from his youth to the present. Graham seems to have come at religion from a political perspective. By contrast Ian Fraser's theology beginning in the church at worship moves seamlessly on to the 'oikoumene', the whole inhabited world, where politics and so much more should contribute to the life of all God's people.

Ian had no intention of publishing his thesis as a book. As the 150th anniversary of Cunninghame Graham's birth approached in 2002, Ian was pressured to produce a book to mark the occasion. A local bookseller in Bridge of Allan, the people who were now living in and using Gartmore House and the folk in the Smith Museum and Art Gallery in Stirling separately approached Ian for a book. He was known to have access to the material.

When Rennie McOwan, a Stirling journalist saw 'RB Cunninghame Graham: Fighter for Justice'[18] he told Ian, 'Just you wait till Lady Polwarth (Admiral Sir Angus Graham's daughter) sees this. She never has a good word to say about anyone who has written about her great uncle.'

In time her letter arrived. 'Marvellous,' it said, 'You have discovered him perfectly . . . It is exactly the sort of work I have always wanted someone to write. I found the task too daunting to put his 'seven lives lived in one life-span' into *one* book. You have achieved the impossible! His portrait (Lowry's study after the Glasgow picture) smiles on me from my sitting room wall, as I write, so I'm sure *he* is pleased, too!'[19]

The early readings in Forres had found their proper place. As George MacLeod was known to say, 'If you think this is a coincidence, may you have a very dull life.'

The Fraser children, now three in number with the arrival of Ian in 1949 were fortunate with school in Rosyth. Not only did they do well in school, Miss Money saw to it that all pupils who wanted to play instruments got that chance. For Anne and Ian this meant violin, for Keith cello. Keith was Marie Dare prizeman in the Edinburgh Music Competition at the age of 12 in the 12–16 category in the cello section. He was asked several times to audition for the National Youth Orchestra. He deliberately failed one audition – the time it would have required was eating into time allocated for football. He got a trial for Southern Scotland schools. In High School Anne turned out to be a sprinter. The 100 yards was her forte. On one occasion she was entered for the 220 yards. She took off as if it were the 100 yards and just went on with nobody able to catch her.

After 10 years of household chores and child-rearing Margaret was delighted to be asked to do a five month teaching spell each year. Primary school children went to secondary school in two batches. King's Road School asked Margaret to take the batch who were ready in December, mature them a bit, sharpen their gifts, enlarge their view of life. It suited her and the pupils perfectly. Ian was talking to the woman in charge of the bicycle shop across the burn from the house and asked her how her son Bobby was getting on. He was known as a bit of a wild card. 'Taking the mickey out of the teachers as usual,' she said, 'except for Mrs. Fraser. She has developed such a good relationship with the class that he would never think of that.' 'Lucky lad,' Ian said, 'that lovely lady has a backbone of steel; if he tried taking the mickey out of her he would soon learn to rue it.'

The male and female teachers had separate staff rooms. One day the women got on to the question, 'How would you know for certain if your man is chasing another woman?' It was concluded 'when he starts to bring you flowers.' 'In that case,' said Margaret, 'Ian has been chasing other women all our married life.'

About ten years after the Frasers arrived in Rosyth, Mrs. Murray, a parishioner responded to a Scottish newspaper invitation to write to them about minister's wives. Her prize winning entry was printed in the Sunday Mail in 1957.

> *'In my opinion, the wife of the Rev. Dr. Ian Fraser of Rosyth Parish Church is second to none in looks, figure and popularity.*
> *'She is blonde with a figure that equals that of any film star. She is serenely beautiful and radiates happiness and contentment.*
> *'One has only to look at the happy and contented faces of our young minister and his children to know that they have a wife and mother who devotes herself to them and yet takes her full share of the hard work and duties which fall to a minister's wife.'*

The paper had the good sense to provide a photograph of Margaret Fraser to accompany her letter. The camera did not lie!

Ian remembers that it was the Methodist minister who took the initiative to found a local Council of Churches. His church building lay almost opposite Ian's Parish Church. In addition to the Methodist and Church of Scotland ministers there was participation from Baptists and Episcopalians. The Roman Catholic priest would have no truck with this group. Ian was hardly surprised for the said priest seemed to be allergic to the company of his own people, never mind unsanctified alternatives.

At first the group spent time getting to know one another and the variety of church backgrounds they represented. At one point the Council of Churches took off. A stream flowing past the primary school had got blocked. Sewage was being washed into the school playground. The stream passed through land belonging to five parties, none of whom were prepared to take responsibility.

A parents' committee got their dander up. The local Council of Churches joined them en masse. The parties were hard to bring to book but the problem was dealt with. It was a good example of churches finding their calling by joining those undertaking responsible work in the secular world. This approach to life and faith is often recognised in the Salvation Army. Although they did co-operate with the Council of Churches from time to time they did not have a strong presence in Rosyth.

Ian found it fun to be involved in a visitation mission to the whole of Rosyth. A Methodist and a Baptist representative might take one side of a street; an Episcopalian and a Presbyterian take the other. If someone said at a door to the former, 'Actually I am an Episcopalian', the visitors would simply whistle over that visitor from the other side of the road. There was no escape!

Probably the biggest risk the inter-church group took was setting up a platform at the entrance/exit to the local park. Successful attempts were made to draw passers-by into a discussion of the Christian faith. At first there was some concern that perhaps lay and ordained folk would put things differently and so the experience might be more marked by division than unity. Would one denomination react in horror at a stance adopted by another church? They took the risk. It came off. What they discovered was that they shared so much in common they could with integrity back one another up. They had agreed to be open about differences even to argue as the need arose. The experience that Ian shared with the folk in the Rosyth Council of Churches focused his ecumenical endeavours and became a basis for the work that he would undertake in Scottish Churches House in Dunblane and beyond.

From time to time the Home Board of the Church of Scotland would be in touch with Ian. By the late 1950s the roll of the church had reached 1100 with combined average attendance at the main services on Sunday being about 750. It was suggested that an assistant minister might be appointed to the parish. Ian's reply was always along the same line: 'Over the past year some eighty (or so) more people have become church members. A church which has 80 plus additional ministers is hardly inadequately equipped for its task!'

When the Kirk Session told Ian they had met in his absence and decided on a raise in his salary Ian corrected them: they had decided to *offer* him an increase – Margaret would join him consider whether this rise would meet mounting expenses or break solidarity with members of the congregation whose income averaged out at roughly their own. Those who knew him best still could be caught out by his independence of thought.

The church door in Rosyth does not seem to have acted as a boundary. It acted as a portal for coming and going. What was happening in the community informed the worship inside the church. What was said and done there found its fulfilment in the community. The Council of Churches was involved in the political awakening of God's people. A report on the World Council of Churches Assembly at Evanston was given in a public hall in the town. Hot issues of the day like the Central African Federation were debated in that hall, jam-packed with a great range of people. This was not to produce a church position in such matters. It was to provide folk with knowledge on which they could make informed decisions.

Ian was a local councillor for 5 years on Dunfermline Town Council. In the preceding years he had much to say with others about the inadequate lighting in Rosyth particularly in the public parks that were used as shortcuts. It was no surprise then when he was appointed 'Streets and Lightning Convenor'.

While Ian was visiting near a polling station, a woman took delight in telling him, 'I'm going in to vote you out if I possible can.' Ian knew she meant it. Clearly this was a challenge for Ian in the pulpit and in the parish. His party politics were open for all to see. He believed that this presented an encouragement to everyone to be more fully involved in the political process locally. David Orr, an Iona

Community member and a minister in nearby Burntisland told Ian that he was convinced that his stance in Rosyth had been the best way. The Tories in David's congregation tended to dismiss him as a socialist while Labour folk were sure he was a closet conservative. Try as he might to represent positions fairly no one seemed to hear him clearly.

Ian gave Independents short shift. He was convinced that while involvement with a party would sometimes cause you to vote for something against your own judgment, a larger programme of action could be threatened if a common mind was not honoured. There was an occasion when Ian was carpeted for voting against the party line. He cannot remember the issue of that day. The leader of the Council was delegated to enforce party discipline. Ian had no sense of foreboding before this meeting. Looking back he felt his liver had been removed, chewed over before being replaced. It shook him to the core. In later days Ian argued that there had been right on both sides. He had been open in his opposition on a matter of conscience. The leader was right to hammer it home that being in a Labour group community carried responsibility for decisions collectively arrived at.

Looking back over his time with Margaret and the family in Rosyth, Ian sums up his experience succinctly as pastor, minister and parson. As a pastor (episcope) he undertook his responsibility of care for the church. It entailed, 'oversight of the congregation's own life so that it may . . . measure up to the range of Christ's universal Lordship.' As a minister (servant – diakonia) it is 'doing what you can . . . to restore and bless people when they are down and out.' It means entering into people's lives and taking the weight from their shoulders. As a parson (that is a person) . . . not the Person of Importance (who was the laird) not the Person of Intellect (the schoolmaster) but essentially as the Person-you-can-turn-to. Ian remembers a number of specific occasions when he was called on as a parson. He went to the door on one occasion to be confronted by the local grocer. 'Dr. Fraser, my horse has bolted: could you come and help me catch him?' One parishioner confronted him repeatedly with a plea that he should find a wife for him! These calls are often inconvenient and beyond the range of things that the office of parish minister normally covers but Ian concluded 'you have infinite reward: and you do the work God gave you to do.'

He reflects finally on the role of a minister's wife who, he remembers, only fell in love with a man who also happened to be a minister, and all too often is called on to serve in partnership with her man. He is adamant that her service should never be presumed on; and so glad that in his case she is 'so well equipped, willing and ready to be of service'. As he says 'We (were) a team. She (was) often the partner who counted most.' In the new millennium this can surely be applied to the minister's spouse or partner without more needing to be said.

Twelve full years in Rosyth! Tough times some of these years were. And Margaret such a support. Her first illness arrived in the last days in Rosyth. She was diagnosed with severe breast cancer. People stopped Ian in the street with 'Terrible that it should happen to her.' He startled them when he replied, 'Terrible if we were above or beyond the suffering that comes to all kinds of folk.' Margaret would have agreed. So in 1958 Margaret was given the heaviest dose of radiotherapy used to that time in the Western General Hospital in Edinburgh. Happily her life's work was not yet complete. She lived for another 29 happy and productive years.

One chapter in the life of the Frasers was about to close and another open.

Endnotes

[14] Bible, Congregation and Community Ian M Fraser SCM Press London 1959.

[15] It was the model known affectionately to the world at large as a 'baby' Austin.

[16] The eldership of course in those days was the preserve of men.

[17] Their family home at Gartmore lies 15 miles west of Gargunnock where Ian has lived 'in retirement' since 1982.

[18] Published privately to mark the anniversary.

[19] Personal letter from Jean, Lady Polwarth to Ian Fraser.

CHAPTER FIVE

SCOTTISH CHURCHES HOUSE

ONLY FIVE OR six times in their married life did Margaret ask Ian to wear his ministerial robes. When the Queen visited Scottish Churches House in 1967 Ian dressed for the occasion. He remembers the monarch – 'she was as nice a lassie as you could ever come across.' He concluded that if she wasn't interested in what had been done in Scottish Churches House she must have been a magnificent actress. Rather it is understood that she was and is genuinely interested in what is happening in the lives of her people.

Scottish ecumenism is usually traced from the Edinburgh Conference of 1910 and the Missionary Continuation Committee for Scotland, which began thereafter. In 1948 when Ian went to Rosyth the World Council of Churches' General Assembly took place in Amsterdam. It was part of the background against which Ian's parish work was undertaken. It was also a spur to ecumenical activity in Scotland. Many of those involved, like Ian, had connections with the Iona Community and the Student Christian Movement.

It has often been noted that the Iona Community, begun as it was in 1938, had an inauspicious beginning with war following the next year. It is perhaps just as significant to note that the ecumenical movement in Scotland had suffered a setback in 1959, in the year before Scottish Churches House began.

Archie Craig who had been the General Secretary of the British Council of Churches during the Second World War, and one time depute leader of the Iona Community, came to public attention in Scotland when he chaired the Inter-Church Relations Committee of the Church of Scotland. The General Assembly of the Church of Scotland in May 1953 instructed the Committee to renew conversations with the Church of England, the Scottish Episcopal Church and the English Presbyterian Church. The Joint Report hammered out over four years drew newspaper headlines that bishops were to be accepted in the Church of Scotland. Dr. Craig eloquently commended the report to the 1957 General Assembly for two years of prayerful consideration. When the matter returned to the General Assembly in 1959 the proposals of the Joint Report were rejected root and branch. Archie resigned as convenor of the Inter-Church Relations Committee.[20]

This is the background against which a group of ecumenical enthusiasts had been working[21]. During the 1950s this group committed to ecumenism had searched high and low across Scotland for premises, which could act as a home for the 'churches together'. Those involved in this included Robert Mackie[22], Archie Craig and Isabel Forrester.

Some ten properties were looked at and rejected for a variety of reasons. When they came to Dunblane it was apparently the worst of the lot. The local Council had gone to court to get permission to demolish the buildings. When questions were raised about a possible use for the property the Council offered as a great courtesy permission to the Civic Trust to look again at the situation. They decided that if the row of buildings were demolished it should be rebuilt to the same plan. The humble row of houses gave the cathedral opposite its proper status. Monaghan, the main builder who was chosen for the renovation of what would become Scottish Churches House, was a Roman Catholic. He was a real enthusiast and supporter of the work. He made tools freely available for the parts of the work allocated to volunteers.

The plan to establish a 'home' for the Scottish Churches owed some impetus to the 'Evangelical Academies' in Europe. This meant that the house was based on a reformed model not just the model of a Roman Catholic retreat house. While the influence of Iona is very evident in these early days it is important to recognise that Scottish Churches House came into being while the rebuilding phase of the living quarters of Iona abbey was still progressing. Only in the later 1960s did the primary function of the abbey become a place of hospitality in a way similar to Dunblane.

Ian was not personally involved in the search for premises for the proposed Scottish Churches House. In 1960 when Margaret and Ian met Robert Mackie they were informed that they had neither money to pay the salary for a Warden nor money to restore the buildings. 'That's for us,' said Margaret. She was at that time undergoing radical radiotherapy treatment for breast cancer. She did not even know if she would be alive at the year's end. Ian accepted the position as first warden of what would in time become Scottish Churches House, doubling up with eight months assistantship in the Cathedral to earn money to feed the family. So the twelve good years in Rosyth came to an end; the Fraser family were clearly missed when they moved on

The choice of Ian Fraser to head up the initiative was, according to Douglas Gay, 'bold but predictable'. He had been active in ecumenical circles in the 1940s and 1950s. His ministry in Rosyth was both distinctive and effective. The combination of pastoral experience and ecumenical commitment with a 'notable intellectual and political edge'[23] was attractive to those who wished to see ecumenism in Scotland deliver through its social and political engagement.

As no accommodation was available at that time for the Fraser family, their daughter Anne moved to Dunblane and was boarded out with two friends, Alison Harvey and Maisie Masson. This allowed her to enrol at the High School in Stirling. In those days Dunblane had no secondary education provision in the town. Anne was not entirely delighted by this arrangement, living as she said with 'two old maids!' The rest of the family had use of the lodge of nearby Deanston House Hotel until their place in Scottish Churches House was made ready. Before the boys left Rosyth they were heard to complain, 'We'll never have any friends ever again!' In half a day in Deanston they had made new friends. In time the two boys went to McLaren High in Callander for their schooling. With the Beeching axe falling on the railway line to Callander, the last years of schooling required travel by bus. This all took time and reduced opportunities for socialising with other teenagers. Keith played the 'cello and had to be transported regularly to Falkirk for tuition. Margaret for her part taught for a time in the Queen Victoria School in Dunblane: it was reported that the boys found it hard to believe that such an attractive woman could be a minister's wife! She also made huge contribution to life in the House.

Scottish Churches House was formally opened in 1960 by no less than the World Council of Churches' Central Committee, which broke off from its meeting in St. Andrews to attend and inspect the work of its own ecumenical work-camp and to conduct worship in Dunblane Cathedral. The supporters of Scottish Churches House saw this high profile beginning as confirmation of their hope that the house might be a sign within the world church. It may also go some way to explaining a later move that would link Dunblane to Geneva.

The restoration of the building was largely completed by the time Scottish Churches House was dedicated in January 1961 by Neville Davidson, chairman of Scottish Churches Ecumenical Committee. The new warden was adamant that Scottish Churches House was never to become just another conference centre.[24] His background led him to view conferences as passive experiences for those attending. He preferred to think of the events as consultations for the participants. He was particularly committed to providing opportunities for the church and the world to interact. The size of the house meant that groups of around thirty could be accommodated for an overnight or weekend event. More could be catered for when a day consultation was deemed appropriate. This size of group seemed to be suited to getting to know other participants in some depth and surely contributed to the success of many of these gatherings.

Ian approached subjects that might be tackled with two questions always at the forefront of his thinking:
- Is anything needed in this field at all?

- Does Scottish Churches House have a role to play?

The subjects that were tackled were often matters that Ian had a personal interest in even before he arrived in Dunblane. He also was good at networking with people who had a breadth of vision similar to his own.

There were five recognisable stages in the consultation process. On any particular occasion some of these stages might be more or less obvious but the pattern became established as one that could be trusted to deliver.

- Programming: the warden worked with Robert Mackie and others in the Policy and Programme Committee to select the key concerns. 150 consultations took place in the nine years the Frasers were in residence in Scottish Churches House.
- Preparation: the warden saw it as his responsibility to approach 'people who matter no matter how busy they are'. He persuaded people to submit materials to him. From the varied contributions he produced a working paper. The consultation process was thus already under way. People arrived to consult with their own experience and with some idea of the thinking of those they would share time with in Dunblane.
- Consultation: Ian became convinced that the key to success at this stage depended on the chairperson. It was not enough just to let everyone have their say. The signs of a growing common purpose or of sharpened disagreements had to be fastened on to produce effective action. A number of outsiders were tried but Ian quickly accepted that he had particular skills in this area. Gillian Carver who joined him as

the assistant warden in 1964 in Scottish Churches House fulfilled this role on occasion.

- Reporting: Ian saw this as an essential part of the process and these reports included both a summary of the proceedings and 'next steps' where these had been identified. As Scottish Churches House had no official standing with other bodies any recommendations or ideas for further work had to commend themselves by their own merit.
- Dissemination: this proved both a difficult area and the least successful of the whole process. Time did not usually permit a write up of these consultations in a way that they could be made accessible easily to people who had not been present in Scottish Churches House. Some seed was sown; some undoubtedly bore fruit. Ian was adept at using the media both in its printed and broadcast form. James Dey, who worked at the time for the BBC as their religious affairs adviser would approach him. Ian took part in discussion programmes on a wide variety of subjects. Nelson Gray held a similar position in Scottish Television and called on Ian's input from time to time. Philip Stalker, the religious affairs correspondent at the *Scotsman* newspaper knew his road to Ian's door. Some particular work was written up in more detail and published e.g. 'Sex as Gift' (1967), which SGM published – Ian himself being the author.

The breadth of the programmes that were organised by Scottish Churches House is hard to comprehend. Significant in the present context are the memories that Ian has looking back over half a century. In his mind one of the great communicators at Scottish Churches House was Richard Demarco, an artist and impresario. He had a tremendous gift. He had more to say about prayer when he was giving a talk on art than anybody had any right to expect. He participated in 'Faith and Doubt' weeks. The groups who participated were always half Protestant, half Roman Catholic; they were also a mixture of doubters and those committed to faith. Richard would take a group of sixth-year students who were participating in such a week and sit them down. He would place a painting in front of them and ask them to examine it carefully. Within minutes the group were deeply involved in talking about the things that really mattered in life. Skilfully the artist drew the different threads of life together and helped the group to weave them in to a coherent pattern.

Ian also vividly remembers a week with William Barclay, the Glasgow University New Testament scholar, and Bernard Haring, the Roman Catholic moral theologian. It took place during the last Holy Week when Ian was warden. Bernard was deemed by some to be generally too welcoming of folk from other Christian traditions. It was a week of great energy. The two speakers helped one another to understand communion more than had been possible previously. At the end of the week there was a service in the Roman Catholic chapel in Dunblane. Ian was away in Glasgow on Good Friday evening and missed the session that Willie and Bernard had with the teenagers. No report of that meeting came to Ian on his return at a late hour. It was sufficient for him to hear that it had been agreed that the group should respect the position that the Roman Catholic Church took at that time. This meant that all could participate but all could not partake.

In the service Bernard Haring reached the point of invitation. His face lit up like the face of an angel. With a sweep of his hand he gave invitation to all who wished to partake. Bernard said later that he could not be part of a Christian community that had become one, and keep some out. One thing had been agreed in the cold light of reasoning. It was quite different in the warmth of that celebration. It can be asked, 'May there be a time for the heart to rule the head? Is it possible that those who partake can allow themselves to be emotionally as well as theologically involved?'

Rumours abounded about the consequences for Bernard with his church but Ian recalls nothing more than rumours. Developments in theological understanding can take place in particular circumstances not least in ecumenical sharing.

A brilliant Policy and Programme Committee included Archie Craig and Isabel Forrester. When the gangs in the wilderness that was Easterhouse in the east end of Glasgow were doing their worst, the committee in Ian's absence invited these young folk to come to Dunblane. Three of the four gangs accepted the invitation.

It was a remarkable time. It was all too easy to imagine graffiti and gang violence descending on the quiet streets of Dunblane. During the discussions the gang members found they could not sit for more than about 20 minutes at a time. They were in and out constantly. Yet for all that, progress was made.

At the end of the process one of the gang members said to Ian, 'You've fairly spoiled things, sir!' Ian asked in what way they had done this. 'Well,' he said, 'You cannae stick a knife in someone when you've spent time under the same roof as him.' There are clear echoes here of what was later done with young folk from across the religious divide in Northern Ireland who spent time in 'seed groups' at the Ballycastle Centre run by the Corrymeela Community.

Ian came to recognise that for such young people violence was one of few things that gave colour to the drab existence of Easterhouse. Did the church stand accused of attempting to remove the colour from life and putting nothing in its place? Life might be different for these young folk who had spent time in Dunblane but nothing much had changed in Easterhouse itself. Therein lies the challenge from young people to the church of our own day.

During Ian's time as warden an annual conference was held on matters to do with the life of the nation. In the days before the establishment of a Scottish Parliament at Holyrood it was clearly important that places existed for such national deliberations. Churches together provided an opportunity for matters to be heard fairly when single churches might have been suspected of having their own agenda. Politicians from the Scottish Office attended to share their thinking and to listen as people offered their own perspectives on the discussions of the day. There was a maturity in these consultations that developed over time.

During the Fraser era there were twice yearly ecumenical consultations on church order under the banner 'Examining the Faith'. These included time spent on the ordination of women, overseas mission and patterns of worship. Lay consultations were held under the general title of 'Sharing the Gospel'. These too were held two or three times a year and tended to follow topics that were also being examined under the 'Examining the Faith' banner.

In the 1960s Professor Erik Routley[25] was at Scottish Churches House during a consultation on evangelism. He noted that hymns, which were being lauded as modern, continued with all the old stereotypes. He encouraged the writing of hymns that really enabled worship in a changing world. It was a job that needed to be done. Over 100 folk made a contribution of one kind or another to the hymn writing in the 1960s, which used Dunblane both as a stimulus and a clearing house.

Gracie King, a teacher in a Bo'ness school tried out some of the material developed with children in mind. If the youngsters took to something she put it away for three months in case the appeal was short-lived. Only if they asked for it thereafter was it brought back into circulation. She encouraged her children to write hymns themselves. The children's hymns found their way into 'Dunblane Praises for Schools.' A primary teacher recently retired on the south coast of England who caught sight of a 'Dunblane Praises' was happy to confirm that she had had her copy when it was produced originally.

Ian notes that 'adoration slush' characterises so many of the hymns that have been written in recent days to give a 'bawl of praise' – not disciplined to give fresh and creative insights into God. People have been too slow in sending such material to the 'recycle bin'. It is equally important to make contributions to the hymnology of the ages from our own time.

Ian and Erik took on the work of keeping people on task between meetings. Neither of them had any intention of writing hymns themselves. Within ten years a number of collections of hymns were published. Items that Ian had included in a sermon or a meeting sometimes took shape and developed into a hymn. Stainer and Bell hold copyright for Ian and for the Galliard Press who published material for the Dunblane Group. While Ian did not consider himself to be a gifted hymn writer there were still hymns that needed to be written.

One example of the work that Erik and Ian produced together must suffice (The words were Ian's, the tune Erik's):

Bright angels thrumming through the air
Announce a royal birth;
Shepherds in answer upwards stare
To hear of peace on earth.

He who all power and might commands
Of time and space the king,
Is cradled in a mother's hands –
Is made a little thing.

To make the whole creation new
He takes the sinner's part
To bring a new-found hope to view
Reveals the Father's heart.

Lord, make our calling high and sure,
Bend us beneath your grace,
That in our lives, like his made poor,
Men see the Father's face.

Full records were kept of the annual music meetings. In time this allowed proper analysis of the process. Ian was challenged to find words that in time could become words that others would own.[26]

Some surprising items appear in the lists of discussions held at Scottish Churches House in the early years: they included road safety, nursing and rural affairs. Other things that were attempted while Ian was at Dunblane appeared to fail. A number of programme initiatives were cancelled through lack of numbers. Ian was always willing to accept that subjects could exist where the input from Scottish Churches House might be very limited. It was equally possible that in some cases the time was not ripe for some of the consultations that had been arranged.

Not everything that Ian did himself quite saw the light of day in the short term. He was invited to write an article for a new magazine, which some dramatists hoped to launch. The publication itself never got off the ground but the article, which Ian wrote, is enlightening.

Under the title 'Allies and Critics' Ian noted that the Spirit is to be 'poured out on all flesh' (Acts 2). It is too easy for the Christian God to become a tribal god made in their image, protecting Christian interests. Ian was convinced that people of many faiths and atheists must be listened to – for fresh illumination about the God one seeks to serve. Ian concluded that 'atheists may speak most vividly to Christians on behalf of those who stand outside the Christian fold; who are essential for its life.' The temptation will be, as always, to stay where we are and as we are, to get whatever is alien to us and deal with it in terms familiar to us. Ian recalls Arthur Miller in a

'View from a Bridge' saying, 'We must ask the largest questions. Where are we going now that we are together, all in the same boat?'

While consultations in Scottish Churches House were much more than pietistic retreats some overlap can be found. Given the foreign nature of traditional retreats to many of the participants the warden developed what he called 'the streaky bacon approach': three minutes input, three minutes sharing and then three minutes silence. He accepted that it was an odd and rather fragmentary approach; he simply confirmed that on occasion it worked.

In addition to the programme developed under the auspices of the Policy and Programme Committee of the house, church groups from the denominations who shared in the House, also used the centre. These retreats and consultations would have been as numerous as the consultations that Ian was directly responsible for. They went some way to maintaining Dunblane in the thinking of the churches and encouraged ecumenical activities both in Dunblane and further afield.

When he was warden of Scottish Churches House Ian continued as an active member of the Iona Community. The principles of the House reflected Iona thinking to a considerable extent. The Iona Community at that time had its house in Clyde Street in Glasgow. Community House in Clyde Street was largely a Glasgow resource. Dunblane was to be for the whole of Scotland. A meeting of apprentices in Clyde Street would have drawn participants from across the city; in Dunblane such a group came from the length and breadth of Scotland. It is interesting that when the first thirty years of the Iona Community were recorded in the film – 'Sermon in Stone'

– Dunblane is mentioned favourably as is the fact that the first warden was an Iona man. Is it a simple oversight that Ian is not mentioned by name? In the fifties and sixties Dunblane, the place, left no real imprint on the understanding of Scotland from the particular perspectives of Glasgow and Edinburgh. The dark day that would imprint the place on the consciousness of the world lay far in the future.

While Ian was in Dunblane the Corrymeela Community was just beginning. It started in 1965 and predated 'The Troubles' as they became known by some years. Ian was nominated by the Iona Community as a consultant who would inform discussions about what might be done in the North of Ireland. Ian did not take a large part in that work but got to know Ray Davey, the founder of the Corrymeela Community, and continues an interest in the work down to the present time.

While Ian was based in Scottish Churches House in the 1960s opportunities further afield came his way. He made a significant contribution to one of the groups that supported the consultation in the Roman Catholic Church that was Vatican II. John XXIII thought of himself a simple man, a peasant's son. In a private conversation with Cardinal Franz Konig during the week of prayer for Christian Unity in 1959, John revealed that the idea had come to him of calling a Council. He became convinced in that week that this was under the prompting of the Holy Spirit.

Vatican II made significant changes to the life of faith in the Roman Catholic Church. It established that the church would indeed be a global church. This led directly to the move away from Latin as the liturgical language: the vernacular was introduced. A second significant theme of the Council was its support for ecumenism. John XXIII invited the non-Catholic observers in 1962 and their number and influence increased during the years of the council from then up to 1965. A third element of Vatican II was the emphasis on the laity. Before Vatican II the Church was perceived as a two-class system, with the hierarchy dominating and the laity passively responding. The new emphasis became the church as the whole People of God – a pilgrim people on the move. The impetus of a Church on the move is hardly better made evident than the way in which the Council survived the death of John XXIII and the appointment of his successor in 1965. And it was no mere matter of survival. Paul picked up and ran with what had been achieved. He took what John had begun and translated it into the action which was required.

When John XXIII got his head together with that of Rosemary Goldie, an Australian nun whom he had appointed for laity concerns, those close to them reckoned that you never knew who had been responsible for a particular initiative. Through her an approach was made to the World Council of Churches. The question raised was whether it would be possible to appoint 15 people, Orthodox, Lutheran and Reformed to meet with fifteen Roman Catholics appointed by Pope John for informal dialogue on matters to be included in the Council's decree, 'The Church in the Modern World'.

Ian Fraser was chosen to be one of the Reformed contributors. One of the Roman Catholic group was Jerome Hamer who became convener of the four-person steering committee of the Decree on Ecumenism. In this way insights could be filtered in to the work of the Council itself. Klaus von Bismark was appointed the leader for the WCC group. There were three meetings; the first group met at Glion on the hillside overlooking the Swiss resort of Montreux; the second was convened in Gazzada north of Milan in Italy and the third meeting was back at Glion. The whole process looked forward to the 1967 Laity Congress in Rome at which several of the group including Ian were invited guests.

The first gathering at Glion lasted 3 days. The first day started with an RC mass, the next with an Orthodox Eucharist and the third with a Reformed communion service, which Ian was asked to take. At the end of the service several Roman Catholics cornered Ian. 'Where did you get that service? How has it so much in it that we want to get back into the Mass?' Ian took the opportunity to explain the Reformed tradition with its input from the early church, with Celtic and Continental influences.

After the first meeting von Bismark had to withdraw. Ian was appointed as co-convener with Martin Work, an American Roman Catholic layman. Ian understood that his appointment had nothing to do with his standing within the group but of having the knack of helping people to work well together. The preparation involved for the meetings allowed Ian closer contact with the participants than might have otherwise have been the case.

The overall effect of these gatherings was not any great ecumenical strides but an opportunity for people to get to know one another. For too long they had been taking their separate ways in theology, worship and church practice. These differences had been distorted or misunderstood by Christians beyond their own traditions. Henry

Docherty, a Scot on the Roman Catholic side was very open and in contact with Ian. He was a creative, quiet, positive person.

The consultation at Gazzada was held from 7th to 10th of September 1965 immediately before the fourth and final session of Vatican II. The theme chosen was 'The Formation of the Laity'. It was intended to give greater freedom for sharing experience on a matter of vital importance to all churches at that time. In the official report of the consultation it was noted that the report had been produced not to become a monument to 'three days of prayer in common, hard work, some fun and much fellowship.' It was intended essentially as a stimulus for further prayer, reflection and for appropriate action.

In his opening statement Martin Work called on the participants to be bold by daring to be honest and not afraid to open up new horizons in thinking. To Ian was given the opportunity to draw some conclusions from the time spent in Gazzada. He recalls attempts at conversations with Roman Catholics during his student days in Edinburgh. These failed because as he says, 'They ended up as attempts, because we bounced off one another like rubber balls.' Each side had a whole background to which the other had no access. Ian contrasted this with the new circumstances he believed they found themselves in, where 'one of the great gifts of the Holy Spirit in our time is the gift of a common language – Christ-centred and world-concerned. It was indeed a new Pentecost!'.

It seems worthwhile to quote in full his concluding remarks:

> 'God has prepared new ground on which we divided Christians may walk together. Instead of 'us' giving in to 'them' or 'them' giving in to 'us' – in some selling out on the truth as we

understand it – we are all being brought forward together, together are given riches of new insight, together are being led in Abrahamic obedience – with God's 'certainly I will be with thee' as our sole security. There are clearly things which God withholds from us until we seek them together. How sad it would be if we were artificially to denominationalize what God offers his Church today as a common inheritance.

'At Gazzada we were of one speech, and were being renewed in Christ's mission and ministry. There was joy and promise at the heart of our work.'

Ian put his name to his contribution and reveals that he was at that time the General Secretary of the Scottish Churches Council.

It should not be assumed that everything that Ian looked for from these consultations was easily achieved or achieved at all. He had argued passionately for a proposal for sharing communion not just sharing worship. This was removed from the final document. Conversations Ian had informally suggested that there was support for the former as well as the latter in the steering committee's notes on the Decree on Ecumenism. He took heart, however, when he overheard a group of the Roman Catholic hierarchy noting with a degree of alarm that John XXIII had 'opened so many windows to let light in to the church, that they could not all be closed.'

A fortnight after Ian returned from Gazzada he was invited to write a full-page article for the *Scotsman* on Vatican II (25 September 1965). He entitled the piece 'Gin ye daur'[27] and this wasn't just an encouragement to himself.

In light of the final session of Vatican II which was about to begin, Ian recognised that different interpretations could and would be placed on the various documents. He placed significance on the Decree on the Church produced at the previous session of the Council in 1964. It began from the holy, priestly and prophetic people and only then considered the hierarchy, which should serve the whole church. Dialogue of the whole church should precede and direct the formulation of the Faith.

Ian reported that he had attended a consultation in Leicester in mid-August (1965) on the 'Christian faith in Modern Society' arranged by Denis Rice. He described him as the imaginative warden of Vaughn College. About 80% of those who attended were Roman Catholics; the remainder came from a variety of churches. Ian recognised that these Roman Catholic lay people there were much more confident in their questioning of their disinheritance in their church than had been typical in earlier years.

Reporting on the work at Gazzada which Ian had expected to be preparing the ground for later work, he was pleasantly surprised at just how much progress had already been made. He recognised that personal encounter is of immense value in itself. He recalled meeting some larger than life characters who were balanced by the more unobtrusive with their scholarly contributions. He remembers that previously opportunities for personal encounters were all too infrequent. What the world needs is a Church made new in reconciliation. He noted that in Scotland with its variety of denominations there were real opportunities for evangelical witness; 'we need not leave our own shores to meet the "world church"'. It was surely with tongue in cheek that Ian said, 'To refuse to have Roman

Catholics participating alongside us in the process is one way of saying there are no serious questions of truth between us which need to be cleared up.'

Ian strikes a very positive note which will be developed many years later when he looks forward into a new millennium. He more immediately states his contention that 'theology is beginning again to capture people's interest, and no longer be treated as a mere academic discipline . . . In a certain way this Age of Doubt is also an Age of Faith.' The ecumenical movement and the renewal of the Roman Catholic Church provide a unique opportunity. 'No chance like this has been provided for centuries.' It is a great time to be alive – 'gin ye daur' It is hardly surprising that Ian has contended that Vatican II was the most ecumenical council for a long time and that it heralded a sea change in the Roman Catholic Church.

Years later in 1981 when Pope John Paul II visited Scotland he was presented with a spinning wheel. He asked that it be given to Scottish Churches House and through it to all Christians in Scotland. On the Eve of St Andrew's Day in 1983 the Apostolic Pro nuncio, Archbishop Bruno Heim and Cardinal Gordon Gray handed over the spinning wheel to the Very Rev. Prof. Robin Barbour, Chairman of the Scottish Churches Council, in the presence of representatives of the churches. Robin Barbour accepted it as a sign of promise for the future and of longing for the time when the thread that is spun by the Churches in Scotland gets woven into one single garment, making visible their unity in Jesus Christ.

It is no easy task to tease out the significant themes of the time Ian and Margaret spent in Scottish Churches House. Douglas Gay has in his PhD thesis made at least a start in the examination of the theological framework within which Ian was working.[28]

It is instructive to compare the content of the programme in the 1960s in general terms with what was being offered through Scottish Churches House 2007. It is helpful too to consider the programme content offered by the Iona Community in its centres on Iona. The classification of consultations can be difficult as they often embrace more than a single category as show in the table.[29]

All figures as percentages (rounded to nearest per cent)	Scottish Churches House 1960–69	Scottish Churches House 2007	Iona Community Abbey and MacLeod Centre 2007
Social Concerns	32	4	6
Church and Religious Concerns	39	63	70
Political and Industrial Concerns	22	4	3
Cultural Concerns	7	29	21
Total	100	100	100

Some conclusions can be reached immediately. The two centres had much in common in 2007. In the sixties Scottish Churches House seems to have made much more of its involvement in the life of the nation and in recent times there has been greater emphasis on the life of the churches. It is open to debate whether Scottish Churches House might have benefited from a return to the emphasis it placed in early days on the *oikoumene,* the whole inhabited world.

The development of Ian Fraser's thinking during his decade at Scottish Churches House can in part be followed through his writing. In 1961 he wrote an article for the Scottish Journal of Theology, 'The Apostle's Doctrine and Fellowship'. He was aware, we can suppose, of the responsibility the position of warden placed on him at 'the heart of Scottish ecumenism'. He recognised the necessary but limited role of top-level inter-church conversations but in echoes of the WCC deliverances from Lund and New Delhi he emphasises the need for ecumenism to be made a living reality in local situations.

The Scottish Churches Council published 'Let's Get Moving' in 1969. Douglas Gay ranks it alongside George MacLeod's 'We Shall Rebuild' (1945); Ralph Morton's 'The Household of Faith' (1951) and Tom Allan's 'The Face of my Parish' (1954). In his book as Ian prepared to leave Scottish Churches House, he reminded his readers that church order in Scotland must serve church mission. He is outspoken in declaring that the churches stand in urgent need of reform. In successive chapters he demolishes claims of Scottish Episcopacy and Scottish Presbyterianism to provide hope apart from ecumenism. He is especially critical of the lack of lay participation in the General Assembly of the Church of Scotland. A proposed merger of the Scottish Episcopal Church and the Church of Scotland he saw as important, but secondary to the essential task of reforming the life of the churches for mission. The Episcopal Church put itself forward as a bridge between other churches but Ian asked 'What is the point of a bridge which has both ends in the water.' Ian rejects calls to abandon the church as institution and affirms his belief in the centrality of the church in God's purposes for the renewal of Scottish life.

Ian concludes that 'reunion without renewal is a pie without meat'. Parishes can start right away from where they are if they are prepared for a renewal and a restructuring of the local church. If not, he can see the churches finding a way of continued existence, but not a way of life. At the last he is almost lyrical: 'A spring in the step, even a jauntiness becomes us as we swing into a future which is largely unknown to us, but which is in the hands of our faithful God. Forgetting the things which are behind we press forward.' [30]

It is perhaps fair to give Douglas Gay a last word on the time the Frasers spent at Scottish Churches House. He concludes that the Fraser achievement was remarkable and Scottish Churches House was indeed a sign set up for Scotland and its churches. Its work deserves to be remembered, valued and learned from. 'For the Reformed tradition so often accused of a pathological obsession with the world's depravity, a churchly theologian who faced the 60s with confidence and optimism rather than fear and loathing remains a key prophetic witness to the Incarnation and a significant part of the story of how we are to be church in the world which is Scotland.'

As a place of 'salt and light' it is clear that Dunblane made its mark on the life of the nation in the first decade after it opened. As important to Ian and Margaret were the marks it left on the lives of persons who participated in the great experiment. In Scottish Churches House there was a consultation on the Kilbrandon proposals for the reform of local government. Some years later a woman approached Ian. 'You'll not remember me,' she said. Ian confessed that he did not remember her name but he did remember her as someone who said very little till they were approaching the end of the conference. Then she had spoken briefly and put her finger on the next steps that needed to be taken. She had left her mark. It was really only in retrospect that the value of her contribution was appreciated.

An occasional visitor to Scottish Churches House, John Calder, a publisher from London, always took part in acts of worship in Scottish Churches House, though he was a professed and convinced unbeliever. In case this was done as a courtesy he was reminded that all those who came to Dunblane had their convictions respected – it was to be a matter of his choice whether he did or did not attend worship. He replied that he was quite aware of this and it was of his own choosing. His questioner could not resist asking how this was the case since he made no secret of his unbelief. 'The things you pray for in the chapel are real. They are important to me too. I can share with you in your worship by making them into meditations.' Acts of worship which do not have hard lines of set belief drawn through them, but open people up with awe to a God who is marvellous and mysterious, can draw atheists and agnostics into participation, without feeling that their integrity is being assaulted. Ian continues to be in contact with John till the present time.

An unnamed social worker said of the Scottish Churches House experience, 'We all meet officially on committees: and I know exactly what everyone is going to say. The great thing about this place is that you never know what anyone is going to say!'

Ian continued involvement with the Glion-Gazzada group right through to the Laity Congress in Rome in 1967. It was the start of this congress that coincided with the Queen's visit to Scottish Churches House. Ian had to be there to welcome her but the timing of the two events meant that he should have been able to be at nearly all of the Congress. Special flights were laid on to get Ian and Margaret to Rome on time. This sadly was all to no avail. The last leg of the journey was delayed by fog. They had to content themselves that they would arrive a day later than planned! The only non-Mass worship session at the Laity Congress was a Church of Scotland communion that was led by Ian. It seems to have been part of a recurring pattern.

After nearly ten years in Dunblane, it was time to move on. Ian and Margaret were to find themselves headed for Geneva.

Endnotes

[20] Dr Craig was, however, still held in high regard in the Church of Scotland and was appointed Moderator for 1961-62.

[21] In the 1950s the 'Tell Scotland' movement struggled to hold its evangelical and ecumenical wings together. In time the evangelical wing would look to the St. Ninian's Training Centre in Crieff; the ecumenical wing would have its centre at Scottish Churches House in Dunblane.

[22] The chairman of the executive committee of 'Tell Scotland' in 1957 was Robert Mackie, former general secretary, first of the SCM and then of the World Student Christian Federation.

[23] PhD thesis Douglas Gay 'A Practical Theology of Church and World: Ecclesiology and Social Vision in 20th Century Scotland' (available online)

[24] A detailed account of the Fraser years at Scottish Churches House is given in 'Ecumenical Adventure: a Dunblane Initiative' (ACTS) 2003.

[25] He was later to become Professor of Music in Princeton Theological Seminary.

[26] Ian also collaborated later with Donald Rennie, a member of the Iona Community living and working in Aberdeenshire. Their work was published in the 'Try it out' hymnbook, which is available from Wild Goose Publications, the Iona Community.

[27] 'If you dare' – the inference is of a challenge to enter into the unknown.

[28] Douglas Gay PhD Thesis. It needs to be realised that the thesis is exploring a particular interest of its author and cannot do justice to Ian Fraser's time before and particular after his time in Dunblane. The links that interest Gay relate more to Ian's theological predecessor and his successor, John Baillie and Duncan Forrester.

[29] The table was compiled from figures in Gay's thesis and from the 2007 published programmes of the Iona Community Centre and Scottish Churches House.

[30] Philippians 3.13,14.

CHAPTER SIX

GENEVA AND THE WORLD

DURING HIS TIME as warden of Scottish Churches House Ian was frequently invited to attend conferences and consultations at home and abroad. On one such visit to France, Ian was walked out by some of the World Council of Churches (WCC) headquarters staff. It reminded him of nothing so much as mafia bosses putting a gun in the back of an outsider 'inviting' him to become one of their own. As far as they were concerned choice did not come into it. It was explained to Ian that he was being 'invited' to join the WCC staff in Geneva. He promised to consider the matter.

Ian phoned home to Margaret in Dunblane unsure of how she would react to this invitation. She told Ian that it was time for him to make himself available to the world church. Ian listened to Margaret. He accepted the position at the WCC headquarters and was appointed as an Executive Secretary in the WCC Unit on Education and Renewal. And a right royal send off they were given in Dunblane!

Ian and Margaret found Geneva a good place to be. It is a beautiful city lying at the western end of Lake Geneva. Some fine bridges cross the river that flows through the city. Margaret and Ian stayed in an apartment. He suffered from sinusitis and was prescribed medication that made him drowsy at night. On one occasion they awoke to find their building deserted only later to discover that there had been a fire in the basement. Smoke had risen up through the flats. The fire engine had been in attendance. Everyone was out in the street. The two of them had slept through the commotion. It might so easily have had a very different outcome given the dangers of smoke inhalation.

Other people in the WCC were less enthusiastic about Geneva. A colleague's wife got a phone call from the police asking if she would want to know that her husband had parked his car in the red light district of the city. The truth of the matter was that he had gone to the dentist and could not find anywhere else to park – a not uncommon occurrence even in the Geneva of forty years ago. The citizens of Geneva are often characterised as rather inflexible in relation to life in general. Ian saw that as an oversimplification. Two days before he was due to go on his first visit to Africa someone asked him, 'Have you had all your jags?' If his memory serves him well, seven were required. In Geneva you are meant to diagnose your own medical condition then find a doctor who specialised in that ailment. Ian being Ian found an atypical Swiss doctor. He administered all seven jags in the one session and provided the follow-up inoculations as required. Ian had to have these carried in the refrigerators on planes as he flew south. He was neither up nor down with this sudden burst of medication.

The main problem on that trip arose when he flew in a terrible Old Russian Illyushin aircraft. It seemed likely that it would shake itself to bits on the flight from Rome to Addis Ababa. Ian was travelling tourist class. They had overbooked so he was offered a complimentary move up to first class. Ian was miffed. After a yellow fever jab, alcohol was the last thing he would be allowed and it was free in first class!

Margaret and Ian had a caravan just over the border in France. They had clearly moved on from earlier holidays in a borrowed tent. The great delight however now was to go to a place where you could check that you had not lost your sense of smell. Even the dung on the farms around Geneva seems to have been sanitised. The whole country is inhumanly 'clean'. A quick dose of France kept the Frasers healthy. One of the staff at the Ecumenical Centre was a skiing enthusiast and was prepared to act as an instructor to those of the staff who were novices. As part of the preparation, he had a look at legs, ankles and feet. When he saw Ian's (and no surprise given his history with his feet) he said at once, 'No downhill skiing for you. Your ankles are so slim, if you make a sharp turn, they would almost certainly give way under you.' Instead he advised cross-country or Nordic skiing. This suited both Margaret and Ian. On a Saturday morning they would go up to Girvine, in the mountains above Geneva and enjoy themselves on the seven mile long cross-country piste through the woods. Ian remembers spending hours at this exhilarating exercise. When they arrived back home they were sometimes so tired that they would have a shower and a siesta rather than eating their midday meal.

In Geneva, Margaret and Ian alternated between the Scots Kirk and the Protestant Church (French speaking) at Petit Sacconneux where they stayed. Niall Watson was the minister of the Scots Kirk when the Frasers were in Geneva. A friendship began when neighbours in the pews mentioned what a pleasure it was to worship alongside such a fine singer. That was Margaret. From such a small beginning began a friendship that lasted over many years.

Margaret participated enthusiastically in the group which was called 'Staff Wives' – at that time nearly all the staff were male. She was one of the 'Femmes de Pasteurs' who took on the task of meeting guest workers from Italy and Spain at Geneva Station. She made sure they had a personal welcome, a hot meal and the opportunity to seek any advice they needed with regard to accommodation before they moved on to a place for work. It is certainly no surprise that Margaret found her niche in the work of hospitality. She was also involved in studies undertaken by the group. Ian remembers they tackled a course on Buddhism.

The Swiss rarely visited one another. Staff members and families in the WCC did visit back and forward but there were few opportunities to meet Swiss folk in their own homes. They seemed to be allergic to the company of others. Such at least was Ian's impression. Sadly this may have been as a result of an old tradition. It maintained that you could not be so forward as to invite the minister to call socially. It can still today contribute to loneliness for those in the ministry and not just in Switzerland. It can be particularly difficult where it is a single person who is serving a congregation.

In theory the three units into which WCC was divided were meant to relate to one another in their work, although the strong tendency was for each to go its own way. In the early days of WCC Faith and Order was the prestigious department although Ian contended that its biggest challenge was to drag some top brass ecclesiastics into the 20th century. The Unit Ian was part of got on with the job of discovering how people were living the truth and how the church was changing in consequence. The person Ian found most eager of all to develop links between the different departments and units was Philip Potter. When Ian had been travelling in some area which seemed to be important for staff or had been embroiled in some event (such as the Munich Olympics) Philip would eagerly seek him out and ask him to share with his colleagues whatever Ian thought to be important for their departmental work.

Ian was ambivalent about the work of the Faith and Order Department. The membership of the committee did not represent the church but rather the officials in the churches. When one began to see signs of a great growth of faith and re-ordering of church life from below their preoccupying concerns remained those in-house concerns – ordination, participation in sacraments etc. These matters deserved attention but not the undue emphasis they were given by those whose own status depended on the results of the debates.

However, Ian found Lukas Vischer, who led Faith and Order, humble and thoughtful, hard-working and well-informed. Ian felt his judgment about the Faith and Order Department was justified in later years. A staff member of that department, Irmgard Kindt, came to the resources centre on Basic Christian Communities at Scottish Churches House. She spent four days studying the material Ian had gathered. She made it clear that she was convinced that it was 'from below' that the main signs of renewed faith and reordered life were emerging in the world church.

Ian still remembers vividly the first General Secretary of the WCC, Visser t'Hooft, telling him about the time when Pope Paul VI arrived for the first visit of a Pope to the Ecumenical Centre in Geneva and announced 'I am Peter'. Visser said to Ian 'I wish I had had a cock at the time which I could have squeezed and got it to crow!'

Ian characterised the WCC headquarters staff as being at that time 'too many men and too many Westerners.' It was the way things were; and the way things were needed to be renewed! Ian worked closely with Hans Rudi Weber. He had been with Ian in the laity consultation which sat alongside Vatican II. Hans was a perceptive biblical scholar with an interest in the history of many countries. He was resource person for many in the WCC. His books were widely read and valued. He wrote particularly on the role of the laity in the life of the church. Hans and Ian had independently come to a very similar understanding of the importance of equipping the laity and drew strength from one another's work.[31] In later years Hans expressed regret to Ian that all this work was wasted. Ian took issue with him. He used the image of a river which goes underground for a time and later reappears where it might be least expected. In time it reaches and contributes to the open sea. The investment of time and effort Ian believed had borne fruit in many places.

There was always the temptation for WCC staff to value their assumed status more highly than the opportunity to effect change. On one occasion HQ staff members were asked if they would be willing to accept salaries more in line with missionaries working in the field rather than being paid as executives. Two staff members agreed. The identity of one of the two is surely not a matter of guesswork. The rest of the staff insisted that that their salaries continue to reflect their *executive* status. Ian's commitment to people across the world clearly had informed his response. The fact that he was recently appointed weighed little with him. He was never afraid to speak his mind whatever the company.

Ian was initially appointed to Laity and Studies when he went to Geneva. The director of that department took ill and made way for Werner Simpfendorfer. He was welcoming and helped Ian to settle into his new post. He was a good companion. The staff in the headquarters tended to be a group of specialists in their own fields. Posts were not advertised. Potential members were identified and then press-ganged into accepting an invitation to join WCC in Geneva. Ian's own experience had been all too commonplace.

When it came time for Gene Blake to retire as General Secretary of the WCC, there were those who said of a successor, 'We must get the best man for the job.' For one thing it was assumed that it had to be a man; for another the words 'known to us' were implied. Those who supported this view had a limited range of acquaintances and knowledge. Up till that point the influences which dominated in the WCC were the USA and Western Europe. There had been brave attempts to take the Third World seriously and through the Orthodox Churches to establish new and creative relationships with Eastern Europe. But it was time then to break the mould. Americans and Western Europeans were well-known and would readily come to mind. A search was needed to bring into the limelight people from the Third World whose potential could be only too easily overlooked, since they lacked the visibility afforded to the people from the 'North'.

In the middle of these discussions Margaret asked Ian if he would take the job as General Secretary of the World Council of Churches if it was offered to him. He reminded her of his conviction that the next holder of that position should come from the developing world. She repeated her question indicating that the circumstances would need to be right. In that case Ian affirmed that he would not only accept but was brash enough to believe that he could make a good job of the appointment.

Ian had two changes in mind which he would have implemented immediately. The first related to the headquarters staff of WCC in Geneva. He would have taken more time to listen to where they were at in their remits. The second related to churches around the world. He would have spent less time talking to church leaders and more time listening to the people on the ground, hearing something of their life and faith. Ian often admits to being a mix of 'intense shyness and brashness' at one and the same time. It is not in his understanding true humility to undervalue your own gifts. Margaret was pleased to know where Ian stood on such matters. She was concerned that he might be too diffident to take on work such as they had discussed.

Ian remembers staying at a Holiday Inn in Utrecht when the decision about the next General Secretary was made by members of the Central Committee. Ian picked up some work that needed his attention and found an empty room right at the top of the building where he could get on with it in peace. The name of Philip Potter had come to the fore. He was a Trinidadian who had served the churches in Britain. The time came when Philip was asked to withdraw in order that his candidature might be debated in his absence. He found himself in the same room as Ian. This meant that when Gene came to tell Philip that he was their choice as next General Secretary Ian was the first to be able to congratulate him. He also wished him the strength that would be required for the heavy burden which would now have to be carried.

In the early 1970s not long after he had been appointed to the Geneva staff, Ian went to Philip Potter and asked if he should resign to allow someone from the developing world a place in Geneva. 'You would be the last member of staff whose resignation would be welcomed,' was the reply.

Denise Goodall was Ian's secretary in Geneva. She had courtroom speed shorthand – no task was too difficult for her. Ian recalls one of the tapes she transcribed for him. It was an interview about the Iroquois in North America. Denise challenged Ian. She was convinced that there was more to learn from that contact than he had recognised. 'Well,' said Ian to her, 'you follow it up.' She did.

Ian referred to Denise as his working partner and in later correspondence to Ian she picks this up: 'It is very difficult for me to express as much as I want to, how much I have enjoyed our years working together. All I can say is that I have loved it tremendously and thank you for being such a super 'partner'.' It was one thing for Ian to call her 'partner' It was something else that she knew that Ian meant it!

At the Bossey Conference Centre some miles north of Geneva Ian was principally interested in matters relating to the laity. He longed to discover how the people of God can be nourished so that they can develop using their own resources. It was necessary to make these insights available through publications and to provide further opportunities to confer. There were important lessons to be learned even in the presentation of the material. Ian discovered early on that publications printed on glossy white paper would not be read by many of the poor in the developing world. The very nature of the paper used in printing spoke volumes about the people for whom writing was intended. By contrast the poorest quality paper said loudly to many – 'this is for you'. Ian encouraged the use of cartoons rather than standard text where this would lead to more effective communication.

At Bossey people from many lands came and shared their experience and understanding of the faith. It was always the intention to draw students from as wide a spectrum as possible to allow sharing to be as fruitful as possible.

The students at Bossey came to work on a particular subject. As the years passed more long term study was undertaken. Their studies were tied into the academic programme of the University of Geneva. Ian reflected that one of the purposes George MacLeod suggested for the renovated living quarters of Iona Abbey when the rebuilding was coming to an end in the 1960s was the establishment of a centre for theological studies.

When Ian arrived in Geneva he was to be responsible for the 'Laity and Studies' project along with a Canadian colleague. They were attempting to discover how lay people could be encouraged to develop studies and action in the world to express their faith. Then Ian was asked in addition to be responsible for one of the five major study programmes decided on at the 1968 WCC Uppsala Assembly which he had attended. Ian worked under a man to begin with on the

'Living with Change' programme whose parents had not survived the Holocaust. This took its toll on him. In time Ian was asked to take over and head up this programme.

A meeting of the Division of Ecumenical Action of the WCC considered the proposed 'Study on Living with Change'. Ian had opportunity to have some input into the process. After discussion it was agreed that some changes were desirable. The word 'study' with its academic overtones was dropped in favour 'action-research programme'. The work was to be led by a 'co-ordinator' rather than a 'director'. The title was also changed from 'Living with Change' with its neutral or negative connotation to 'Participating in Change' with an altogether more positive outlook.

It was this programme that Ian was required to coordinate with a view to submitting a report to the WCC Assembly in 1975. The general guidelines given were that 'the process should aim at involving a broad constituency of ordinary people who were struggling to cope with change in issues which faced them locally so that they became more aware of where and how to adapt to, resist or initiate change.' WCC speak at its best! When Ian consulted senior colleagues on how to fulfil his assignment, all he got was, 'It's for you to find out.' The world can be a very big place with no marked path to follow. Prayer for light had a note of desperation in it as Ian strove to find how he might fulfil his remits. While the tasks were reasonably clear no one seemed able to help. This was not just because other members of staff were unwilling to help it was just that they had no more experience or expertise than Ian had.

Very early on Ian rejected the development of the 'Participation in Change' programme using the WCC's standard approach. What tended to happen after an Assembly fixed its major programmes? People from Western Europe and the USA within reach of Geneva had a first run at the theme. People in these two areas tended to have the money to travel to Geneva. This material was then sent out world-wide with a request for reactions and comments. That put a Western stamp on the material from the start and people from parts of the Pacific with travel and postal difficulties might not be able to make any contribution at all.

Ian came to the conclusion that he should begin by gathering material for this programme by making visits to Third World countries. He lived with the poor and brought back to the West insights related to Christian belief and practice. In this way people were educated who so often are expected to take the role of instructors.

The 'option for the poor' was a central concern in the WCC. But it tended to be a concern not lived out in the way staff went about their work. Ian pointed out that if you took a flight to some part of the world, went by taxi to the hotel which was like any hotel anywhere, held a conference and then retraced your steps, you lost all the value which contact with local people might have provided. Ian's way was to find how ordinary folk travelled – by bus, jeepney, bicycle, rickshaw or whatever and brush shoulders with them as he went about his allotted task.

A message normally preceded Ian's visits. It said that he would not be living in a hotel – so could they give him a corner of a shanty to curl up in at night – he didn't even need a blanket; and would they share some of their food with him? Jim O'Halloran, a notable promoter of small Christian communities was amused when Ian spoke in his hearing of the different merits of sleeping spaces: bare earth was fine, never rigid; wood was often warped a bit and you could adjust; concrete in the Third World was almost always hand-laid and your body could adapt to that; worst was teak – it was quite unyielding. But in fact Ian learned to cope whatever the situation.

If the family meal in the Dominican Republic was four potatoes per day and in Venezuela was one big dish of vegetable soup, food could not be easily spared from meagre rations. Yet it was important for people to share what little they had. The people were thus identified as the honouring hosts, Ian their honoured guest. This preserved their dignity. In no time they were entrusting Ian with their life stories as they would never have done had he stayed in a hotel and merely visited them. He found what a feast is to be enjoyed in stories of faith and hope against all odds.

So the 'Participation in Change' programme was developed through sharing stories rather than by abstract thinking. Ian had been in conferences on 'The Shape of the Church of the Future' which were so theoretical that they lost all touch with reality. All the time the Church of the Future was emerging, concretely! Small Christian Communities have operated clandestinely in China, in Hungary, in the Czech Republic under Maoist and Marxist regimes. Pruned back by persecution, they pared down church life to essentials. Ian found similar communities throbbing with new life in the developed west and in the developing world of the Americas, Africa and the Far East. He focused on stories which spoke of reality and hope. His report to the Nairobi Assembly in 1975 was published as 'The Fire Runs'. It is a collection of stories linked in such a way as to point up the theological insights they embodied. Lessons Ian had learned working in the paper mill and walking with his people in the Parish of Rosyth were bearing fruit on a global scale. The discovery of theology had been a revelation and a joy to Ian in his student days: he believed that it provided a faith basis for life. As such it needed contributions from people from all walks of life - just as Jesus in parables offered a theology that could be accessed by people, both the learned and the unlearned.[32] Over the years this approach to theology made headway. The risks that Ian took paid off.

So Geneva became the base from which Ian visited the five continents to listen to what the people of God were doing in their Christian communities and in their wider communities. Ian was careful to record in detail these visits and the discoveries he made have been made available both in the recordings he made of conversations and in much of what he has written. The first visits and his reflections on them formed the basis for the report he presented to the 1975 Nairobi WCC Assembly as coordinator of the 'Participation in Change' programme. Highlights from these and later visits with other life experiences feature in 'Strange Fire' and 'Salted with Fire' published later.

In the penultimate chapter of Ian's report to the Nairobi Assembly he has a significant parable. In summary it runs along these lines:
> 'In his own way he was happy. He had been blind and deaf since birth. He had a place to sleep, food sometimes sufficient for his needs and company to get him through the long hours.

The trouble started when the 'Healer' arrived. He asked the man, 'Would you like to see?' When indication was given that the answer was 'Yes', ointment was placed on the man's eyes. The Healer left. Sight began to return. On a later visit the Healer asked the man, 'How is it with my friend?'

'Bad!' he is told.

'Has he lost his sight once more?'

'Oh, no his sight is completely restored, more's the pity!'

'Why do you say that?'

'He is no longer the happy man he was. He has seen the rich and the poor – the injustice of life. He is no longer contented as he was.'

The Healer met up with the man. Through an interpreter he asked, 'Do you want to be able to hear?' The villagers tried to interfere. They clearly believed enough damage had been done. The man, however, indicated that he would like to have the ability to hear.

When the healer returned some time later to the village he was met by a hostile crowd. 'Was it not enough to rob him of his peace, that you had to rob him of his faith?'

'What do you mean?' asked the Healer.

'Well,' they said, 'he has learned of other religions, other understandings of God. He no longer has something to hold on to. He has become a disturbance to us all!'

The man saw the Healer in the distance, ran to him and hugged him. The Healer turned to the crowd. Then he looked again at the man. 'They tell me I have robbed you of your happiness and security by giving you sight and hearing.'

'It is partly true,' said the man. 'I am no longer as happy as I was. I am no longer as secure as I was. Only, now I am alive!'

The reports of the visits Ian made to Christians around the world are often disturbing as well as enlightening. Those who would prefer to imagine him as an icon should perhaps skip the remainder of this chapter or seek an immediate refund on the whole. Time and space prevent a detailed account of all these visits. The usefulness of such repetition would be dubious. Rather a selection of reports from the visits in the period from 1969–75 will allow some key themes to be identified.

Ian's first visit to the Iberian Peninsula took him to the Ecumenical Centre for Reconciliation in Figueira do Foz in Portugal. When Ian arrived he thought he had stumbled on one of the last outposts of Christian civilisation, of civilisation as he knew it. Breakfast was programmed for 8.30 a.m. with the first session due at nine that morning. By nine o'clock the breakfast table was beginning to be laid. He enquired, 'When does the session start?'

'Half an hour after they intend it to.'

'Well then, when do they intend to begin?'

'Nobody knows yet!'

The Sabbath was made for man and not man for the Sabbath. The Portuguese clearly believe this also applies to the rest of the week. Time was not allowed to dominate human life.

With time on his hands, Ian walked out into the surrounding community. The women he saw around the town were not so much dressed as huddled up with clothes. Everything was carried on the head – baskets of fish, vegetables and fuel; water was carried in an earthenware jar as had been the case in first century Rome. The men were mainly peasant farmers or fishermen. It took Ian back to his farming relatives struggling through the Depression of the hungry Thirties.

In the Portuguese Ecumenical Centre Ian discovered alliances of evangelical churches existing in a minority situation, with all the defensiveness that this implies. They were in a country, on paper overwhelmingly Roman Catholic, but quietly and firmly anti-clerical. A quite new Roman Catholic and Protestant relationship had developed which was both exciting and upsetting; how does any establishment of whatever side, deal with an ecumenical conference in which Roman Catholic and Protestants were combining to tackle problems of farmers and fishermen? Ian experienced the beginning, the very beginning of church people coming alive from the roots up.

In 1972 Ian visited the San Miguelito Community in Panama. He was aware that in the struggle of everyday life Christians were working out new ways of life which were still evading the 'wise'. People were binding faith and politics together, experimenting with many types of lay ministry and tackling the biblical and theological understanding of their faith. They were making life a liturgy which was both locally rooted and yet belonged to the universal Christian family.

In a recorded interview Ian asked:
Q: How did the parish of San Miguelito start?
A   People from the interior and from poor areas of Panama City were forced to find space to live. The people came with a real

sense of adventure. Legally they were outlaws; they were squatters on land they did not own.

Q: What about the church. How did it move in?

A: It was the result of a partnership between the diocese of Chicago and the diocese of Panama. Three priests from the USA were invited by the Bishop of the City of Panama. The Americans were unsure as to what to do for the best. They had to ask the local people; this sat well with the culture of Panama – dialogue, conversation, dance and music. Together the conclusion was reached that they were on to something truly great. A willingness to adopt radical change laid the basis for the church in San Miguelito.

Q: Do you have deacons?

A: A sizeable number of people were trained as deacons but the bishop lost the paperwork that should have gone to Rome. When this happened repeatedly the people finally said, 'Let's cut this out. Let's have a lay ministry.' The people set apart the folk who would minister to them and they just got on with the job. About 250 trained volunteers were carrying substantial responsibilities, supported by the core group of full time priests and laymen.

Q: How are these ministries developed so that they relate to actual needs?

A: People take on themselves a ministry based on what has been their own personal experience of resurrection in a particular area of life. Fidel Gonzalez who had miraculously survived a car crash is extremely adept at talking to people who are sick and dying. It is a fantastic experience to hear him talk about death and resurrection because it is something he has lived through. Modesta Contreras is a man who was illiterate. Fascinated by scripture he determined to learn to read and in a reversal of the usual man-woman roles he learned from his wife. This changed his whole life. His love of scripture and his ability now to express himself are wonders to behold.

Q: Do the people see a theological dimension to the discoveries they are making?

A: People have experienced physical change but they have gone on to discover that profound, definite, personal change has become important in life. This includes change in family life, community life and change which God intends for the whole world. To the question 'What are we really living for?' has come the answer, 'We live for other people.' Two other theological understandings are people's preoccupation with the incarnation and the presence of a creative spirit in a community which is conscious of its responsibility as something able to change the world. God is present in their lives and this represents the potential for change.

Q: Do people build up worship in the parish themselves?

A: People prepare themselves in small groups in the parish. They deepen their understanding so that when prayer is made to the Lord who is present, the community must begin to look for ways to live it out. The innovative contribution to the liturgy found its roots in music. The instrumentalists on guitar, drum and *bocina* (a local folk instrument) felt that the music in traditional worship was alien. They began to use folk melodies to express basic ideas e.g. penitence.

Given the brief nature of Ian's visits to churches and small Christian communities, time could not be wasted. Every experience was an opportunity to look, listen and learn. One night when a planned engagement fell through, Ian wandered among the houses in the community. He met a man, Bill, washing a car. Nine moths previously he had been a hopeless drunk. He found Christ. Now he lived by doing odd jobs. Ian wondered if there was some meeting he might attend. The man was a lay minister and was shortly to conduct a 'liturgy of the Word'. Ian was welcome to join him. The man went to the meeting in the same creased shirt and trousers in which he had washed the car.

The simple house where the people met was really just one small room with parts partitioned off for a bedroom and a kitchen. Two children cried intermittently during the service. Outside dogs howled competing with a transistor. On the kitchen table was a cross with a lighted candle on either side. Over his open-necked shirt Bill placed a stole and was ready to start. About ten neighbours pressed in, some bringing their own chairs or stools with them. Most of those who took part were in their twenties or early thirties.

After an introductory session of singing and responses, a passage from the Acts of the Apostles allocated for use across the parish that week was taken for study. Almost everyone participated in building up an understanding of the passage. At one point Bill seemed to be emphasizing too strongly God's presence in the midst of life. The people would not have it. They said, 'We know that God is in the thick of things where we are. We believe that. But that is not all. God is also beyond us. We don't know how he can be with us and beyond us. But that's the way it is.'

After about forty minutes of Bible study those who took part were asked to offer prayer and all but two responded. Another song was sung, there were one or two more responses, and the service ended.

The immediacy of that event is captured by Ian's description. It remains fresh almost 40 years later. So do many of the insights that came to him in the report he wrote about his travels from his base in Geneva. Some are emphasised not least the creativity of the laity in the face of clerical failure. But the readers are also left to draw their own conclusions. Truth was finally discovered not just in Bill's ministry but in the participation of all who were present. In this way the mystery of God is revealed.

With the Nairobi Assembly in mind Ian visited a number of African countries.

In Nigeria[33] a local group met to contribute to the 'Participation in Change' programme. They were asked, 'What should be prominently on the agenda of the 1975 Fifth World Assembly of the WCC? They replied, 'Christianity came to us from the West. But Westerners are not acting at all like Christians. One of the group reported 'I went to a church in Germany; it was obvious no one wanted to sit with me; the church in the west is full of racism. The West has money and power but it needs to learn what real humility means. The big question for the Assembly is how can the World Council of Churches begin a mission to the West to evangelise people there in all their dealings with other countries. Nothing is more important.'

When the first grants as part of the Programme to Combat Racism were announced, African Churches hailed this as a sign that the WCC was becoming genuinely a *World* Council of Churches.[34] Many churches in the West reacted defensively, imprisoned by their history and culture.

In the north-west of Kenya[35] the Council of Churches assisted a largely nomadic people affected by drought in a mainly Muslim area. One group, given a bag of maize for sowing, dug a hole, buried the sack full of grain and waited for a harvest! Education was clearly required. Missionary agencies offered this as they saw it as an opportunity to proclaim the light of the gospel in the face of the darkness of Islam. But the local African church was in brotherly relationship with the Muslims. A split threatened. The local community made it clear that technical assistance was welcome; propaganda was not. The view that evangelisation was being rejected was false. An adviser noted, 'The people are open to evangelism but it must be evangelism by quality of life. Evangelisation that meant a wholesale and uninstructed condemnation of Islam and local culture would not be tolerated.'

In 1973 Ian attended the Annual Assembly of the Council of Protestant Churches of Cuba as he brought to an end the first series of visits to churches and small Christian communities around the world. He was part of a small delegation of three from WCC who went to suss out the situation in Cuba after the revolution. He felt that this Assembly would offer him an opportunity to meet folk from many small churches within the context of their national conference.

The last warning Ian was given before he set out was 'Remember, it is a police state.' In fact his experience of officialdom in Havana was of an administration in the Latin American style but with accompanying efficiency. It is true that Cuba was under a military regime. Ian observed a country living in a state of relaxed vigilance. But there was no reign of terror.

There Ian re-discovered a pace of living that is not dominated by the clock. The programme said the Assembly was due to begin at 2.30 p.m. – in fact it began at about 4.30 p.m. – and no one seemed either surprised or concerned. The missing hours seemed largely to have been used to renew old relationships and establish new ones.

Before he left Cuba Ian had the opportunity to meet a member of the Central Committee of the Communist Party. His host encouraged a free and frank exchange of views including a discussion of a pilot scheme for local government freed from close Communist Party control.

People in developing countries are supporters of the United Nations Declaration of Human Rights but many see it as very Western in its approach. In many developing countries the human rights that are required are more fundamental. Everyone should have access to justice – but it is of little use if a person does not have enough to eat. There should be freedom of the press but what of the vast numbers of people who cannot read or write?

Emphasis had been placed in Cuba on providing people with an affordable home. Health care was universal; free and good. Education was open to everyone. In 1973 tourists were not treated like gods. The best hotels were kept for workers who performed well in their place of employment not for tourists at all. As Ian explored the open society he discovered in Cuba his memory drew him back to the tiny church of Lecropt which stands high above the motorway which by-passes Stirling, in mid-Scotland. There the main entry led straight into the laird's gallery, where he could warm himself by a fire and sleep through the sermon in a comfortable armchair in the presence of his family. The congregation had to go down to a side door and enter the church from below. The session clerk long frustrated by the way the church had been built expressed his delight when a new entry was driven through the laird's gallery into the heart of the church. He realised something theological had been done. It was an architectural way of saying that all human beings are made in the image of God and all are made to worship. For Ian to see workers enjoying their holidays in fine hotels in Cuba seemed to him to be similarly a theological statement about the dignity God gives to all.

Ian was interested to hear of the political results of the revolution. It was pointed out that massive Soviet aid had funded development but concluded that aid had been used as Cuba saw fit and that it had particularly benefited the poorest 40% of the population. The flagship development in education in Cuba was, of course, the claim by Fidel Castro in 1960 that he would eliminate illiteracy in a year. The story of what was then done belongs elsewhere but the United Nations no less recognised that in 12 months illiteracy was reduced from 24% to 4%!

Since 1966 a new national goal was added to the goals of economic development and social justice – the goal of a new humanity. Che Guevara[36] wrote, 'To build communism, you must build a new man as well as a new economic base.' Ernesto Cardinal[37] who was living and working in Nicaragua in the 1970s spoke recently of a 'new breed of men who live for each other.' Ian reflected that a window of opportunity existed in Cuba to look afresh at Jesus Christ. This New Man not only provides encouragement and support but also turmoil and judgment. Is he likely to commend himself to Cuban society? He may be too much to take. On the other hand his suffering love and his identification with the lowest and the least may make their impact.

When the Revolution came the Protestant Churches' pastors had often come from the USA. They returned home. The churches more or less emptied. In time those who were left had to find a different way of being church. Finance that would have gone to the support of the ordained ministry was now freed for works of care and outreach. A corporate ministry of the whole congregation was developing, in which lay people preached, visited and conducted many of the Bible studies.

Change was also the order of the day in the Matanzas Theological Seminary. Students were now spending one day each week working in the sugar fields or on community projects. Ian recognised three significant strands of work in the seminary. They were attempting to develop a biblical theology which related closely to everyday life. Space and time was being given to think out the basis for Christian attitudes to social and political questions. They were encouraging interchange between the clergy and the laity, and laity and laity about the significance of life as they saw it.

Ofelia Ortega in 1973 was an ordained women minister who was pastor of a congregation, a teacher in the Theological Seminary, Dean of Education of the Presbyterian Church of Cuba and a wife and mother[38]. Her first venture out of Cuba was to Scottish Churches

House where she spent several weeks before going on to the Uppsala Assembly. She was disarmingly frank when she noted that the Cuban Revolution was developing a great advance while the churches took little steps behind. For all that she remained convinced 'that Christians have something in their faith that is needed. It is for them to help establish a community of real love.'

Ian cautioned in his report, as he considered the Council he attended, that there was a danger that it might become too closely identified with the regime. The regime itself needed the churches to keep their distance so that they could continue to speak prophetically into an ever-changing situation. Cuba in the 1970s raised questions for countries in the West such as the United Kingdom. In contrast with Cuba Ian concluded that 'ours is a dishearteningly class-structured society with acres of privilege and poverty. How can we build a just human order? What contribution would be made by a Thatcher-led government which pronounced with glee the end of society in the lemming-like charge to individualism? To what extent would the reality of the poor in our country be bettered by a Blairite government afraid to speak the name of socialism? And where would the churches be in all this? Tempted to turn in on themselves and protect their own or be enabled to rouse themselves and adopt a prophetic role to help us live in a world community by a thorough-going social, political and moral repentance and renewal of national life?'

The conclusion of the report of the six years of visits and consultations is instructive:[39]

> 'Why in the end, look to the church, which has let God and men down so often? Because of the life of Jesus Christ at the

heart of it. It draws from him a capacity for repentance and amendment of life, and a capacity for self-criticism. The one who is at the heart of it keeps calling it to its true vocation. It must become what it is.'

If it is true, and it is, that earlier stages of Ian Fraser's life were a basis for more learning with each new opportunity, it is surely equally true that the lessons of earlier times can be informative even essential for the growth and renewal of each succeeding generation of Christians in every place. 'Things written afore time are for our learning.'[40]

The mid-70s WCC Assembly was originally planned for Djkarta, Indonesia. It proved necessary to move the gathering to Nairobi, Kenya. Ian paid several visits to Nairobi. He argued for a 'sleeping-bag assembly'. It would have been very economical and a sign of a church really concerned for the poor in the shanty towns if halls were hired and enough space provided for a mattress and a sleeping bag for each delegate. When it was argued that distinguished church leaders would not come to Nairobi if that was the only kind of accommodation offered, he asked, 'Who complains about getting two advantages instead of one?!'

Ian's personal preference was for working with small groups of people, so he had no desire to go to the Nairobi Assembly; when other people were trying to make themselves as visible as possible in the hope of being invited, he made himself as invisible as possible in the hope of being overlooked. In the end Lesslie Newbiggin attended and Ian was left to get on with the work he was by then undertaking in Selly Oak.

The one WCC Assembly which Ian attended on behalf of the Scottish Churches Council, of which he was then General Secretary, was Uppsala in Sweden in 1968. Ian retains only vague memories of it. He remembers Ofelia Ortega from Cuba and her warm clasp when she recognised Ian's voice in the middle of the Assembly. Ian also remembers remarking on the Scottish connection when he saw that the police cars were all marked 'Polis'! He recalls attractive women journalists who moved around the Assembly with the label, 'Press', on their shirts without anyone being brave enough to take up their invitation! And he recalls the workbook which he turned out very quickly on his return home entitled 'Live with Style' which had to serve the whole of Britain for some time since there was a printing mishap delaying the main British report. He found that one of his early hymns had been adapted and adjusted without his agreement under the 'Live with Style' theme and realised the importance of copyright – the changes made were not acceptable to him.

During his time in Geneva Ian was frequently asked to undertake additional duties as the needs of WCC arose. One such duty of note was his appointment as the Ecumenical Chaplain to the Munich Olympics of 1972.

A German newspaper carried the news of the infamous massacre of Jews and Israelis under the headline 'The Blood Bath'. At the previous Games in 1968 in Mexico City an unspecified number of demonstrators were massacred outside the city. So absorbed were the athletes and the sporting world that Christopher Brasher remarked to Ian that 'for all that the world and the athletes seemed to care, these killings could have taken place on the moon.' In 1972 the terrorism moved into the Olympic village itself.

Ian regretted that the incident had taken place in Germany. He saw clearly that the nation that had used the 1936 Berlin Olympic Games for Nazi propaganda was anxious to make reparation. It might even have been that the more relaxed security in place in the Olympic Village was a determined attempt to make the Games less Germanic. On the morning of the break-in people were more curious than anything else. By the next morning, when everyone knew about the killings there was a sense of bewilderment rather than the shock and grief that were spoken about in the memorial ceremony. Some felt that the Games should have been abandoned. But most were glad to take part in the memorial ceremony as it gave a focus in difficult and dark days. The killings made them face the larger human questions including the purpose of life. It was difficult for the remainder of that day to know what else to do. It was announced that the village theatre would remain closed for the rest of the day. However, the cinema programme was to continue and subdued music was to be played in the venue for the disco. Dancing was to be permitted.

People took the opportunity to sit about and talk not so much about the killings but about the questions thrown up by the Olympic Games. It has been noted that while athletes are required to nourish their bodies to compete at the highest level. No such nourishment is regularly provided for their minds. One such discussion focused on the statement by the IOC President Avery Brundage, an American at the memorial service. He linked the raid of the Black September Group with the exclusion of Rhodesia from the Games which he called 'naked political blackmail'. Ian concluded that the most mature people in those days were the Africans. They could have walked out of the memorial ceremony but refused to allow the indiscretion of an ill-informed President to rob them of the opportunity to remember the athletes and coaches who had died.

When he returned to Geneva Ian wrote up a report of his visit to Munich and made recommendations based on his experiences there. He suggested that there should be greater lay involvement in the provision of chaplains and they should be well-briefed and in place before the athletes arrived in the village. He also tackled questions relating to the inequalities faced by athletes from the Developing World and considered in detail the problem of drugs in sport. Above all he recommended that chaplaincy people should have the best of listening skills. He noted that there would be a temptation for some religious groups to view such events as opportunities for crude proselytising.

Then after three and a half years in Geneva out of a six year appointment, Ian was approached by the Selly Oak Colleges in Birmingham. They wanted a dean who could co-ordinate the work of four colleges with a teaching centre and head up a new Department of Mission. Some pioneering preparations had been undertaken by another Scot, David Lyon.

Ian went to Philip Potter and said, 'I have been asked to consider another job.'
He put his head in his hands. 'What job?'
'They want me to head up a new Department of Mission in the Selly Oak Colleges in Birmingham.'
'That is the one job in the world you must accept . . . of course you must finish the WCC job at the same time.'

Shortly after it had been agreed that Ian would move to Selly Oak he passed Philip Potter in a corridor in the Ecumenical Centre. Philip stopped and said forcefully, 'You must never underestimate the contribution you have made to the WCC!' Ian had cause to ponder for some years what he meant specifically. Some years later the Faith and Order department of WCC were holding a consultation in Scottish Churches House. Ian was invited to a social occasion. A colleague from WCC days was there with his wife. When he saw Ian he said to her, 'Dear, I want you to meet Ian Fraser who changed the whole way the World Council tackled its work.' Again Ian was left scratching his head as to what was meant by this statement. No further opportunity presented itself to allow Ian to clarify the statement.

When Ian was asked by the Friends of Dunblane Cathedral in 1998 to write about the changes he noticed when he moved from Dunblane to Geneva he thoughtfully considered his contribution and the opportunities the move gave him. He came to the conclusion that four elements might have been behind such comments:

- The change in methodology which Ian employed in his consultation with the world church – no longer were they expected to travel to Geneva – he went to stay with people where they were to hear their stories.
- The option for the poor became more than a slogan and was adopted as a lifestyle by Ian not least as he lived with the poor and ate their bread.
- Ian's discoveries about a renewed church were shared through their stories not by abstract speculation.
- Then Ian dared to suggest that theology cannot be done behind desks and within walls. Reflection and life had to

interpenetrate one another if the product could in any sense be called 'theology'.

So Ian accepted the position of Dean in Selly Oak Colleges and did a double job, continuing to work for WCC until he had completed his report to the Nairobi Assembly.

The family and friends were not forgotten during the years in Geneva. By Christmas 1970 after sixteen months in Geneva Margaret wrote in their Christmas letters[41] that all of the scattered family except son-in-law Gene had visited their home in Chemin Champ d'Anier, Geneva. While Gene was in south-east Asia, Anne and granddaughter Alison spent three months with Ian and Margaret in Switzerland. By that year end Anne and her family were settled in Charleston, North Carolina and she was doing a year in paediatrics in the hospital where Gene was working. Ian Junior also pursuing his medical training spent some weeks on placement in the same hospital – the collective noun for a group of Frasers is not recorded.

Keith meantime had completed his teacher training in Dundee and was teaching Geography in Riverside School in Stirling. Not all the family news was good that Christmas. Ian's mother had died in the June of 1970 at the age of eighty. Margaret notes she was 'a blithe spirit to the end'. On a happier note she intimated that they were planning to spend Christmas with Granny Stewart in Scotland. She had visited Geneva for six months during the summer of 1970.

Ian records a variety of visits in Europe and Africa the latter in a period of six and a half weeks which he notes as being short for such a vast continent. His main concern was for the powerful influence of western culture which he fears is cramping indigenous initiative and life styles. The following Christmas (1971) mentions a ten-day visit to Israel and a month in Barcelona for an intensive beginners' course in Spanish. As he wrote he was on the verge of flying out for a seven week visit to the Caribbean, Oceania and Asia - not too difficult as long as you say it quickly. He planned to visit his daughter Anne in Laos, where she was supporting her husband Gene who was participating in a Medical Aid Programme.

The following year which was to bring Margaret and Ian to their final Christmas in Geneva found Ian and Margaret together on a visit to Laos. Margaret wrote, 'Gene's working hours are still totally absorbed in hospital work with refugees up country; Anne, working part-time with a Lao doctor, runs a clinic for the rehabilitation of drug addicts in Vientiane, the capital, and Allison trots along daily and happily to nursery school.'

Ian Jnr had been married the previous year to Hedvika, his charming Czechoslovakian wife. In November 1972 Keith was married to Hazel in the Chapel of Scottish Churches House. The date was determined by the time of Ian's visit to Scotland on a WCC assignment. Margaret was able to fly over from Geneva at short notice. Ian officiated at what Margaret describes as a 'simple, beautiful and deeply moving service.' Meanwhile Ian Jnr qualified as a doctor and was working long but satisfying hours in one of the surgical wards in Edinburgh's Western General Hospital.

Margaret takes time to recount some of Ian's globe-trotting noting without comment his presence in Munich for the Olympic Games in August 1972. In his section of the letter Ian broke the news about the impending move to Birmingham. He noted that he would be undertaking a dual role working both for the Selly Oak Colleges and continuing his work for WCC for two years through till 1975. As he said, 'So we move and we stay!'

Endnotes

[31] See 'Immanuel' Hans Rudi Weber 1984 WCC pp 67,68 where Ian's poem 'The Magi' is discussed.
[32] Matthew 13:34b 'indeed he (Jesus) said nothing to them without a parable.'
[33] The Fire Runs p 60.
[34] The Fire Runs p 97.
[35] The Fire Runs p 64,65.
[36] An Argentinian revolutionary Marxist who served under Fidel Castro after the Cuban Revolution.
[37] Revolutionary Nicaraguan poet and Roman Catholic priest.
[38] Rev. Dr Ofelia Ortega, of the Presbyterian-Reformed Church in Cuba, was the first Presbyterian woman to be ordained in Cuba. She served as the rector of the Evangelical Theological Seminary (SET) in Matanzas from 1996-2004, leading it to a multi-faceted ministry of social service and community involvement. Ortega worked at the WCC from 1988 to 1996 as executive secretary for Latin America and the Caribbean in the Programme on Theological Education, and before that, from 1985 to 1988, as professor at the Ecumenical Institute, Bossey. In Cuba, beyond her responsibilities with the seminary, she served as volunteer in the rural areas during the national literacy campaign, as well as for the Ministry of Public Health. At the time of writing she is the WCC president from the Caribbean/Latin America area.
[39] The Fire Runs p 152.

[40] Romans 15.4 .

[41] The annual Christmas Letter gives interesting personal and family insights, a tradition which Ian continues to the present.

1. Alex (A.B.) and Annie Fraser, parents of Alex, Ian and Margaret

2. Ian, Margaret and Alex Fraser

3. The family business then . . .

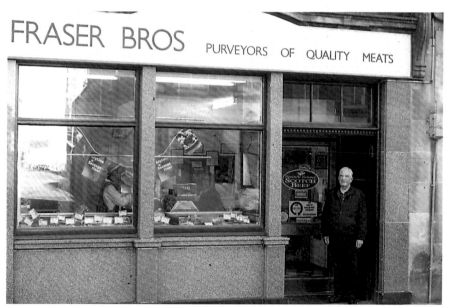

4. . . . . now (Ian on a recent visit to Forres)

5. Margaret Stewart (Fraser), head girl, Dumfries Academy 1937-38 (seated next to Rector Lodge)

6. Edinburgh University Association Football Club 1940-41 Winners of Lothian Amateur League; Ian Fraser 2nd left, front row

7. Ian M Fraser Graduation

8. Margaret Stewart (Fraser) Graduation

9. Alex (RAF); Margaret (ARP) Ian (Home Guard) in Forres during wartime

10. Ian M Fraser (Industrial Chaplain) with the 1943 Permanent Staff on Iona: Ian M Fraser, Lex Miller, George MacLeod, Robin Martin, Bill Amos, George Wilkie and upstage John McMillan (Copyright unknown – printed in The Coracle February 1944)

11. Wedding of Ian M Fraser and
Margaret D.D. Stewart

12. Ian M Fraser during a recent visit to Tullis Russell paper mill,
Markinch/Glenrothes

13. Ian and Margaret Fraser, Rosyth

14. Ian Fraser with Admiral Evershed
conducting Lady Mountbatten during a visit to Rosyth

15. Ian Fraser with Tom Fleming recording a programme for the BBC in 1961

16. Rev. Ian M Fraser conducting HRH Queen Elizabeth during her visit to Scottish Churches House in 1967

17. Ian, Anne and Keith Fraser

18. Ian at his WCC desk in Geneva

19. Ian and Margaret, Selly Oak

20. Ian and Margaret at Ferndale, Gargunnock

21. Launch of 'Caring for Planet Earth' in Gargunnock Primary School.

22. Ian in a discussion group at an Iona Community plenary

23. Ian with the family: Hazel, Ian Snr, Gene, Ian Jnr, Kathy, Anne

24. Some of the Fraser generations

25. Launch of Jubilee Appeal for Scottish Churches House and celebration of Ian's 90th birthday (2007): Alastair Hulbert (Warden Scottish Churches House), Margaret Brisley (Provost, Stirling Council) Ian, Mary Buchanan (Convenor, ACTS)

26. 2007 portrait of Ian by Ruth Goodheir, member, Iona Community

CHAPTER SEVEN

SELLY OAK

IAN WAS APPROACHED from the Selly Oak Colleges in Birmingham. They needed someone to establish a new Department of Mission to coordinate the work of four colleges representing a number of missionary societies.[42] The appointment was to be as Dean and Head of Department. Bishop John Taylor asked to see Ian when he was passing through London. Evidently he thought that Ian would do.

Margaret as usual was clear. 'It has been a bit of a mountain top experience here in Geneva. It is time we got our feet back on the ground.' Ian had too much on his plate to return to Britain to consider the situation. Margaret went on her own. It was early December 1972. She was met at Birmingham's New Street Station by a yellow, dripping, pea-soup fog. It accompanied her all the way as she travelled out through the semi-derelict Selly Oak village by bus. There had been the intention, never realised, to make Bristol Road into a dual carriageway. Shops and houses had been bought up by the Council and left boarded up.

Margaret talked with people when she arrived on campus. She was shown the Hawthorn's house which would become their home. She was also told that it would be suitable for student gatherings!

Margaret reported back to Ian in Geneva. 'It will be a real sacrifice to leave the beautiful city of Geneva for Birmingham but I think there is a job to do here.' In May 1973 Ian and Margaret moved from Geneva to Selly Oak. They arrived in the picturesque Cadbury area, full of cherry and hawthorn blossom with the singing of birds; they fell into one another's arms laughing and saying, 'Some sacrifice!'

So it was that Ian took up his position as Dean and Head of the Department of Mission in Selly Oak. The word 'dean' can indicate a power position or a coordinating role. At Selly Oak Ian chose to emphasise the latter. The word derives from the Latin *'decanus'* leader or instigator of 10 people. As Dean Ian had a double portion – he was responsible for about 20 staff during the years at Selly Oak. David Lyon, another Scot, had been invited to Selly Oak in 1967 to bring into being a Centre for Training in Christian Mission. The whole development was worked out closely with college president Paul Clifford to whose warm cooperation David paid tribute. In the summer of 1972 David returned to Scotland to serve the Mission and Unity Enterprise in 121 George Street.[43] In the second half of 1972 a decision was taken to appoint a Dean and establish a Department of Mission. By that time Ian was about halfway in time between Uppsala and Nairobi. He received an innocent looking request from Selly Oak. 'Would he mind if, in the light of a development they wanted to make, his name was brought into their deliberations?' There was no mention of timing or that he was the only person they had in mind, so Ian raised no objection.

The year between David's departure and Ian's arrival seemed to have obliterated much of the preparatory work which had been done. Ian found it necessary to test out deliberately and without undue haste the elements of a programme which would serve everyone. It was necessary to coordinate the work of all four colleges with the teaching centre. Ian's involvement in the 'Participation in Change' programme for the WCC meant that what had essentially been a mission programme enriched and informed the Selly Oak experience. Not that everything Ian offered was welcomed with open arms. He remembers one and another bursting into furious criticism of the agreement to develop cooperation.

Ian gave himself to invest in prayer for the work to which he was now committed. He taught himself to waken at 5 a.m. and from them till 7 a.m. he took people from all over the campus by the hand, brought them before God and led them into the day. It was then time for breakfast and he was able to be at his desk by 7.30!

In the first year at Selly Oak one of the most important duties for Ian was to set up the annual consultation between representatives of the Missionary Societies and the staff of what was now the Department of Mission. Ian discovered that the event was popularly known as 'the circus'. He believes that nicknames are significant, especially those which are attached unconsciously and which stick through common consent. He put some effort into the first of these consultations for which he was responsible. He drew satisfaction from the preparatory work that he had done. When it was all over he concluded, 'This is doing nothing of significance at all.'

The following year the whole process had to be repeated. The same careful preparation was undertaken. In addition an outside facilitator was invited. Ian had met Paloma from the Paris Paulo Freire Centre and had an animated discussion with her. She was from one of a number of centres worldwide based on a philosopher and educator of the same name. Freire thought in terms of teacher-student and student-teacher; that is, a teacher who learns and a learner who teaches, as the basic roles in classroom participation. This was an attempt to implement mutual learning as an educational method and not merely a goal. The staff in the Paris Centre prepared people who had been working overseas in some form of Christian service to make a self-examination of their activities and the effect of these activities in the year before their return home. Then at the Centre they were invited to criticise and challenge one another and so advance the process of understanding.

Ian made up his mind before the second consultation that if the whole event broke down, he would not lift a finger to save it. If the whole process was really an empty exercise leaving basic questions unanswered, then that would be allowed to come out. Paloma's contribution was searching. The consultation did break down. Lesslie Newbiggin[44] and others were furious. They knew that, even at that point, Ian could have put everything together in a face-saving exercise. It is very hard to let things fail and come to bits in your hands if you seem to be letting your friends down in the process. Ian was convinced that he had to persist in what he had decided. Everything ended in disarray.

At that point Ian and the staff at the colleges entered a dense jungle. They were far from sure where they were going and yet at the same time had to go on carrying through a training programme as best they could in the meantime. Ian cannot speak too highly of his colleagues who bore with him during that period. It was a time when the different Missionary Societies and Boards were asked to think deeply about the kind of equipping which was needed for people who would undertake service in the world church at home and abroad. This would then be applied to the redesigning of the Selly Oak programme.

Once they entered this process of reassessment, Lesslie was as patient as the rest of the staff, and he it was who noted the point at which they had worked everything through and could begin the process of reconstruction. As the whole staff had been involved in the negative process it meant that they could all now share in what was positive. They now knew the aspirations of the Missionary Societies as well as anyone could. The staff in the colleges were given a clear mandate to take things on from there. Every member of staff contributed, every member of staff listened, every member of staff shared in the construction of the new programme. They worked with conviction and the end result grew out of a common struggle. Mutual respect and trust were immeasurably increased. The sense of responsibility was enhanced.

When it was agreed to have a certificated course this was not to be limited to some academic attainment level prescribed beforehand. People were to be accepted into the programme who had no strong academic qualifications where this related to a lack of opportunity or a lack of provision in the area where they grew up. What mattered more was that their own church, wherever in the world that was, was convinced about their potential. The certificate would be a sign of growth in understanding and commitment in terms of world mission. Thus it would be possible for someone who had had only primary schooling but was wise and quick of mind and perceptive about the faith, to be awarded a certificate, while someone with degrees could be refused it if they showed lack of application and growth during the whole process.

Another decision of importance was that the students should be able to provide their work in whatever form seemed appropriate to them. Thus, for those who were used to a spoken culture, essays could be offered on tape rather in written form. If they found English very difficult as a second or third language, they should exceptionally be able to present work in their mother tongue. It would be the responsibility of staff to obtain translation for assessment purposes. No medium for presentation was to be rejected out of hand. Two girls provided a Christian reflection on Marxism through music and dance. As there was an Indian in the Communications Centre who had been accustomed to teaching Indian girls to announce the gospel in song and dance in his home area, it was possible to have a professional judgment on the presentation given by the two girls.

Ian concluded that the traumatic time spent in the 'jungle' without a clear path to follow resulted in fruitful developments in the life of Selly Oak Colleges, both in the imaginative work invested in the programming and in the development of trust and solidarity in staff relationships. The task Ian had been set of bringing together the work of the separate colleges was far from easy. This coordinating task had clearly not been avoided.

Ian was involved in teaching while at Selly Oak. One of the subjects he was responsible for was Marxism. Given the breadth of his experience of the new developments in Christian life and faith around the world this was surprising. It reflected perhaps his willingness to meet whatever need was uncovered. Almost thirty students opted for his class. At least half the class had Marxism developing in their home areas. Every session began with input from a student. Each shared insights on the national varieties of Marxism they had experienced. Only then did Ian bring in the 'book stuff'. There followed opportunity for general discussion. The international experience of the class went way beyond what the books covered.

Others had lessons to learn at Selly Oak! One day Ian crossed the Bristol Road to go to his office in Selly Oak. A man stopped him and asked directions. He was looking for a road or street he believed to be nearby. He had a pale, thin face with protruding bones. There was evidence of sleep at the corners of his eyes; there was green snot at his nose. Ian said he was sorry he did not recognise the street name. He could not help and continued on his way. It was then that the man threw after him, 'I was only asking a civil question!'

Had Ian turned away too quickly? Had he shown some revulsion? Perhaps he could have paused for a moment or two, called on the assistance of another passer-by. At least his questioner might have felt affirmed. As it was he clearly felt rejected. The teacher had learned a lesson but at what cost? Living may be for learning – but learning is always for living.

Ian knew that what was considered to be the most difficult college to work with would be the industrial college, Fircroft. It was popularly called 'Marxist' but he believed it was simply radical. It tended to be left to go its own way. Fircrofters would not have wanted truck with mission students. Ian took time and developed good relations with the staff and through them some leading students. He waited to see what the Holy Spirit might throw into the mix. It turned out to be the Lucas Aerospace workers' campaign.

Lucas Aerospace was an arm of Lucas Industries, a British-based multinational firm manufacturing a wide range of components for the motorcar and aerospace industries. In the 1970s this group employed 13,000 workers on its seventeen sites across the United Kingdom. They were a significant employer in the Birmingham area. The Lucas Aerospace Combine Shop Stewards Committee (the Combine Committee) was set up in 1972 in the year before Ian arrived at Selly Oak. In 1974 at the Combine Committee's request they met with Tony Benn, the Minister of Industry. It was concluded that in the light of possible cutbacks on defence spending, other products should be considered as a basis for diversification within Lucas Aerospace.

While other factors played their part the threat of redundancies was clearly the factor which triggered this process. Ian recognised that workers were also saying, 'Here we are, a trained skilled workforce, serving the war machine. If we were to use our gifts constructively what might we produce?' They identified and outlined no less than 150 products which they could produce to meet the needs of the wider human community. The Corporate Plan was published and presented to the management in January 1976. In discussion it became clear to Ian that Fircroft students were prepared to work with Mission students if a day conference could be arranged. Ian was mandated to invite the management and trade unions to take part in such a conference to which the two groups of students would be invited to participate.

Ian asked Lucas Aerospace for a meeting with management and Combine Committee representatives to explore possibilities. He discovered that his meeting with them would be the first formal occasion when the two sides would meet and dialogue. The management did not want to acknowledge any virtue in ideas which came from the shop floor. In time the day event and its programme were arranged; the questions, which were to be addressed, were agreed. They did not realise that they were letting themselves in for theological thinking. Ian intended that they should be focused on the questions, 'What is human life for?' and 'How should human gifts be used?'

On the day Ian confined himself to inserting appropriate biblical material. He took five or ten minutes at the start of the presentations by the two sides to point out relevant biblical passages. He also made sure that a session never finished without serious concern about all that an industrial enterprise had to take into account if it were to survive in the modern world. Idealistic proposals were hammered into the ground or hammered into shape. The participants were left to take it from there. The lessons learned in Scottish Churches House had not been forgotten.

The impact on the student participants was very positive; the whole process was very much appreciated. The Marxist and other left wing ideologues were left scratching their heads – how could material that they had dismissed as 'the opiate of the people' have such a lively relationship to what they had to think through in their time? And, with them, Mission students got fresh enlightenment about the relevance of biblical insights to the present day.

Ian recognised that the long-term effect of the day would be limited. Separately, the General Manager of Lucas Aerospace and the chairman of the Combine Committee took Ian aside. The General Manager told him that he was a churchman but despaired of getting any help, facing the difficult decisions he had to take, from fellow members of the church. They had shown no interest. He asked Ian if he would be willing to do this kind of Bible Study with his management team. The Marxist/atheist chairman of the Combine Committee said that they needed these insights into what life was for – 'Would Ian be willing to do bible study with them?' Ian made it clear to both parties that he was more than willing. Neither knew that the other had drawn him aside. He was convinced that these requests would not be followed up. As he said, 'It takes immersion in such an experience as we had had to want it. It was a fond hope but wishful thinking that workers' committees or management teams might respond without having been through the kind of experience gained by those who had attended.'

In time the Lucas Aerospace Corporate Plan died the death; it had been more or less rejected out of hand by the management. Some elements of the Selly Oak day and the wider project survived. These included:

- The desire to use skills constructively and to establish the right to work on 'socially useful and needed projects' remained as an impetus. Events can live again as they inspire and empower later generations.
- Fircroft and 'Mission' students were no longer such strangers to one another, nor were the staff members who participated in the process.

- An openness of management to shop floor workers had begun to develop if somewhat reluctantly, like a creaking door – it was only ajar but the potential for future progress could not be denied.

Reflecting on these events in recent years Ian concluded that he was able to establish trust in part because of his pioneering work in the 'manual-working industrial chaplaincy' at the paper mill, 'I knew to some extent what it was like to be on the shop floor. This harked back also to my experience in the family shop in childhood which robbed me of some of my childhood but provided compensations. Life is all of a piece!'

From 1973 till 1975 Ian was also busy as we have seen with his visits around the world as part of the 'Participation in Change' process towards the Nairobi General Assembly of the World Council of Churches. His travels went on beyond that Assembly. During his early years at Selly Oak Ian developed a concern about mission from, and mission in Europe.

In 1980 Ian was invited to attend a conference in Romania of the World Alliance of Reformed Churches. Margaret was able to accompany him. Their visits together became an increasingly frequent occurrence when Ian retired from Selly Oak. The conference was due to be held in Poiana Brasov a hundred miles north of Bucharest, the Romanian capital. This place was to become in time Romania's premier ski resort.

On the way to the conference Ian and Margaret spent a few days in Istanbul. This gave them a few days holiday together but the main purpose of the visit was a consultation with Demetrios, then the acknowledged head of the Orthodox Churches. Ian had been received with great warmth and understanding on a previous visit. On this occasion there were Turkish soldiers all over the place with rusty bayonets on their guns. It was shortly after a military take-over. When Ian and Margaret reached the building which was the seat of Orthodoxy in Istanbul there was a palpable atmosphere of fear. This visit was a short one. Ian was given some support as he voiced his encouragement for the laity within Orthodoxy to be drawn more into the whole movement for recovery of the ministry of the church by the whole people of God.

Thereafter Ian and Margaret had a couple of days to explore Istanbul together; its marvellous museums, mosques and its superb location with water and land and sky answering one another in a joyful play of light.

On the day of their departure they already had their tickets for Poiana Brasov but still went to Istanbul station early. There were huge queues for information, tickets etc – especially in every place where someone might have understood English, French or German. Officials that Ian and Margaret stopped were no help. They indicated that they did not understand what was being asked. The travellers persisted and eventually managed to ascertain which platform their train would be leaving from. Of the train there was still no sign. The platform itself was a nightmare. It was not just the crowds of waiting passengers. There were huge bundles of what looked like laundry or bedding. They were clearly destined for their train.

Then the train arrived. Ian tried every carriage but none indicated that it was for Poiana Brasov – Moscow. The train stood for a long time although gave every indication of impending departure. Having decided that perhaps the extra coaches would be added somewhere en route the Frasers squeezed on to the nearest carriage. They mentioned their destination to some of their fellow-travellers. Some pointed back at the platform. The message was rather late; the train was already in motion. They wondered where they were going to end up. They shrugged their shoulders and sat down on their luggage.

But not for long! The train reversed and returned to the very platform it had left. Whatever the reason for the manoeuvre our intrepid travellers, with some relief, got off. They valued a second chance to see if something could be made of the situation. At last they found a railway official who spoke some French. He let them know that there were three carriages to be added to the train. He did not know whether they would be added at the front or the back. An eye had to be kept on the whole length of the train. In time they realised that they had in fact been added at the front. The new carriages had their destination clearly marked – Moscow and Poiana Brasov.

The man in charge of these coaches was Russian. He looked at the Frasers' tickets, made out in the West, and dismissed them with an airy wave of the hand. He made it clear that they had no right to be on the train and there were no sleeping berths reserved for them. A stream of people approached him seeking information and directions. When Ian and Margaret insisted on more of his time to attend to their predicament he continued, dismissive as ever. At that point one element in Margaret that people often failed to notice rose to the surface. Margaret was never hard; but she could be exceedingly tough. Her hackles rose, and, in English, she bombarded the official to such effect that his arrogance was quite deflated. He then made a gesture of hopelessness in the face of the situation. They realised he could do nothing for them.

Their attention was drawn to another official who seemed to be responsible for sleeping berths. They approached him. He quickly recognised their tickets and sleeping berth bookings and took them to the appropriate compartment. It was already occupied by a woman from the USSR who insisted fiercely that she was not a Russian. She had got on early and every bit of the compartment was filled with treasured consumer goods and bedding which she was taking home. It was as well that Ian and Margaret were travelling light. They found just enough space for themselves and their rucksacks and cases.

The ticket collector arrived as they approached the frontier of Bulgaria. Passports were produced. At one point Margaret and the lady had tried to communicate with one another. Their travelling companion had taken out her official documents and conveyed something to Margaret that the officials were unable to understand. Somehow through the language of gestures Margaret was able to ensure that the stranger's papers were accepted.

The train had left Istanbul hours late. They slept through the night, surveyed the countryside in the morning and read and chatted until the train arrived in Sofia. The train stopped. Nothing happened. It kept on happening. Eventually an announcement came. The train would be remaining overnight where it was. Evidently the train had arrived so late in Sofia that the connecting train had left without them. They would have to be hitched to the connection for Moscow and Poiana Brasov the following day. No food was offered. It was assumed that travellers had emergency rations for the journey.

When they were sure that the train was going nowhere for the time being Ian and Margaret went into the city. Ian had been there as part of his consultations in the WCC Participation in Change programme. On that occasion he had been received with respect and he was allocated a room in a hotel as a guest of the Orthodox churches. It was a good hotel and Ian was allocated an English-speaker to make sure the short time of his visit was used to the maximum advantage. From that previous visit Ian had maps and money. He was carrying them with him, not expecting to use them; just carrying them in case. Ian and Margaret headed straight for the Alexander Nevsky cathedral. They were fortunate. Evensong was being sung and most of the service was still to come. There was a mixed choir. On his earlier visit Ian had taken a recording of the singing in the cathedral to share with Margaret. Being in the Cathedral was something else. It was a most enriching experience; an undreamt of bonus – all thanks to inefficiently operated train timetables.

After the service they poked around in the city and came across a restaurant. Many of its patrons were young people. It appeared to be serving good food. They went in hoping that the money they had would be sufficient for a meal. It was. They had a good meat course with a dessert to follow. They felt well set up for the extra night they would need to spend on the train.

The train arrived in Poiana Brasov early the next morning. The Frasers spent some time in the waiting room and Ian went out from time to time to check on the situation. Those who had been travelling with them on their train seemed to know what they were doing. They had found the taxi rank and continued on their way. It took some time for one or two taxis to return. In time they reached the hotel where the conference was due to take place. At the end of the conference they had a day at leisure in the town and were concerned to see what poor thin pieces of meat and chicken, if any, were on sale in the shops. Their hotel, part of the ski resort, had provided them with good food, well cooked, in over-abundance. There was an unhappy feeling not unlike colonial times of being counted among the rich and powerful, living in luxury among people who had to live with very little.

Ian's responsibility was to develop the process of the conference. He was given a free hand. There more than 200 members attending. The main languages were French, German and English. Ian proposed 7 French-speaking, 7 German-speaking and 7 English-speaking groups. Each language section would have a coordinator attached and Ian himself acting with them would draw the whole conference together. When participants actually assembled they discovered they only needed two French-speaking groups. The problem was easily solved; additional English and German-speaking groups were formed.

People in their small groups of about ten were asked to share what they were discovering about the Christian faith, what was new to them, what they were unclear about, what worries they had in their lives. They had been asked to consider some themes before travelling and were asked to identify what they believed would be the most significant to share with others. This meant that people began by speaking about matters which were familiar to them. The leaders of these small groups met with their coordinators at the end of the morning to share the main themes, questions and common concerns which were emerging.

In the afternoon the three coordinators met with Ian. They spread out the matters that had come to the fore in the morning session. A selection was made of issues to be shared with the whole gathering. Having established the main points they spent time developing a variety of dramatic dialogues to illustrate them. These were presented to the plenary session that evening. The following morning the small groups were invited to work on the matters highlighted the previous evening. The option remained for small groups to set their own agenda. The only requirement was that they should do so responsibly. In this way the matters about which there was general interest and concern and matters specifically of interest to each small group would be worked on. In this way people were free to build one another up.

It worked. Ian was confident that the process worked extremely well. But some people were ill at ease with his method. People who lived in hierarchies were accustomed to work being laid out for them and expected a final report to show what had been accomplished. At one point a message was conveyed to Ian that the Orthodox felt that their rather top-down way of meeting and consulting was not being given enough attention. He tackled the matter in an open session of the assembly. He encouraged people to believe that new ways of working were bringing new opportunities for learning and sharing. At that time there were few opportunities for Orthodox believers and their leaders to meet and consult with their 'separated brethren'. Holding the conference in Poiana Brasov Ian affirmed was a particular opportunity for the people from Orthodox churches. This plain-speaking by Ian was not appreciated. The Orthodox hierarchy continued to keep their own company. They mingled little and moved around in convoy rather than mixing with the company as a whole. Progress is often slower than our plans for it.

Margaret and Ian had, as usual, taken the most economical method of travelling. On this occasion that meant a flight to Hungary and onward travel to Poiana Brasov via Istanbul. After the conference they needed to return to Hungary by train and had booked overnight sleepers. This time the train was up to time. But when they tried to get on to the carriage in which their sleepers were booked their way was barred by the attendant. He indicated that it was not the right carriage. Ian persisted and got on to the train. He found the compartment they had booked only to discover that it was already occupied. He returned to the attendant and showed him the tickets but he just shook his head. Margaret and Ian thought it prudent to board the train anyway. Ian attempted to take over the compartment and found himself violently ejected. He was promised further violence if he continued in his attempt to enter the compartment. The attendant was unwilling to see justice done. He explained that when the train was leaving Bucharest it was always possible to bribe attendants and gain access to still unoccupied compartments. That was the end of the matter as far as he was concerned. This was what often happened to accommodation booked by foreigners for a later part of the journey.

When the ticket collector appeared the Frasers used gestures to explain their predicament. He was sympathetic but felt unable to confront the violence. So he took them to another carriage. He unlocked a door and allowed them to stretch out on two padded benches. They made the most of it till the early hours of the morning. At this point they were roused and told to present their passports. This was standard practice in East European countries. The passports were taken away. Ian and Margaret felt pretty vulnerable without them. After about threequarters of an hour the officials came back and at great length explained that there was a problem that the travellers could not understand. They stood at the door as if waiting for Ian and Margaret to leave. They sat tight. The officials left only to return a short time later. This time they lifted the Fraser luggage on to the platform. They were ejected with their luggage. It transpired that the train was halted at a small town still inside Romania. It later became clear that the problem was with the Hungarian visa. Their visas allowed for a single entry and exit point. What they had asked for was visas allowing them to leave at one border crossing on the way to Istanbul and to re-enter Hungary at a different crossing point. Lack of language earlier had led to this problem.

So there they were, Ian and Margaret stuck about five or six in the morning, and with no idea what to do. The station was dirty; the toilets filthy. There were hard seats. There was nothing more to do than wait around and see if someone might appear who could throw light on their troubles. Two hours later a man arrived, who seemed to be the stationmaster. He spoke French. He was able right away to explain about the visa problem. His advice was that they should take a train to another border crossing where a new entry visa could be obtained. They were assured that there would be taxis that could take them from that station to the immigration office where the new visa could be purchased.

It was all largely fantasy. There were no taxis. The office was 5 kilometres from the station. There was nothing else for it. They had to walk carrying their luggage through a deserted no-man's land with nothing but military installations. When they reached the office they were pleased to discover that a new visa could be obtained at a price. Ian had a habit of carrying additional passport-sized photographs for such emergencies. He recalled trying and failing to enter Laos from Thailand on one occasion and having to wait while daughter Anne crossed the border to visit him. No visa – no go!

Margaret and Ian were required to take their place at the back of a queue to have matters dealt with. Requests were dealt with in order of arrival. That meant there was a trailer truck, two cars, a lorry, two more trailer trucks and then it would be their turn. They did finally get the necessary documentation. Without too much delay they got their train to Budapest. The frontier crossing went without a hitch. They even had two hours for last minute shopping before making their way to the airport for their flight home.

Such then from time to time was the travelling. And then there was the writing. Ian had been asked for material for publication from the time he had been in the paper mill in Fife. He had never stopped writing but something very particular was now to come from his pen. 'Reinventing Theology as the People's Work',[45] first published in 1980 towards the end of Ian's time in Selly Oak, takes as its starting point the failure of traditional theology, when left in the hands of the professionals, to meet the needs of the whole people of God. He bases his assertions on a life lived with people and on a commitment to risk-taking. He characterises his understanding of theology as a 'theology for the road' – 'the faith-basis for living'. Ian draws widely on his experiences of the Kingdom of God he encountered on his travels and the theological understanding he discovered as he moved among people in small Christian communities.

Ian draws strength from his understanding that at the heart of the Christian faith is the belief that change is possible. He gives a definitive place to the Incarnation as giving us clues as to how we should live our lives. He is particularly interested in new ways of doing theology in Europe the traditional heartland of Christianity. Two assertions underpin Ian's understanding of the role of the specialist theologian; the theological specialist has no *special* access to God and no *separate* access to the knowledge of God. He balances his judgement that too often theology has suffered at the hands of the specialist, who makes it an abstract exercise, with his conviction that the theological specialist does have a role in recognising authentic faith in an increasingly diverse world. He or she has a distinctive role in providing tried and tested knowledge of the scriptural text and the tradition as signs of God's hand in history up to the present time.

The second part of 'Reinventing Theology' is entitled Tools and Techniques for the Reinvention of Theology. Ian was committed to developing partnerships between theological specialists open to new ways of thinking and the whole people of God who are challenged to demand their birthright to develop theological thinking and action appropriate to their own day. He recognises that new ways may be more easily developed beyond the supposed theological heartland of Christianity in Western Europe and its satellites. He quotes the example of Fr. Ed de la Torre in the Philippines who argued with his own people:

'You say I am the one who knows because I have been ordained a priest: right? Then listen to the one who knows . . . you have a ministry to fulfil which is more significant and complete than mine.'

Giving people confidence to do theology is the starting point. It requires that tools and techniques are in fact provided.

Ian considers the work of two of his colleagues in Selly Oak – Walter Hollenweger and John Davies. The former is associated with 'narrative theology, the latter with 'The Bible Workshop'.[46] There follows an explanation of Ian's own method of dealing with 'social, industrial and political' concerns from a theological perspective.

Ian Fraser's process for theological work is careful
  a) not to transpose a struggle for light and justice into some alien sphere of thought
  b) never to impose unrelated language from outside the context
  c) always takes seriously the complexity of situations – avoiding giving 'easy' answers to 'difficult' questions.
  d) never to give experts the only or the last word.

A three-stage process is identified
  a) There is recognition of a concern of one member of the group or community which is shared and owned by the whole study group.
  b) An in-depth probe is undertaken into the underlying realities in the particular situation being examined. This leads to a theological analysis of the problem. Input is sought from a diverse group of expert theologians. Practice suggests that a

point may be reached of real enlightenment – sometimes identified by Ian as a moment of 'conversion'.

c) A search continues for an alternative theological basis for dealing with the situation. A strong sense of community is important for further outworking of a situation as required. People who are involved in the thinking but not in the situation examined may offer to be present at a crisis point with those who are, to give them support.

Ian finds no need to seek common ground within these three approaches. The alternative tools are able to speak for themselves and will surely need to be tested by faith communities. These three techniques are not prescriptive. It can be assumed that tools will be honed in practice and that different circumstances will encourage participants to find new ways to do theology. But this at least is certain – theology that is authentic will be a process involving the laity – the whole people of God. Interesting examples of theology in action can be found widely in Ian's other writings. From within Selly Oak he offers an example of his own method at work.

On one occasion at Selly Oak colleges Ian had a group of about a dozen mature students with varying backgrounds with whom to develop an exercise designed to help them get theological resources for issues faced in the world. This had to be done in a two hour period.

Each was asked for a brief description of a life situation. They chose to work on the one given by a nurse. She came from an evangelical background. In the laundry of the hospital where she worked the staff had gone on strike. She felt vaguely that her faith required her to do something about this, but she did not know what. She wanted some help. So they stripped down the situation to find

a) what factors had led to the strike
b) what pressures those on strike were under
c) what effects these events were having on those involved
d) what major powers were at work shaping the events
e) what 'entry points' or 'handles' existed which might provide some concrete leverage on the situation.

The group examined the main policies promoted or advocated. They identified values underlying these policies. Then they laid an alternative biblical/theological basis for action and identified policies which should result. They finally checked on the relevance and realism of their proposals.

When the others left, the nurse remained behind. Her face was radiant. 'I thought what I had to do was to do something about that strike,' she said. 'I have also been attracted and puzzled by the doctrine of the Atonement. Today I learned how to act in relation to the laundry strike by getting deep into the meaning of the Atonement. It's incredible! I can hardly take it in!'

Sometimes there is a reminder that to be a teacher/enabler is the greatest privilege any human being can have.

Margaret flourished in Selly Oak. The Fraser home did indeed become a place of hospitality. Every member of the colleges, staff and students, was in time invited during the course of every year. In the wider community Margaret became an elder in a Weoley Hill United Presbyterian Church.[47] She got involved with an inter-faith group,

'All Faiths in Selly Oak and the City'. Margaret headed up 'Tools for Self-Reliance'. Ian fetched and carried for this group finding unused or unwanted tools in huts and garages and bringing them to the refurbishing workplace. Margaret was in charge. She had found retired craftsmen who were willing to give their services on Saturday mornings. Complete chests of tools, sufficient for the needs of a carpentry industry in a village or a small town, could be provided for countries where such items were poor in quality and in short supply.

One winter Margaret and her team were given the use of the cricket pavilion at Selly Oak Colleges for the reconditioning work. It was there the unexpected happened. Two Tanzanians walked past the pavilion. They stuck their heads round the door and asked what was going on. When they were told they became animated. They had seen the fruits of this project in their own country. A chest of tools had been delivered to a village. Up to that point the carpenters had been struggling with substandard equipment. Now a proper business could be established and orders for basic furniture fulfilled. 'The kind of thing you are doing *here*,' said the Tanzanians, 'can revitalise a whole area *there*!' It produced apprenticeships, led to development and proper harvesting of trees.

On an evening in early March 1981 Margaret went to an All Faiths meeting and found the door locked. It was a dark wet evening. Pointing fingers directed her round to the back of the building. In the dark she fell down a dozen unguarded cellar steps, breaking her left leg and doing damage to her foot. She spent two days in hospital, and in all was twelve weeks in plaster. There followed a three-month period of physiotherapy. X-rays showed that the healing had left her with a stiff ankle which gave her pain on occasion. In all this

Margaret showed her usual courage, seeing the humour in the fact that the worst case in her physiotherapy exercise group was a woman who had fallen off her platform shoes! A claim for compensation was settled out of court. Margaret was able to bring into play her gifts: intelligence, imagination, attractiveness and a generous and resilient spirit in the face of such difficulties.

While this life story of Ian Fraser is no academic thesis when the opportunity presented itself to have a considered view of his time at Selly Oak it seemed prudent to make it available.

Representing the Department of Mission of the Federation of Selly Oak Colleges, Ian was on the appointing committee when Bishop John Davies was called to the post of Principal of the College of the Ascension, one of the four participating colleges. The appointment was made in 1976. John's background was in South Africa from which he had been expelled during the apartheid era in 1970.

In his description of the Department of Mission John identifies it as Ian's department. He gives valuable insight in a recent written reflection on these days which is included here as an interesting view on Ian's time and influence at Selly Oak from one who valued the time shared with Ian but is prepared to present particular and personal insights.

'The Department of Mission's students were men and women, lay and ordained, including some married couples who had been selected by UK Missionary Societies for service in churches overseas. Some were at Selly Oak for a full year's course; others were there for only a few weeks. They were from very varied Christian traditions.

'Then there were students, mostly older men, sent by overseas churches for theological study to equip them for leadership roles in their own countries. They were mainly from Asia, Africa and Latin America. Another group of students were some Germans and Scandinavians who were preparing for service in churches in the 'Third World' who had been sent to Selly Oak for the English-as-a-Foreign-Language course run by the Colleges. Their competence in English was sufficient for them to spend some of their time in the Mission Department. There was, in addition, a bewildering range of individuals in what must be understood to be a small department with some 50–60 students at any one time. Some were at post – graduate level while others had few literacy skills.

'Ian as Dean had the responsibility for holding together a staff of about twenty. Of these only Ian and Lesslie Newbiggin were directly employed by the Department of Mission. The others were staff members of the missionary colleges along with several leaders of the one-person institutes which had developed under the Selly Oak umbrella. Ian depended on the goodwill and cooperation of a varied assortment of individuals each with loyalties which lay outside his Department. The Chairman of the Governors of the Selly Oak Federation was Sir Robert Birley. He said that a federation was the most responsible form of government which human beings had ever devised, but that it was also the one which made most demands on its administrators. This was certainly true for Ian. It may not always have been evident to folk who were not directly involved in the management of the Colleges and the Department. There was always room for some misunderstanding.

'The staff of the Mission Department had all come from a university tradition. For this reason 'subjects' tended to dominate. A meeting of staff took place before the beginning of the academic year. Each member of staff was encouraged to offer a subject they might teach and to bid for a slot in the overall programme. Ian was anxious that students were not sent out into the world with their customary ignorance of Marxism. Lesslie clearly had a vast store of wisdom which was relevant to the central core of what the Department of Mission needed to offer. By its very nature the course offered in the Department was somewhat unsystematic and subject-orientated. A number of the staff were anxious to have their courses recognised as being of university standard. Students and missionary societies felt the need for some certification, which they could use as some justification for their time spent in the Department. This ran into difficulties with the students who were anxious to use this time of preparation before going overseas on issues, which they felt would be of immediate benefit and relevance.

'This problem was exemplified in a number of ways. The new President of the federation, John Ferguson, after many years at the Open University with its emphasis on distance learning, came to Selly Oak longing for direct classroom contact with students. He offered a course from his profound knowledge of Greek philosophy. He was deeply disappointed that this course had so few takers. Most of the staff in the colleges found it difficult to recommend it to students as a preparation for service in Tanzania, Pakistan or Brazil. Ian's major concern did not lie in mere academic excellence. He held this in tension with his personal passion for a theology which would be 'of the people'. He believed this would arise from people's experience and from their confrontation with the darknesses of this world, rather than from academic categories. This was what caught the imagination and commitment of many of his staff colleagues and students. Lesslie already had an international name. He was inspired by the criteria which applied in the studies which a nephew of his was following in architecture, and he wanted students to become good practitioners of mission, not just to pass exams. Together Ian and Lesslie increasingly focused on the kind of issues which a person in mission service would have to meet and respond to. If, among the staff, they were able to find someone who could lead a study on an issue of this kind, well and good. If not, they would work something out from scratch, often with the resources from the students themselves.

'A sort of certificate was provided to satisfy the requirements of those who needed such a thing. It had a limited status. Ian hoped that the Department of Mission might be able to offer a theological qualification for which literacy was not the sine qua non.'

To clarify the intention of the work of the Department of Mission Ian led the staff into articulating a set of Aims and Objectives. Like most such documents, it represented a lot of argument and compromise. It does however, Bishop John believes, give a useful and valid window into the leadership which Ian provided at Selly Oak.

Aim. The aim of the course is to enable participants to assist as effective agents of Christian mission in the community in which they are to serve, whatever their task, and wherever it may be. (Note: we hope to send people to assist the local church, not to govern it or to act as agents of an outside organisation.)

Objective. *To this end, the objective of the course is to help students to understand and accept for themselves the implications of commitment to Jesus Christ as Lord of all creation and within all cultures, in proclamation of the Gospel, in seeking God's kingdom and justice within the contemporary world, and in sharing in the life, witness and renewal of the churches to which they are sent.*

The document took the risk of saying that the programme will include opportunities for participants to grow as men and women in Christ, and in particular

a) *to grow in their experience and practice of worship, prayer and discipleship.*

b) *To broaden their awareness of Christian traditions of spirituality.*

c) *To identify what is good and true in the created order.*

d) *To appropriate the resources of Christ's atonement and resurrection in handling conflict and guilt, including corporate guilt.*

e) *To be willing to live in frontier situations without familiar landmarks and to be prepared to experience alienation.*

f) *To be sensitive to the spiritual problems involved in making decisions, especially in times of crisis, and identifying what must be abandoned and what must be retained.*

g) *To handle questions of their own successes and failures with the resources of the Christian Gospel, to define their own needs, and to seek out the resources to meet them.*

To make such a list is clearly a statement of hope and intention. It would be impossible to guarantee success or award marks. But students did recognise that this was a serious agenda, which invited genuine commitment.

John quotes at length from this document because he thinks 'that it does encapsulate the ethos of the whole Department of Mission. It was a combined effort from a big team, but Ian was the convener and enabler. It represents his priorities, his enthusiasm and his ability to enable and encourage'. Alongside the work Ian did as Dean of the Department of Mission John places the work of hospitality that Margaret led in their home. He notes that given the wide range of 'personalities, structures, and of backgrounds, this personal support was absolutely vital'. In a somewhat apologetic way he seeks to remind those who will listen 'that in these Selly Oak days life continued to be centred in the Colleges rather than in the Department of Mission'. Some might sense that the coordinating function of the development was fulfilled at least to some extent by drawing diverse groups together but at the same time leaving them the best of their own culture and practice.

Now it is true that as Ian's 65th birthday loomed he had the opportunity to retire or go on for another 5 years. Margaret and Ian found that they were of the same mind. For nearly a decade Ian had been at the heart of bringing into being a new department. He wondered if he had put too personal a stamp on it. He decided that it would be better if someone else was given the opportunity to test that out.

Lesslie Newbiggin said to Ian, 'You retire on a certain date but you are only discharged from working for the Kingdom on the day you die.' Ian certainly seems to have taken this to heart. As the time of his retiral drew near Ian felt drawn to return to work in Scottish Churches House. He was reluctant to impose himself on the people now in charge. Ian asked Horace Walker, Secretary of the Home Board of the Church of Scotland whether it might be useful when he returned to Scotland to serve in some capacity in Scottish Churches House. Horace said, 'Don't even think of it, Ian. You would be far too much of a threat to the people there now.'

But Kenyon Wright, then the Warden of Scottish Churches House came to Birmingham. He telephoned and invited himself to the Frasers. During his visit he encouraged Ian to be involved in work that needed to be done on small Christian communities. He indicated that Scottish Churches House could act as a base for this work. Ian accepted this as confirmation that he should take on the task. A house for Ian and Margaret to make into a home was required; proximity to Dunblane would clearly be an advantage. They did not have a house. They had never had a house of their own in almost 40 years of married life. In all that time they had lived in houses tied to Ian's employment.

Ian and Margaret looked in on Grandma Stewart in Thornhill on the way from Birmingham to Tillicoultry, where son Keith and his wife Hazel lived. They intended to check out properties in the Stirling area. On the way north Margaret's mother was adamant that they should not look at a house, which would have room for her. She was determined to stay in her own home, in her own village, with her own neighbours.

A property was inspected not far from Keith and Hazel's home. It was on the market at a knock-down price. There was some question about the stability of the building; it was on or near a fault line. Nothing was finalised and Margaret and Ian called in at Thornhill on the way south. Grandma had had a giddy turn; it had given her a scare. She hoped that in any house they acquired there might be space for her! The option on the house in Tillicoultry was given up; it had no possibility of providing a 'granny flat'!

Shortly after these visits Margaret's mother died. She left them a legacy. This was added to the compensation Margaret had been awarded after her fall in Selly Oak. Some money that had been due to Ian at the end of his time in Geneva had been invested. The policy, which they had both forgotten about, matured just at that time. Keith had continued to watch for a property in the Stirling area. When the house in Gargunnock became available there was just enough to buy it, putting cash on the table.

Ian was unable to return north to look at this property. He had to leave Margaret to visit it without him. She saw the property one day, talked to Ian on the telephone about it the next day and was required to make an offer on the property the following day. It was accepted. But she was concerned. Since they always did things together she was worried that Ian might not like it. She should not have worried! The house became their home together for the next five years. Ian is at home there still.

Endnotes

42 St Andrews College – Baptist and Reformed; Ascension College – United Society for the Propagation of the Gospel (USPG); Crowther Hall – Church Missionary Society; Fircroft College.
43 The headquarters of the Church of Scotland.

[44] A Church of Scotland missionary who became a bishop in the Church of South India.

[45] Originally prepared for the European Woudshoten Conference in April 1981 – 'A Theology for Britain in the 80s'.

[46] These methods are given in detail in 'Reinventing Theology as the People's Work'.

[47] It was in this church that Ian preached a sermon broadcast on BBC Radio. He might have been at the Nairobi Would Council but chose rather to preach in the church where Margaret was an elder. The text of this sermon is included as Appendix B.

CHAPTER EIGHT

HOME AND AWAY

WHILE IAN DID not reach the customary retirement age till his 65th birthday in December of 1982, it made good sense for him to leave Selly Oak at the end of the summer of that year. The nature of the work that would occupy him with Margaret for the next period of their lives was beginning to take shape.

Margaret took considerable delight in meticulous planning to turn the newly acquired house into their home. Lists were produced of those items already in their possession which could serve in the new place, while other lists noted items that were surplus to requirements that could be sold to help with the purchase of items outstanding.

Ian was also busy. He was approached by a number of enquirers with ideas of what he might now turn his hand to. He made it clear that he would no longer require a salary but he was equally clear that this time of working in partnership with Margaret would mean that he would take on nothing that failed to provide two sets of expenses. Ian became a voluntary research consultant to the Scottish Churches Council and later to its successor body ACTS, Action of Churches Together in Scotland. It was therefore a real delight to them when the British Missionary Societies and Boards asked Ian and Margaret to accept a joint appointment, initially for two years with the possibility of extending the work for a further three years. The autumn of 1982 was to be given over to a 6 week visit to small Christian communities in the Philippines. This would be a taster for Margaret of Two-Thirds World developments and would allow Ian to re-visit people and situations he knew. The purpose of this visit and later visits to small Christian communities in Europe was to bring back insights for the renewal of the church in Britain.

Ian had memories of earlier visits to the Philippines. On his first visit in 1973 during the programme of encounters around the world which informed the 'Participation in Change Programme' for the World Council of Churches, Ian visited with great interest a community of farm workers in Tarlac La Paz. They had suffered disaster after disaster. It started with a plague of rats, which like locusts, ate right through the crops. The following year a virus destroyed the whole crop. The year after that typhoon and flood ruined everything. 'For forty-five days,' said a mother of nine, 'it rained day and night. I gathered my children and said, "Children, this may be the end of the world". All we had was one cup of rice per day for the whole family.'

In May 1974 Ian visited them when they were just beginning to get on their feet again. He asked them whether they had come to feel that God had laid a curse upon them, as catastrophe had followed catastrophe. 'We felt that God was punishing us for our sinfulness and carelessness,' said one farm worker. His interpretation was challenged by others. 'God does not act like that. God never acts like that. It wasn't a punishment; it was a time of testing. We had to go through a time of testing.'

The result? They had developed a new communal way of living. The few who owned fields decided to offer them to the farm labourers after the rice harvest to plant *mongo* (beans). They took common responsibility for the productive land. If one was ill or away from home, neighbours stepped in and saw that the land was tended. They became a caring and sharing community and none was left out. Even those who for one reason or another could not work got their portion.

It was on his 1973 visit that Ian had the opportunity to meet Ed de la Torre, a priest who was willing to pay the price of serving Christ's people in these dark days of the Marcos' dictatorship. He interviewed Ed in a safe house while the priest was on the run from the police. As was his custom Ian taped the interview, always anxious to have record of experience in the words of those he met.

Ian was keen to meet up again with Ed de la Torre. He discovered that he had been jailed by the authorities for his open support of the poor and the oppressed. Ian called on Mommy de la Torre and wondered if he might visit Ed in jail. She seemed to live constantly in prayer. As she went about her daily work and life it was as if she was picking up signals all the time about how to manage the way ahead.

Ian went with her to the prison camp. At that time visiting was restricted. He had no permit to get in. Mommy seemed to be looking for directions about what to do. Finally her brow cleared. 'We are to play this straight.' They went to the reception room at the jail without more ado.

Whenever the commandant set eyes on Mommy he concentrated all his attention on her. She reared pigs. He wanted one of the piglets as a gift. He was so intent on this that when she said, 'I have this other friend with me,' he waived Ian aside to a table where passes were provided, without shifting his attention from Mommy. Ian's credentials were not required. Without questioning, he was given a pass. Ian was unsure whether a piglet had been promised. This he knew: he got safely through to spend some time with Ed. The blindness of greed was their ally that day.

On occasion Ian accepted that some of his planned visits and meetings would just not be possible. In 1977 it looked for example that he would have to return home without having an opportunity to interview one person he particularly wanted to meet, Senator Jovite Salonga. He was the man who later after the revolution, was entrusted with the business of tracing the Marcos' millions squirreled away abroad in secret accounts. He was lawyer, lecturer and Baptist lay preacher. He would take up the case of anyone who got rough justice from the Marcos' regime, knowing that this made him a political target. He had suffered in jail.

During Ian's visit the senator had gone to an island off the coast of the Philippines. He was not due back until after Ian was due to leave. Ian had been interviewing Trining Herrera, the leader of the Tondo Community and was in the office of her lawyer. The phone rang. The language used in the conversation was Tagalog. It wasn't a language Ian was familiar with but he could not help hearing some words he thought he understood, including the name 'Jovite'. Ian asked whether by any chance the person at the other end of the line was Senator Salonga. To his delight he was told that it was.

Ian asked the lawyer to send Salonga his regards and to say how sorry he was that they were out of reach and that they would not be able to meet. 'But he is back on the mainland,' Ian was told, 'He did not intend to be back but he has just been telling me that he felt under very strong pressure to return early – that something was required of him.' Ian was able to take the phone and speak to him directly and he was then able to meet the senator for two hours – exactly the time which he had to spare before leaving for the airport.

One thing that Senator Salonga said remains with Ian. The senator spoke of 'the evangelical necessity of research into transnational corporations. Lest the world fall into a powerful grip, which is other than God's.'

Ian's own safety was at risk from time to time. The nearest Ian came to getting jailed in the Philippines was in 1977. Ferdinand Marcos had decided on a period of special vigilance. He attempted to seal all exits from the country of information which might be detrimental to his unjust regime. Evidence had been assembled about imprisonments, torture and assassinations but the channels for getting them to justice and peace organisations in different parts of the world had been blocked. Ian volunteered to try to get them delivered.

Taking his cue from Edgar Allan Poe's story, 'The Letter', Ian decided that the safest place for the documents might be the most obvious – in his hand luggage. At the airport he was picked on for a spot check. The woman, who looked through his bag instead of examining it just for bombs, hand-grenades and such like, demanded what the packets were. Ian replied that they were friends' letters which could reach their destinations more quickly if he posted them in Britain. She asked what was in them. He replied, 'I do not read my friends' letters!' She retorted, 'You are getting no further until I find out what is in these letters!' They stood facing one another across the table, the bag between them.

At that point a group of Japanese tourists came up behind Ian, some pushing from the back because they were late for their plane. Those at the front swept Ian off his feet and past the point of search. He grabbed the bag with the documents before the woman could. She held up her hands in defeat and gave up any further attempt to challenge him. Discovery would surely have meant jail.

At the next stage another obstacle appeared – the screening chamber in which all tapes and films could be scrubbed. During that visit to the Philippines Ian had recorded 32 interviews including that with Trining Herrara, the leader of the Tondo Community speaking about the severe torture she had suffered. What a loss these tapes would be! When Ian returned to Britain tape after tape proved to be unimpaired. Trining's voice went out on the 'Sunday' Programme of the BBC, telling of her torture and giving direct testimony to what she had endured.

So it was with this background that Ian and Margaret undertook their visit in 1982 to the Philippines. They entered that country when Ferdinand Marcos was in the USA, being feted by Ronald Reagan. Extra care was being taken to vet all who sought entry to the Philippines. The queue moved very slowly towards passport control.

Ian's turn came. The man looked at his passport, frowned and consulted the black book at his side in which all manner of undesirables were registered. Ian slipped round to the other side of the desk when he was distracted. The page was open at the letter 'F'. There Ian was in all his glory. Ian quickly returned to where he should have been. The official gave his attention afresh to Ian's passport. His face cleared. Ian and Margaret got through without delay.

Ian did not tell Margaret what he had seen until they were safely back in Britain. In the black book he was 'Rev. Dr. Ian M. Fraser, MA BD PhD, Dean and Head of the Department of Mission, Selly Oak Colleges, Birmingham'. On the passport he was 'Ian M Fraser, educationalist, Gargunnock'. What connection could there possibly be between the two? The fact that on a previous visit Ian had taken out reports of tortures, imprisonments and assassinations and sent them to Justice and Peace organisations in different parts of the world must have become known. Ian is of the opinion that the most the authorities would have done would have been to keep tabs on him. But he was glad to slip through the net! His prayers that night might have included thanksgivings that 'while God did not intervene to prevent the rise of dictatorships, she also did not intervene to insist on their competence in keeping records up to date.'

What a variety of experiences the Frasers had as they visited widely around the Philippines. Zamboanga City is a significant city on the island of Mindanao, the second largest of the islands of the Philippines. There Ian and Margaret were invited to meet with Carmelite nuns. They wondered what to converse about, for they are a contemplative order, 'confined to barracks', concentrating on meditation and prayer. The meeting was memorable on both sides. When later the nuns heard of Margaret's death they wrote to tell Ian that they would remember her in a mass year by year on the anniversary of her passing. They have done so faithfully.

On the day of the visit the nuns assembled behind iron bars to meet Ian and Margaret. They spoke through the grilles. What struck the visitors was their understanding of developments in the Philippines. Ian had cause to reflect later that in the course of their six-week visit to the Philippines they met with researchers, analysts, social workers and political activists. None of them seemed to have the rounded appreciation of events which the nuns exhibited. It was a mystery, for these people were shut away from the traffic of humanity. Ian was left musing as to whether 'prayer provides a kind of chute down which knowledge comes to those ready to receive it, who look to God for light.'

On their visit to Mindanao Ian and Margaret met Bishop Escaler of the Ipil diocese. The city of Ipil which gives its name to the diocese lies 3 hours north-east of Zamboanga City. It is a strategic centre and capital of its district. It was there that they saw how a hierarchy can be both flexible and dynamic. The secret, Ian was convinced, was that you take a pyramidal structure and make a spiral of it; then press down on the spiral – it becomes a spring!

In the diocese 1200 basic Christian communities met each week to find biblical resources for living the faith in local situations. Their discoveries were drawn into a chapel service on Sundays. Every month there was a *zona* gathering, lasting two days. The leaders present had been chosen by the members of the church a) to get further training in handling the scriptures and b) to challenge one another if it was thought that forms of leadership were becoming manipulative. *Parishes* covered a wider area. There were three *districts* in the diocese. Finally a *Prelature Assembly* of 150 people took an overview of the development across the diocese. Four times a year the spring gathered dynamic from the basic Christian communities and tightened its coils into that assembly; it then unwound to nourish the Christian community all the way to the grass roots. The people were well represented all the way through to definitive decision-making.

There was a lay majority in the *Prelature Assembly*. Bishop Escaler did not even chair the gathering – that was left to one of the laity. The bishop took a seat among the other representatives in the main body of the hall. Bishop Escaler just had authority: he did not need to pull rank, as is so often case with those whose authority is shaky. His authority was like that exhibited by Jesus; you can give that kind of authority away and still have it.

The peasants and workers who came together in the basic Christian communities would identify situations they faced which needed to be addressed. With their growing knowledge of the Bible they would identify texts which might help them to deal with these issues from a faith perspective. Only then would the professionals come in. Almost inevitably they would be greatly enlightened by hearing the biblical texts which the people considered to be relevant. They might then go on to say: 'You suggest consulting this part of the bible. But are you aware that there is another part which seems to speak in flat contradiction to it?' 'Then we must study both!' would come the reply. Thereafter they would work together. It became a matter not of specialists building up the church, but of the whole church building itself up in love (Ephesians 4:10) – preparing ahead biblical resources for nourishing and directing lives.

On their 1982 visit Margaret and Ian saw one of the effects of holding the SE Asian Games in that country that year. There was an area which was deemed to be an eyesore by the authorities. It would disgrace the country if competitors from many nations saw it. So, although the tenants had legal right to their property and could not be faulted on payment of money due, bulldozers were sent in and their shacks demolished.

The residents of Manila were dumped on the outskirts of the city. Many children were included among those evicted. The folk had no resources. There was no opportunity for work. The families drifted back into the centre of the capital city. A husband, worn out by malnutrition and worry, coughed up his life-blood. There was no money to bury him. The body was put in a plastic bag and lay around for two weeks. Neighbours at last sacrificially raised enough to secure his burial.

These neighbours then built a lean-to against a wall and covered the framework with plastic (from the bag that had been used for the body) to provide minimal shelter for the widow and the children. The dimensions of the lean-to were some three metres by just over a metre. A low platform kept the family up out of the mud and had to serve as a sleeping space. Five plastic bags acted as wardrobe for the children's clothes. That was what had to serve as home.

When a small boy gently took Margaret's hand and pressed it to his brow, seeking in this way her blessing, she was totally broken up. The visitors felt that they should be on their knees before these people, seeking their blessing.

Margaret and Ian visited the fishing village of Bagakay in Negros. A sister of the Order of the Good Shepherd had offered to act as guide and interpreter. The people of the village numbered about 50 and the visitors gathered with them in one of their larger rooms.

The village seemed a prosperous place. To the right were fish ponds, to the left were a harvested field and grain drying in the sun and in front was the open sea. But the villagers did not own the fish ponds. They did all the work for a pittance while others got the profits. They did not own the land and a large proportion of the crop, produced solely by their efforts, had to go to the landowner. Japanese trawlers were using the latest technology to scoop out great quantities of fish at the same time destroying the sea bed. The villagers were no longer prepared, as they had been previously, to accept their situation fatalistically.

What produced the change? Until the early 1970s the people thought of the church as being for rich people in the towns, not for the likes of them. Then one of the younger members of the community was given the chance of education. At school he encountered the bible. The villagers would gather round when he returned and he would read and explain it. They found that Jesus' world was their world! In it they met repressive landlords, questions of tenants' rights and responsibilities, the tough business of finding and catching fish, uncertain harvests, the lighting and cleaning of houses, the baking of bread. Hope developed as they listened. Then they began to use their own minds, and draw more on their own experience, challenging the interpretations of the instructor. They discovered the dignity God gave them as people made in his likeness. They became awkward people, no longer prepared to fit in tamely with the schemes of the powerful.

The authorities labelled the challenge to their power 'communist' although the people did not even know what the word communism meant. It was the gospel that had given them fresh life and hope. Pressures on them mounted. An old lady summed up their situation to the nods of all around, 'To tell the truth, we are afraid. But God's word is more powerful than our fears. We will all have to die some day. We have decided we may as well die for a worthwhile cause.'

In just six weeks Ian and Margaret had accumulated many insights. While they were visiting and later, each made notes and these were compared on return to their Gargunnock home. No table was large enough so they used the floor. They laid out their notes and tried to bring them into some kind of order. To begin with they frequently wondered whether they had been on the same visits! In time one of them would see a connection between seemingly disparate items. Slowly the big picture would begin to emerge. Ian referred to this process as seeing in stereo – two pairs of eyes, two heads, and two hearts being better than one.

It was from their Gargunnock base that Ian and Margaret now set out to visit basic christian communities in Europe. The plan included communities in west, central and eastern Europe. As they travelled they continued to make notes and to record interviews which were later transcribed and placed in the Baker Library in Scottish Churches House.[48]

At the end of these visits Ian wrote and published 'Wind and Fire'.[49] This detailed record gives a dozen glimpses of bccs in Spain, France, the Netherlands, Switzerland, Austria and Italy. These were followed by thematic insights from fifty communities across Europe considering their struggle for new life as they came into existence; the sustenance they draw from the word and sacraments; their new patterns of life together and their service in the wider world.

It is clearly invidious to select individual threads from such a rich tapestry of experience but Ian himself selected one encounter by way of introduction to the rest.

Natalie led Margaret and Ian across the Dom Luis I bridge over the River Douro to the main part of the city of Oporto in Portugal. The crags they faced were topped by the magnificent former Archbishop's palace, speaking of the lordly power the church once exercised, and reminding them of the extent to which ecclesiastical power is still in evidence. They reached the other end of the bridge. Natalie gestured downwards. At the foot of the palace lay the dwellings of the poor, with cramped quarters, broken roofs.

'Every day,' said Natalie, 'there is set out before the eyes of the people of this city this visible sign of what the church stands for. What wonder then, that we have been called to contradict that sign to live a countersign'.

The countersign was the lifestyle of basic christian communities in Oporto. They were small in number. They looked frail. They were pregnant with the future. And yet, sometimes their guests had to shake themselves to make sure that they had not slipped back into the first century. The apostles' teaching, the fellowship, the breaking of bread, the prayers; the holding of everything in common and the distribution of possessions as the need of each required; the sharing with unaffected joy – for the Frasers these became a living experience.

Spiritual athletes, these? Anything but! Ian and Margaret listened when with broken bread and wine poured out, the folk told of their own brokenness and poured out their hearts. They heard of frustration and failure in relationships, illness and depression, stresses in the workplace – in searching for employment and alternative work. 'Cast down but not destroyed!' When they met the members of the community did not leave until they had consolidated plans for the political and social engagements to which their faith directed them.

In October 1984 Ian and Margaret met up with Alice Amrein in Switzerland. The record of their conversation includes this sharing:

Q   You (Alice) worked in Columbia for four years before returning to Switzerland. What kind of work did you do?

A   The work was pastoral in character, and was with students and also with peasants in the countryside.

Q   Why return after only four years?

A   There were several reasons, but the main one was that we belong to Switzerland and it is important that a country such as ours becomes far more aware of the situation in the Third

World. We have enough experience to be able to do something in our own country about that.

Q   Are there links with other groups in Switzerland?

A   Until three years ago, there were no links. But then we started to hold an annual reunion. Last year there were fifteen groups and over a hundred people.

Q   And what would you call the main feature of (your) group?

A   Our meeting with one another is very important. We have meals together as families, from time to time in one another's houses. We have the reading of the bible and prayer. We have involvement in the life of the people in this area. Every Friday we have a gathering of all the members of the group.

Q   I am on my way to Turin to share in the preparations for the second European Congress (of basic christian communities). If you were to suggest issues which the Congress has to face from your own situation, what would they be?

A   (Firstly) the need for a vivid relationship with the Third World. Secondly there is a need to take the measure of the role of capitalism in the world today. But the main thing may be to discover the kind of liberation we need in Europe. I have the impression that people (here) suffer from a kind of psychological marginalising.

Q   What about contacts with church parishes in Switzerland?

A   In different parts of Switzerland the possibility for this varies. Our group illustrates one kind of difficulty which is experienced because we are Roman Catholics and Protestants. We are associated with two parishes; the Roman Catholic priest shares in the group and is a good friend – the

reformed pastor knows about the group but has simply
shared once in one of its activities.

Q   When you have a eucharist, who presides?

A   From time to time it is the Roman Catholic priest. But when
he presides it is not in his own name but on behalf of the
whole community. At other times, we have people who are
theologically trained but are not ordained . . . a man or a
woman may preside.

Q   How do you think this will affect the church in the future?

A   I think that ecumenism develops properly from the grass
roots upwards.

With the contacts that Ian had with basic christian communities
around the world he clearly valued sharing between groups as
opportunities arose. Equally he became convinced that the growth of
these communities in Europe was not a simple transplant from Latin
America or anywhere else but a spontaneous work of the Spirit. He
frequently returns to his contention that the early Iona Community
was a 'John Baptist' sign of the new thing God was doing in the whole
world.

It had always been the intention of Ian and Margaret to visit basic
christian communities in Eastern Europe as part of their programme
in the early 1980s. Unfortunately the Polish Congress of bccs which
was to have taken place in June 1984 was postponed and attempts by
the Frasers to make the right contact with Hungarian and Czech
groups proved unsuccessful at that time.

In 'Wind and Fire' the hope is expressed that 'Opportunities may
occur for visits to these (Eastern European) countries in the years

ahead. As has become clear the hope was fulfilled not least on a return visit that Ian made to a Polish new town near Krakow called Nova Hutte. The church Ian encountered there seems to have exhibited the kind of spirit he encountered widely on visits to basic christian communities. On this visit in the late 1980s the government was very cooperative with the churches with regard to erecting buildings but in the early 1970s it seemed to be very different.

The inhabitants of Nova Hutte sent a delegation to the communist Town Council and requested that five churches be built to meet the needs of the inhabitants of the new city. They were told that there were far too many churches already in Poland, and that they would get none. They returned several times, making their case. Each time they were rebuffed. Finally, they erected a cross on church ground and had a sit-in round it.

Eventually, the persistence of the people wore down the local Council, and they said, 'O.K., you can have one church building but you will have to build it yourselves'. It did not seem to strike the authorities – a building which people built themselves was much more precious and significant than a building constructed for them. Also, no size of building had been specified, and the people decided on a church to seat 5000 persons (6000 cramming in for service after service on a Sunday running through the day so that all could be accommodated.)

On the later visit Ian was taken under the church where there was quite a substantial hall-space. The people told him that they had gone back to the Town Council repeatedly with the complaint that damp was getting through the floor and they needed an air-space under the floor. Once again they were refused. Once again they wore the Council down. 'Oh, have your air-space, then!' 'They did not specify the size of the air-space,' said Ian's main informer, 'and we just happened to make it large enough to be another very useful meeting place for 1000 people.' They illustrated the importance of having a God not only of Abraham and Isaac – but also of Jacob, the godly twister!

Reviewing 'Wind and Fire' Jim Wilkie, a member of the Iona Community commended the book and its record of basic christian communities, noting that after the interviews 'comes a chapter on 'The Marks of the Church . . . One, Holy, Catholic and Apostolic'. It should be noted . . . that the bccs do not claim to be true church, only to be forms of the church. They do not look on themselves representing pure and primitive Christianity – they know that they are sinners.

'In these groups ordinary Christians can re-appropriate theology for themselves, can escape from the domination of the establishment and while remaining in real relation with the church universal, can work out their ecumenical, evangelical and economic commitment. In these groups the ordained are again finding their true place of importance and usefulness **alongside** as opposed to **above** the laity and as a result all can develop their vocation – their calling to be church together'.

Alongside the programme of visits to basic christian communities in Europe Ian was involved in the 'Shalom Project' which saw Ian based at Scottish Churches House from 1982 under the auspices of the Scottish Churches Council. It gave him the responsibility to 'help

Christians to examine critically and prophetically the views and presuppositions of our society, bringing faith-resources (theology) to bear.' Rather than seeking to support a group of like-minded individuals or individuals on their own Ian sought to resource basic Christian communities to gee up

a) bible study groups that do not act
b) contemplation groups which do not stand attentive before situations which must be understood and dealt with
c) action groups which do not reach for faith resources.

What God has joined we must no longer put asunder![50]

Three very different public issues were addressed by Ian – the poor, giftedness and monetarism.

Poverty

Ian encouraged groups to share an investigation of biblical references to poverty and to explore its developing understanding from the Old Testament through to the New Testament. Ian reminded people that the Biblical words for poverty refer to something more than material need. Those who are physically poor can be rich-in-faith. Poverty biblically is more about folk made in God's image being refused place and voice in God's world. The poor are thus 'answering people' forced to respond to the initiative of others and the future they plan; and to adjust, as best they can, to decisions which they had no part in shaping.

The response to poverty needs not to be so much compassion (giving from surplus) as justice (sharing what's there). Ian notes that the Bible is clear that people do not just happen to be poor – they are *made* poor. Poverty involves violence – the poor are robbed of what is *due to them* in God's world. Gandhi said, 'Poverty is the worst form of violence.' The policies of rulers should have two main objectives – to preserve a nation from idolatry and to honour and protect the poor. Being rich and 'trusting in riches' are too often near neighbours.

The Jubilee provisions (see Leviticus 25) demand that, instead of yet more researching into the cause of the poor, we need to break the cycle of poverty and set the captives free. The study guide asks groups whether they agree that Jubilee points to the need for times of significant redistribution of wealth and power.

Gifted Children

Gifted children are considered to be the top 2% of a country's children, while clever can be applied to the top 10%. Gifted children are taken to merit selective treatment, extra provision for being stretched with additional access to educational resources. It is this that makes the question of giftedness significant in a society where the children born into have-not families with minimal resources can be shown to suffer from real deprivation.

Ian encourages members of communities considering this question to find responses that will lie within the whole range of education offered within state comprehensive schools. He is particularly interested in the deprivation likely to be experienced by those provided with what he perceives to be a lop-sided 'hot-house' education cut off from the mainstream of life.

Ian considers what the New Testament has to say about gifts.[51] He concludes that in the Christian community not 2% but 100% are gifted. These gifts find their true expression in relation to the community. Those who try to make these grace-gifts serve selfish purposes find that they die in their hands or become corrupt – much as manna did in the desert when more than was needed was collected. But it should be noted that the gifts are not just to build up the community of Christians – they strengthen the whole body for service in the world.

Monetarism

Professor J.K. Galbraith considered Britain as a good place to test Monetarism. This economic theory aims to restrict bank borrowing to dampen down demand by restraining wages and this reducing inflation. Monetarist policies led to unemployment as a means to control wages and prices. The theory is justified on the grounds that 'the market' produces a healthy economy. It requires an ample reward for the rich to encourage their productivity while at the same time reducing money available to the poor to ensure that they do not dodge their responsibilities.

In the 1980s the actual fruits of monetarism included
    a)   the doubling of unemployment
    b)   the decimation of manufacturing
    c)   the collapse of house building
    d)   business failures reached a 50-year high

Ian returns to the two fundamental responsibilities of government a) the protection of the poor and the restraint of the rich and

b) deliverance from idolatry. In 1983 the Church Poverty Action Group showed that tax cuts for the rich roughly equally social security cuts to the poor. The one was at the expense of the other. Is monetarism not just in fact a modern form of idolatry – a trust in a theory to regulate life? Surely people should take personal responsibility for this and acknowledge their blindness in accepting the wisdom of such trust. Biblical writers after all did not bother their heads much about atheism, but attacked idolatry relentlessly.

Ian concludes his action-pamphlet by noting that he finds nothing anti-biblical in wealth creation. God is always providing not just sufficient for the human family but a feast. Biblical hostility is reserved for wealth gained at the expense of other human beings and wealth accumulated rather than shared. 'It is good that human folk should have abundance, bad that some should feast while others are in want, when God is the giver of all.' Groups using the material are invited to comment on what is provided. Ian seeks sharing of insights of others and their relevant biblical references. The prophetic nature of this work done in the 1980s is made clear as these issues are revisited at the beginning of the 21st century.

The Miners' Strike from March 1984 to March 1985 was a major industrial action with consequences far beyond the coal industry. On one occasion during the dispute Ian acted as a representative of the Iona Community and was pleased to support an expression of solidarity with the National Union of Mineworkers and which condemned the action of the government in refusing to facilitate negotiations. They condemned the withholding of benefits and the use of the police as a weapon against the miners, their wives and families. Ian believed the miners' struggle was Kingdom material, though it was not identified as such by those involved.

Ian believed that the country was deliberately being divided. The division took many forms. One was the distinction between those who know how things should be run – the natural decision-makers, and those with no such nous – who should be content to be the grateful beneficiaries of the wise policies worked out for them. Decision-making by the enlightened, compliance by the masses is the way to efficiency; and outdoing rivals is the name of the game of life in a competitive world.

In such a situation, constraining power gets in the way – of government, police and other 'good and legitimate forces'. The ploy is to use words such as 'freedom' and 'democracy'; use the media to develop an image hostile to constraining power; then put in the boot; appoint hit men. At Mrs. Thatcher's insistence and against arguments even of her own party, MacGregor was appointed to 'Coal'. A unilateral definition was given to the future of coal, in place of a plan produced by consultation. It was safe wicket to play on. Coal stocks were enormous. Miners were high in the wages league. They had been wrong-footed and would be on a hiding to nothing if they rebelled.

Deep in the dispute was an evangelical, inarticulate assertion that life's priorities must be human and wrought out by human agreement and cooperation. Ian did not pretend that the violence was all on one side, though he was convinced that is was presented as if this was the case. Ian did not want shop floor power re-established 'just like that'. The old British Leyland factory at Longbridge was too power-weighted in favour of management; a later one was too power-weighted the other way. But what is needed is to find new forms of cooperation.

Ian was of the opinion that it was the miners not the lauded technocrats who were the seers, discerning the future; watchmen on the wall alerting us to the danger. For Ian it was not just a matter of grand gestures in statements of solidarity. Within the local Iona Community family group he could see at first hand the hardship on the human face of the national strike. He did not stand idly by then and he continues to suffer with those for whom life continues to be blighted almost a quarter of a century on.

In June 1986 Jim Wallis, the founder of the Sojourners' Community in Washington D.C. undertook a nationwide tour of the United Kingdom. In the space of 30 days he and his team travelled 3000 miles, allowing Jim to speak some 100 times to a total live audience of 20,000 people. Through the media millions heard Jim 'Announcing the Kingdom'. Some months before Jim's visit Ian had been approached. The proposed tour appeared to be on the point of foundering for lack of direction and management.

Ian and Margaret had visited Sojourners in Washington and were committed to a wider understanding of the insights gained there. Ian encouraged those already involved and drew in others who laid the foundations of what was later deemed to be a successful tour. Ian noted, 'This was not something I could have done on my own but I was pleased to have had the opportunity as 'national moderator' of Jim's visit to establish a framework which enabled the Good News to be shared.'

Reporting to the British Council of Churches Executive Committee, Dr. Roger Williamson noted that the tour was both ecumenical and evangelical. As preached and lived by Jim Wallis this gospel requires an almost inevitable and continuing conflict with the American powers-that-be. It challenges both evangelicalism and a 'social action' gospel with no room for the activity of God. For Jim, American prosperity (6% of the world's population using 50% of the world's resources) is not a sign of God's favour but rather evidence of 'organised theft on a global scale'. The involvement of British black churches, marginalised in the early days of planning, found their rightful place with Ian at the helm.

The message preached by Jim Wallis is that social and political issues are not just social and political issues. 'Is not this the fast I chose: to loose the bonds of wickedness, to undo the thong of the yoke, to let the oppressed go free, and to break every yoke? Is it not to share your bread with the hungry and bring the homeless and poor into you house; when you see the naked to cover him, and not to hide yourself from your own flesh? Then shall your light break forth like the dawn, and your healing shall spring up speedily; your righteousness shall go before you, the glory of the Lord shall be your rearguard. Then you shall call, and the Lord will answer; you shall cry, and he will say 'Here am I'.[52] For Jim Wallis to find Jesus and to know Jesus, one has to find and serve him in 'the least of these'; to visit those in prison and so set at liberty the captive'.

The 'kairos' nature of Jim's visit was noted by many. The interest in his visit was greater than many had anticipated. Something seemed to have been bubbling up in the churches. Ian Fraser noted that

Clodovis Boff (Brazilian theologian and brother of Leonardo of liberation theology reputation) had used the expressing 'bubbling up' about the communities, groups and movements in Western Europe, – their being like water, just before boiling point, as the first bubbles break the surface.

If we can tell something of a person by the company he or she keeps, it is surely instructive that Ian committed himself to the preparation for Jim Wallis' tour. Jim writing to Ian in January 1987 thanks Ian both for his leadership and warm friendship. He notes that only one matter was still giving him cause for concern, namely finance. The report makes clear that in this area too Ian had left no stone unturned to ensure all the costs were met.

Jim was accompanied in Scotland by Catherine Hepburn minister at that time in Gargunnock. Meetings in Glasgow, Edinburgh and Perth were deemed by many to be among the highlights of the visit. Parish minister and parishioner working together in the cause of the good news for the nation! Can any good thing come out of Gargunnock? The answer is surely a resounding 'Yes'.

Ian and Margaret were invited to visit the SCM centre in Norway at Easter 1987. Ian reflected particularly on those who at the first Easter had sought an audience with Jesus. His reply seems to have spoken to Ian in the depth of his being. 'Except a seed fall into the ground and die it remains alone, but when it dies it bears much fruit.' (John 12.24) It was in Norway, that April that Margaret told him that she had found a lump in a gland under her arm.

On their return home the doctor who examined her saw no reason against them taking on the next assignment. Together they were to be resource persons during a consultation on 'Models of Renewed Community' at Bossey in Switzerland, the WCC Centre of Study Research and Encounter which had featured in their time in Geneva.

They arrived on the 10th May for the consultation which was due to begin on the 13th. It turned out to be unusually comprehensive in membership in the balance between men and women, the different backgrounds of the participants and the different levels of society represented.

As the conference started Margaret and Ian shared in the leadership during an opening act of worship. The director of Bossey, Professor Dr. Adrian Gemse introduced them 'I have worked with Ian previously and have known him as a person. But I became more aware of him as a partnership. Now that I have met Margaret I realise that it is knowing the partnership that counts.'[53]

The first few days in Bossey were apparently uneventful with regard to Margaret's health. By the second half of the week it became clear that she was far from well. Cheerful and out-going as ever in public, she flopped exhausted on returning to her room. On Friday 15th May, Margaret was the chairperson of a main conference session. It took the form of a panel. She was complimented for the way she enabled all kinds of folk to make their own particular contribution.

On Monday 18th May Ian was wakened at 3.00 a.m. and told, 'You will have to get Margaret home.' Before others were up Ofelia Ortega and her husband, Daniel Montoya, joined Ian to consider the options in the light of the deterioration in Margaret's condition. Margaret was all for soldiering on till the end of the conference as long as she could take plenty of rest in her room. The others agreed without hesitation that the programme would have to be adjusted to allow Ian and Margaret to make their main contribution at the beginning of the next morning session. A flight home around midday would be booked.

On the Tuesday morning Margaret was not able to take part in their usual 'double act'. Ian felt affirmed that what he was saying was being said for both of them. He noted in his presentation that the Basic Christian Communities and the official Churches live together in a certain tension. Anything which is not ephemeral needs institutionalising. This is recognised by the bccs. What is opposed is the inflexible institutionalising and especially forms which characterise 'the church of power.'

Ian noted that regional congresses of bccs
   a)   show that a new way of being church is a present reality.
   b)   show that bccs develop strength through living in community
   c)   provide mutual support and criticism to help towards maturity
   d)   allow the sharing of resources.
Ian made clear that as 'a new way of being church' bccs need to be reminded
   a)   that communities can be inward-looking, escapist and superficial
   b)   that it is folly to seek a perfect model to adopt from elsewhere.
   c)   that the ministry is the priesthood of all believers.

d) to honour the 'local' and the church 'built from below.'
e) that theology is not wrought of studies, but in kingdom struggles.
f) to emphasise the ministry of the whole people of God.
g) that we are a pilgrim people (as on the Emmaus Road)[54]

A few questions were taken and Margaret joined Ian in responding to them. At 10.45 a.m. Ian indicated that the time had arrived when they must leave without delay. He apologised for their hasty departure without proper farewells. The folk were having none of it. They arranged themselves along the central aisle then in a moving wave swept them out to the waiting minibus in a procession of songs of the Kingdom. They gathered round the departing couple, got their luggage on board, still singing, and blessed them on their way with this tangible outpouring of love.

Margaret was taken directly to Stirling Royal Infirmary. On word of her mother's illness daughter Anne came from the USA immediately. So the family gathered round Margaret, sustaining her with their love, reflecting the love with which she had so often sustained them. Alex and Nan, brother and sister-in-law came down from Forres representing the wider family. From Australia Margaret's sister Garland and her brother Andrew with their families made themselves present through gifts of flowers and words of love. As a family they celebrated Margaret's 67th birthday on 24th May gathered round her in Stirling Royal.

In the first few days back in Scotland as they waited for the results of tests the family wondered how many months they might still have Margaret. Months changed to weeks then days till the time came when they wondered if she would see out the day itself. In Stirling Royal Infirmary the doctor in charge met with the nurses each day to hear grumbles and complaints from patients. Each day against Margaret Fraser's name was the one word 'nil'. When asked whether she suffered pain, her unfailing answer was 'Not pain, just discomfort'. Anne and Ian, the two medics in the family agreed, 'Discomfort is mum's word for pain.'

Two days before she died, Margaret said to Ian in some distress, 'I love you, but I am not able to show it.' That same day the treatment was stopped and medication given to bring some relief. The following day Ian had a few minutes with Margaret. They embraced and opened their hearts to one another. Ian recalls that time. 'What an incredible grace to have been granted that time before we parted.'

The day of release dawned. Margaret when asked how she felt replied, 'I have no pain. I am surrounded by family and love. What more can I want?' Later to Catherine she confided, 'The love which is sustaining me is coming from both this side and the far side of death.' Catherine, by this time one of the family, offered to hold a communion service that evening. Her timing could not have been better. She arrived early before the appointed time. Margaret was given the energy required to fully attend to the service. Keith, Anne and husband Ian were present to participate. Communion was their parting action.

The service in celebration of the life of Margaret Davidson Dow Fraser was held in Gargunnock Parish Church in the afternoon of 3 June 1987. It was Ascension Day. It was led by Margaret's minister

Catherine Hepburn. They had only known one another for a few years but had shared deeply during that time.

Catherine characterised Margaret as a 'Kingdom person, a Kingdom worker.' Her reflection on that occasion cannot be bettered.

'Through her childhood in Thornhill, as headgirl at Dumfries Academy, in her studies at Edinburgh University and Moray House, above all in her marriage with Ian, in her partnership and companionship with him, step by Kingdom step, through industrial chaplaincy to parish ministry in Rosyth, the beginning and building up of Scottish Churches House to the World Council of Churches in Geneva; in the Selly Oak Colleges, as elder in Wooley Hill United Reform Church; in retirement here in Gargunnock, working on the Scottish Churches Council Shalom/Basic Christian Communities Project; visiting basic communities of the world church family in the Philippines and throughout Europe, editing, translating, publishing material, in seminar work, setting up the Resource Centre; in her contribution to the Iona Community – in the family group and on Iona; in the Women's Guild and the World Day of Prayer, in her teaching; in her commitment to the ecumenical movement and the world church family, to peace and justice, as a member of the local church congregation and community – singing in the choir; washing her windows, as wife and mother and grandmother, as relative, friend and neighbour, the hallmark of Margaret's life was her loving, thoughtful management of the practicalities and details of living which freed others to grow and be themselves, and her capacity to form deep, significant relationships quickly.

To know Margaret for 2 hours, 5 years, 40 years or more was to know a person of Kingdom quality and life.'

In the prayer of thanksgiving that day Catherine noted God's goodness to her in her marriage with Ian and her joy in her children and grandchildren; for the gift of her whole life and especially for the gift of the past 29 years since the first cancer. Margaret waiting for results of tests in Stirling Royal Infirmary and expecting a diagnosis of a virulent cancer said, 'Whatever happens, for me there is nothing but thankfulness; I have had a bonus of 29 marvellous years.'

And so Margaret's mortal frame was laid to rest in the new cemetery in Gargunnock on the way between the Fraser home and the parish kirk. In a secluded corner just over the burn from the community garden those loved and lost for a little while are never far away. The stream runs on and summer and winter Ian tends that sacred space which marks Margaret's last earthly resting place.

In the immediate aftermath of that day Ian found himself immersed in the love of friends and family. This sustained him. In the following week Ian was asked to report on the Scottish Churches House project to the June meeting of the Scottish Churches Council. In no mood for business meetings he had produced a one page update of progress. He was minded to miss the meeting but on reflection realised that those who would gather were just the folk who had sustained them as a couple over the past five years. Ian changed his mind. Circumstances conspired to create a space which allowed him to give a full report of the work he had shared with Margaret. He found himself enabled to speak out of the deep conviction which they had shared; Margaret was livingly remembered.

There followed an opportunity to report to the sponsoring bodies of the Conference for World Mission. They might have been expected to ask for a report towards the end of the year. As it was in the week following Margaret's death Ian was able to share the common mind they had reached in the light of their five years of working together. Ian recalls the meeting. The financial report dragged on into the time allocated for his report. He began to fret. In that moment he was conscious of Margaret's presence, a living reality right there with him. 'It's all right, love. This is something we are still doing together. It will need your voice, but it will be our mind. You'll see, it'll be all right, my love.' Ian records simply, 'it was! I was given the necessary time. We signed off together.'

Endnotes

[48] These interviews are now held in the University Library in Edinburgh.

[49] 'Wind and Fire' – The Spirit reshapes the church in basic christian communities. Margaret and Ian Fraser (sic).

[50] Choose Life. Material for groups seeking faith resources for tackling public issues April 1983.

[51] I Corinthians 12.8-10.

[52] Isaiah 58.6-9.

[53] Catherine Hepburn writing in 'A Time for Trumpets' by Nansie Blackie (Scottish church movers and shakers of the 20th century) perceptively entitles her chapter 'Margaret and Ian Fraser'.

[54] Luke 24.13-35.

CHAPTER NINE

THE POLL TAX

THE CASE THE Rev. Doctor Ian Masson Fraser, the Pursuer, brought was against Andrew R. MacCorquodale, the Community Charges registration Officer, the Defender.

'The Pursuer craves the Court to set aside the Civil Penalty imposed by the Defender on the pursuer in terms of Section 17 (10) of the Abolition of Domestic Charges, etc (Scotland) Act, 1987.'

One can almost hear Ian smacking his lips in anticipation. There is nothing like a good fight in a just cause to get his pulse racing. The case came to court on 12th December 1988, a few days before Ian's 71st birthday and was heard before Sheriff Henderson in Stirling.

The facts at the centre of the case were not in dispute. On the 12th September 1988 the Defender imposed a civil penalty of £50 under the Act quoted above which states that 'where the registration officer is satisfied that a responsible person

a) has failed to comply with the duty to provide the information required within the prescribed period, or

b) has given false information

unless satisfied that the responsible person has a reasonable excuse, shall impose a civil penalty of £50 which shall be a debt due to the Regional Council recoverable by them as such as if it were arrears of community charges'.

Now we might ask how had Ian reached the point of taking his local council to court?

The Community Charge (universally known as the Poll Tax by its opponents) was introduced by the government of Margaret Thatcher to replace the rates that were based on the notional rental value of a house. The intention to abolish the rating system which had become increasingly outdated was in the manifesto of the Conservative Party in the 1979 general election. The details of the replacement were proposed in the Green Paper of 1986, *Paying for Local Government.* The new charge was a fixed tax per adult resident, but with a reduction for the poorest people. Each person was expected to pay for the services that they used in the local community. This new tax was included in the 1987 Conservative Manifesto for the 1987 General Election. It replaced the rates in Scotland in April 1989 and was introduced in England one year later.

A Victorian encyclopaedia defines Poll Tax as: 'An unjust regressive tax, long since abandoned and incapable of resurrection.' Odham's encyclopaedia (1953) says of a poll tax: 'A tax per head of population, not graduated, imposed in primitive communities where it appears impossible to ascertain capacity to bear the burden.' Mrs. Thatcher seems to have had limited access to such knowledge or was convinced that she knew better.

The Poll Tax was in large measure a flat rate tax. Everyone over 18 was liable. Rich and poor paid the same. Officially called the Community Charge it was dubbed the 'poll tax' because of the tax introduced in 1381, which led to the Peasants' Revolt. The Guardian reported, 'The Duke of Westminster who used to pay £10,255 in rates on his estate has just learned his new poll tax: £417. His housekeeper and resident chauffeur face precisely the same bill.'[55]

It was introduced on the back of three general election victories by the Tories and unashamedly sought to redistribute wealth from the poor to the rich. It was part of the trickledown theory of wealth creation and the need to encourage people to be active in the improvement of their financial position rather than relying on state handouts.

The Poll Tax depended on a register being compiled under the control of unelected officers of the council (Community Charge Registration Officers). By 1991 it was estimated that as many as one million people had removed their names from the electoral register due to the suspicion that this was a major source of information for these new registers. Since those least able to pay were most likely to vote Labour it suited the Tories to disenfranchise them.

Even some Tories, however, saw the Poll Tax as iniquitous. 'The government has declared war on the people,' said Anthony Marlow, Conservative MP for Northampton in March 1990.

While many people were opposed to the Poll Tax there was no consensus on how to challenge it. The Labour Party in Scotland opted for a protest campaign. They were committed to making themselves electable. Others determined on direct opposition to the Poll Tax. Donald Dewar was of the opinion that the Labour Party could not afford to have selective amnesia when it came to the law of the land.

The 'Stop It' campaign produced posters, leaflets and stickers and was led by Brian Wilson MP who challenged the fairness of the Poll Tax. A number of groups campaigned against the Poll Tax without ruling out civil disobedience. Real resistance to the tax began in May 1987 when the 'Community Charge Bill for Scotland' received the royal assent. The Anti-Poll Tax Union coordinated active resistance to the tax across Scotland. They called both for non-registration and non-payment. Resistance meant confrontation. They chose to be non-partisan in terms of party politics preferring to be community based and a mass movement of ordinary people although it was clear that the base was largely working class.

The resistance had a four-pronged strategy:
- Non-registration – with no register the Poll Tax would be stillborn.
- Non-payment – the central focus of the resistance
- Non-implementation – councils were encouraged to refuse to be involved in the process
- Non-collection – a call to trade unionists to refuse to be part of the process.

The third and fourth elements of resistance hardly saw the light of day; non-registration and non-payment would have to battle on. While the Labour Party pursued its protest campaign under their

'Stop It' campaign the Scottish National Party threw their weight behind a non-payment campaign.

In an attempt to limit the level at which the poll tax would need to be set, the chancellor, Nigel Lawson, made favourable adjustments to the block grant which came to Scotland at that time. This allocation of money provided most of what was required to run local government in Scotland. Considerably less than half of the monies came from local people. Lawson clearly believed that his nifty footwork would 'save the day'. In fact his action was almost certainly seen as a sign of weakness and merely acted to strengthen the resolve of those who rejected the poll tax in principle.

Ian was upset by the law which introduced the Poll Tax, which he deemed to be unfair to the poor. He sought to use the courts to challenge the government for what he consistently described as 'bad law'. Unlike most of the court cases across the country relating to the Poll Tax, Ian was not in court as a defendant refusing to pay his tax. Such cases were all too often heard in a few minutes and judgment given forthwith against the defendants. Rather he brought a case against those implementing the law which introduced the poll tax. He had refused to fill in the forms sent to him so he could not be assessed for his Poll Tax. By contrast, a friend in the local Iona Community family group, Helen Steven, went to court to answer a charge of non-payment. This put her on the defensive from the outset.

The local council phoned Ian and asked him to meet with those concerned. They were convinced that they had met all reasonable demands. Ian maintained that it was still the poor who would suffer.

They had no answer to that assertion. Increasingly he believed that secretly the council were cheering him on. Perhaps they were early in deciding that the whole scheme was unworkable.

Ian maintained a respect for the Council and its officials, aware that they acted as humanely as they could within the law. Ian remembers a local woman who was visited by council officials. They made the point that they had no desire to cause her anxiety but as they said, 'Surely you could afford to pay something?' In fact they had fastened on the wrong person. All her food was in a bottle. Her problem was with alcohol not her poll tax. It is easy to see why the members of Central Regional Council in Stirling, who were seeking in every way they could to minimise the effects of this tax, must have found it galling that it was one of their council officers now stood in the dock.

One person who helped Ian greatly was the head of the University Library in Stirling. He was a Mr. Peacock. His wife was a keen ecumenist. He retired soon after the Poll Tax episode. Some might surmise that in the time before retirement he had that freedom that comes to those for whom the exit door is clearly visible. He directed Ian to legal books where as a layman he could educate himself about due process. Ian never employed a lawyer to represent him. It was perhaps the most important decision he made in the whole matter. That was equally true later, when Ian appeared before the Law Lords in the Court of Session, in Edinburgh.

And so it was that Ian Fraser found himself seeking redress through the courts for what he believed to be an injustice due to bad law. He had come to terms with the legal language of the court. As was reported later in legal circles 'The Pursuer in court claimed that he had a reasonable excuse for his failure to supply the required information and he listed three grounds. The Pursuer (himself) having a reasonable excuse for failing to comply with his statutory duty to provide the information required by the Defender within the prescribed period is entitled to have the civil penalty imposed by the Defender set aside.' Apparently all Ian sought was freedom not to pay the fine imposed; in fact he sought a judgment that would lead eventually to the removal of the Poll Tax from the land if the court found in his favour.

Ian had two main strands to his argument although the second had two significant components. He began by taking to task the language of the Act. He affirms his understanding that what is designated a charge is in fact a tax or excise on people. The key argument, which followed, was that no tax should be differently levied in Scotland as compared with the rest of the United Kingdom. This would he argued be in breach of article XVIII of the Act of Union. It became clear that his argument was that the so-called community charge was in fact a tax precluded the possible argument that as a 'charge' the Act of Union did not cover it. In the first instance Ian concludes that the Poll Tax is illegal.

Concerned lest the early introduction of the Poll Tax in Scotland might be seen as insignificant (after all the charge was always planned to follow in England and Wales) Ian argued that the Tax should not be imposed at all as it was both immoral and impractical. As to the former he based his argument squarely on the Bible and God's demand for justice. Key to this is the protection of the poor, which he argues, is just what the Poll Tax by definition fails to establish. With regard to the impractical nature of the Poll Tax he argued that the collection of necessary data would be an infringement of civil liberties. He went on to call on the support of the Equal Opportunities Act, which was much in vogue at the time.

In his summary Ian was at his impish best. He quoted the Association of District Councils observing that the Poll Tax is 'quite unacceptable' and that he was 'anxious to relieve his adversary of an impossible task of collecting such a tax.' The Sheriff reserved his judgment on the day of the hearing and a written judgment was give on 6 January 1989.

In his ruling the Sheriff made it clear that he could not find in Ian's favour on the grounds that the Poll Tax was immoral or impractical alone but that he had to have principal regard to application of the law. He was of the opinion that he had two questions to consider

a)   whether the 1987 Act which introduced the Poll Tax did contravene the Act of Union and if so

b)   what powers if any he had to apply such contravention in the case brought before him.

He concludes that the Community Charge is not a tax and therefore not covered by the Act of Union. He visits case law but does he rather muddy the water by seeking support from a case with which he only partly agrees. He also argues that while the UK government under the Act of Union 'may' act in a particular way it is not duty bound so to do. In this at least the Sheriff and Dr. Fraser were agreed that his case had raised 'far-reaching' considerations. The only comfort that Ian was able to take from the judgment immediately was that no costs were sought or awarded against him.

Correspondence a few days later from Central Regional Council reminded Ian that he had a month to appeal the decision of the Sheriff. Until it was clear whether he would appeal, the fine of £50 would be held in abeyance. He was reminded 'An appeal shall be to the Court of Session (Scotland's Highest Court) but only on a question of law, from the decision of the Sheriff as an appeal to him under this Act.'

The Poll Tax business started soon after Margaret died. Ian was convinced then and remains convinced to this day that she would have been completely behind him in all he did.

If the sheriff's officers had arrived to sell his possessions, as was possible, Ian knew that the neighbours would agree to offer say fifty pence for his settee. No one would offer more. The offer would have to be accepted. The furniture would simply be carried round the side of the house and be brought in the back door. As he is wont to repeat, 'You need to be in the line of Abraham and Isaac but you also need to be in the line of Jacob – the godly twister!'

Ian has always been an active correspondent so it was no surprise that he had many letters of encouragement during his 'poll tax days'. Stanley, a fellow member of the Iona Community wrote, 'to assure you of our solidarity, love and prayers.' In a later communication he reminds Ian that 'laws can be 'legal' but not 'just'. Linda, a speaker for the Green Party 'highlights and supports Ian's contention that the Poll Tax is illegal because it contravenes the Act of Union of 1707'. John wrote recalling 'days spent with Ian on the Lucas Aerospace Combine at Selly Oak'.[56] Another John from Balloch wrote: 'Congratulations, Sir. I'm glad to see that there are still people like you in Scotland. I have been fighting the same fight as yourself for a long time, and alone I thought, until reading (in the *Scotsman*) about your stance.'

A correspondent from Stronachlachar near Aberfoyle notes: 'Clearly it will be left to the man in the street to oppose the Poll Tax; it is fairly obvious that Donald Dewar and others of that ilk wish to make political capital nothing more.' Ian remembers that on the 19th of December 1988, a week after his case was heard in Stirling, Maria Fyfe, a Labour MP wrote, 'You make a fine statement of the principles involved . . . the powers-that-be think legalistically not morally.'

Of course, not all of Ian's correspondents thought well of him. An irate Stirling widow, a pensioner, wrote, 'Dr. Fraser, I am fed up of hearing your views on the Poll Tax. Stick to your sermons and your visiting and leave politics alone. You have probably lost more members of your congregation because of your biased (sic) views on the Poll Tax than by anything else.' We are left to wonder if she ever heard any of his sermons, knew anything of his faith and politics stance in Rosyth or the rate of growth in the only congregation he ever had!

Ian saw his involvement with the campaign against the poll tax as part of his response to the Peace and Justice Commitment of the Iona Community. He has never been personally involved in the anti-Trident peace campaigning at Faslane. Others were called to that. The Poll Tax was both something he was passionately opposed to, and he believed it was a concern where he could either make a real difference or at least try to. A widower as he was then, he was free of pressing financial commitments, and he considered himself able to be involved and take what consequences followed in a way that was not an option for the poorest in Scottish society. No one can do everything. Everyone should act where they can effectively. To deplore injustice is not enough; injustice has to be opposed.

A plenary of the Iona Community declared its opposition to the Poll Tax, characterising it as an inadequate and unjust method of financing part of local government. The Community sought to tackle the perceived injustice by encouraging family groups (the name given to local Iona Community groups) to balance winners and losers under the new tax. Where a family group as a whole was either a winner or a loser, there existed a framework within the Community to redistribute monies. This might be seen as more symbolic than effective and of course the life span of the tax was thankfully short but it does indicate a very real rejection of the Poll Tax by people who have a commitment to faith and action.

Ian attended two consultations in Durham which examined the response of churches to the Poll Tax and the actions being taken by Christians to oppose it. His early active opposition was clearly an encouragement not least to those south of the Border. Equally it is evident that he drew strength from these meetings to continue even when knocked back by judicial decisions against him.

For Ian the court was an appropriate place for a discussion to take place about the biblical basis for rejecting the poll tax. In fact he judged that another appropriate place was even nearer home. The Gargunnock Inn, just down the hill from his home, was a place where such discussion took place. He left a copy of his case on the pub counter and the punters debated its theological basis.

Now in his campaign of non-registration and in the legal case which followed, Ian acted beyond the way determined as politic by the Labour Party. Ian's membership of the Labour Party goes back to his Rosyth days. When he returned north to live in Gargunnock in 1982 it seemed natural to him that he should reaffirm his support of the party by involving himself in the local branch. It stretches from Stirling to Strathblane along the north side of the Campsie Fells. He continues this membership still. When it came to the poll tax Ian was willing to act independently. He still maintains that he would have gone against the party if the need had arisen. This much at least is clear – Ian was in a different position vis-à-vis the party as compared with his independent action in Rosyth for he now held no office elected or otherwise. It was perhaps equally significant to him that many of the grassroots membership encouraged him in his actions.

With some legal help Ian lodged his appeal promptly although the case was not heard in the Court of Session until Thursday 17th May 1990 in Edinburgh. Much had transpired in the period between the hearing before the Sheriff and this later hearing.

On 31st March 1990 a national demonstration was called by the non-payment campaign. 200,000 marched in London; 50,000 marched in Glasgow; Ian was one of the marchers. Widespread civil disorder occurred particularly in Trafalgar Square. The nation was shocked by the events witnessed on its TV screens but the perceived over-reaction of the police meant that the non-payment campaign flourished. The time would come when 17 million people would be involved in non-payment.

By April 1990 official figures for Scotland showed that nearly a million people had not paid a penny in Poll Tax. Anti-Poll Tax Unions remained small local groups by and large but they operated with growing self-confidence. Window posters were printed and displayed. Poll tax bills were ceremoniously burnt as an act of public defiance.

The hearing in the Court of Session in May 1990 came before the Lord President sitting with Lords Grieve and Kirkwood. Ian took the opportunity to once again represent himself. The basis for his argument remained largely as had been presented in Stirling though he called on a statement by Sir George Young a Conservative MP who had stated bluntly '. . . it is not a charge for services at all; it is a tax.' Ian proposed to continue to call it for what it was.

In the intervening 18 months Ian had not been idle. He sensed that it was expected that he would simply restate his position as he had given it in Stirling when he appeared before the Sheriff. He argued that the provision of the original Act of Union with regard to tax required that there be no variation in tax geographically, comparing Scotland with England. He picked up on the Sheriff's lighting on the word 'may' as if it was not binding but merely a possibility.[57] Ian offered their lordships a Latin lesson no less. *'Edimus ut vivimus'*, which he helpfully translated – 'We eat that we may live'. His point was made it was no mere possibility that was involved even when the word 'may' is used but a life and death matter. Ian concluded the legal argument by reminding the eminent Lords 'while in England parliament is sovereign, in Scotland it is the people.' The prophetic nature of Ian's ministry is here clearly seen. Such a point was much in evidence during the later 1997 referendum on the proposed Scottish Parliament.

In the Court of Session when Ian turned to the immoral nature of the Poll Tax in the light of recent events he focused on the violence done by legislation to the poor over against violence occurring in the protests, which were increasingly focusing other minds. Ian identified violence caused to families – forcing older folk to move from family homes into eventide homes and forcing younger people out on to the streets. He identified a violation of human rights as people were disappearing from electoral registers and thereby being disenfranchised. Ian's quirky sense of humour surfaces again as he comments that promises of increased employment by the Government made no mention that the new jobs would be an increase in the number of sheriff officers who would enforce this unjust law!

The Opinion of the Lord President was handed down on 24 July 1990. He rehearses the facts of the case which were of course undisputed and then considers the judicial process in the Sheriff Court. In his opinion the Lord President argues that the case brought by Dr. Fraser could not properly be brought in law to the lower court. The power to review 'the decisions of administrative bodies' rests exclusively with the Court of Session as the Supreme Court in Scotland.

That said the Lord President went on to say, 'But I do not accept that this is a satisfactory basis for the disposal of this appeal. In my opinion the appellant is entitled to be told whether or not he had a reasonable excuse within the meaning of section 17(10) for refusing to provide the information sought.' He continues by making the following assumption 'that what he seeks in these proceedings is not a declaration that the 1987 Act is contrary to law but rather a finding that his own views and beliefs on these matters give him a reasonable excuse for refusing to comply with it.' Having made this assumption the Lord President proceeds to reject what he has assumed is the argument being presented to him. He says 'the appellant's reason for non-compliance was confined entirely to his own views and beliefs.'

Now it is risky in the extreme for a lay person to question the judgment of such an eminent legal figure but one might hazard a contrary opinion that what Ian Fraser was actually seeking from their lordships was in fact a ruling by them that the 1987 Act was in fact 'bad law' and that it contravened the Act of Union.

In his concluding remarks the Lord President indicates that he has some difference on a point of law with the Sheriff but upholds his decision. Again a mere lay person might wonder if he is of the opinion that the Sheriff had no right to pronounce on the matters in question how his opinion can simply be supported not least where his argument is deemed either to be flawed or suspect.

It would ordinarily have cost Ian £2000 (at 1990 prices) to have taken his case to the Court of Sessions but necessary costs were met without charge to him. In this action at least, justice for 'the little man' was seen to be done when all too often there is the appearance that cases are not heard because the big battalions know that those with a case against them cannot afford to seek ultimate legal redress.

Ian was impressed by the sympathetic attention given to him by the law lords, unversed as he was in court procedures

And so the verdict was given by the highest court in Scotland but the matter seemed too important to Ian to let the matter rest. He concluded that his application in both cases had failed on a technicality and so he sought leave to take his case to the European Court of Human Rights.

The Bible makes it clear that justice is a major theme to guide the way we live – just relationships with God and others lie at the heart of the Christian faith. Jim Wallis, founder of the Sojourner Community, whose visit to the United Kingdom Ian helped to facilitate, recounted an attempt to cut out of the Bible references to justice; the residue could almost have floated away on a breeze. Some of his books were among those Ian cleared out recently to placate a son with an eye on reducing the things accumulated over a long lifetime!

Ian saw his opposition to the Poll Tax as an apostolic act in the cause of justice. Professor JY Campbell in 'A Theological Word Book of the Bible' speaks of the word 'apostle' as having an original sense of 'one authorised to speak out and act for the person who sends him.' Ian sees this as inadequate. The particularity of the word depends on its naval origin. 'Apostle' relates to an expedition sent, with such authorisation, but other nuances are included. Those participating in the expedition may or may not know its objective to start with. They have to set out whether they do or no! They may be under sealed orders which may not be opened till a certain geographical point is reached or a certain time has elapsed. It is sufficient that the sender

THE POLL TAX are you serious

knows the purpose and reveals it at the right time. The expedition is to go beyond recognised, familiar territory, taking on the risk of unmapped shoals, rocks and other impediments. The sender's will and knowledge needs to be trusted.

Ian freely admits that he did not know what he was letting himself in for. He knew nothing about the way law courts worked. It was in every sense a venture into unknown territory. Once he had taken the step of challenging bad law he had to be instructed and be quick-witted to fulfil the mandate.

He saw himself as one of a crew who encouraged one another. All kinds of people are called at times to step out in faith and act as apostles. We can never sit back and say, 'Over to you, Holy Spirit'. We need to accept help offered by those who have instruction to give us. But always we will have homework to do to determine if the offered help is to be useful to us.

In an article entitled, 'The Poll Tax: Some Biblical reflections' Ian draws a distinction between 'power' and 'authority'.[58] Jesus, he contends, was clear that the kind of power exercised by the 'kings of the Gentiles' has no place in 'Kingdom' living. One of the Hebrew words for the 'poor' has to do with 'having to fit you life around the wishes of others'. Choice is removed from life. Ian highlights from Isaiah 53 an alternative way of exercising power. Jesus was making use of the power entrusted to him when he went to the cross. As the Suffering Servant, he suffered as the people suffered, bore the burden of their lives and set them free from their own sins and the sins of those that kept them in poverty. One of the litmus tests for the legitimate use of power is whether the poor are respected and given their share of what is needed for a full life. In this way they have access to the abundant life promised in the Good News. (Luke 4.18-19; 7.21-24) The Poll Tax pushed through by the power of an elected dictatorship in no way passed this test.

All people have been made in God's likeness. What drives them into debt and despair, as the Poll Tax did, defaces that image.

In the public sphere the face of sin is injustice. (Amos 3.10; 4.1) The oppression of the poor, for instance their being taxed to subsidise the rich, is an affront to the Lord (Habakkuk 2.6-8). The Poll Tax is just such a repressive tax so designed that the poor will maintain and enhance the financial lifestyle of the rich.

In the New Testament the word for truth, '*alethia*' means to 'blow the cover' on the propaganda of those who try to cover up offences, and show what is really going on. For instance when there is a claim made in relation to the Poll Tax that local councils will be made more accountable – it needs to be shown that power is in fact being transferred to central government. This became clear when the government in London resorted to capping local government expenditure when they discovered that people would on occasion choose to pay higher local taxes rather than see the quality of services in an area greatly curtailed.

The essence of the Kingdom in a biblical sense is the whole fabric of created life structured in God's way. The church is called to be a sign of the Kingdom. We are, Ian asserts, called upon to be co-workers with God to make life on earth as it is in heaven, indicated by the forgiveness of debts and the satisfaction of basic needs. Thus while 'equality' may be dismissed by some as an impossible ideal, the move towards it is a recognition that all people are made in the image of God and are to share in the Kingdom.

Throughout the Bible it is clear that the requirements of discipleship sometimes demand conflict and confrontation. As Jesus said, no one can serve two masters. People have to choose and accept the consequences of that choice, whether they entail gaining the whole world or saving their souls. Faced with unjust legislation what we do will depend on whether we have come to the point where we stand with Peter and John and say, 'Judge for yourselves whether it is right in God's sight to obey you rather than God' (Acts 4.19). Of course, there are questions as to the extent of the wrong and of timing in this. Remember that Joan of Arc when challenged over whether she acknowledged church authorities answered like this: 'that they are obedient to Christ, my Lord, I do'. Oppressive top-down power has often to be challenged in the Bible and in more recent history so that genuine authority may replace it.

Ian further notes: 'It is true that God does astonishing things with the poor material put in his hands. Who would have thought that in Reagan's last phase he would have wanted to initiate major moves for world disarmament? But the Word is God entering history and our own lives, to do through these lives what He wills for the world. We are never left passive, we are left committed. In God's economy we have no right to choose the options which suit us (e.g. prayer rather than politics or politics rather than prayer) but at each stage in life we have to invest that life with whatever is needed to realise, to make real on earth, Christ's kingly rule. Whatever we do in an ill-judged or wrong way in our attempts to be obedient is amply covered by God's forgiveness'.[59]

Ian is quick to recognise that Christians have no monopoly of the concerns for justice in human society. He recalls the involvement of the wise men in the Incarnation stories as people who knew the truth more clearly than the faith community of the day. Did not Isaiah apply the term 'messiah' to Cyrus, a Persian despot? Standing outside the Judeo-Christian tradition others have their part to play. The converse is also seen to be true. In the 'road to Emmaus' Easter story in Luke's gospel the stranger on the road reminds the two disciples of the 'things concerning himself' in scripture – what we know as the Old Testament. From this Ian draws his particular conclusion. He suggests that we have to sort these out from other materials, which are outside the teaching and mind of Jesus. For Ian the end of Psalm 137 is just such an example:

'Happy is he who repays you
for what you have done to us –
He who seizes your infants
and dashes them against the rocks.'

In contrast Jesus rather says, 'Love your enemies. Pray for those who despitefully use you and persecute you'. You have to choose what belongs to the gospel. Ian concludes that the gospel will include insight from beyond the received tradition and other insights, which claim long to have been accepted by the faithful. Cyrus may have returned the Jews to their homeland on the basis of his understanding of compassion possibly taught by his god, Marduk. In this Ian may have come to some understanding of those in Matthew 25 who say, 'When, O Lord, did we . . .' Surely it is the case that the whole of the human race are not limited by Christian tradition but illuminated by it. This much at least is clear – scriptural tradition has a focus on justice for all.

During these poll tax days, Ian visited 'Big Mags' from the Raploch on one occasion.[60] She was a notorious character in Stirling. She was secretary of the Tenants' Association who were fighting the Poll Tax. Ian got on well with her. He spoke about the theological basis for fighting the Poll Tax. 'What would that be?' she asked. He told her that it was not only heaviest on the poor; it was designed to be that way. The Bible is a book which seeks justice for all and especially for the poor. 'You're right enough,' she concluded, 'There is a theological basis for our fight.'

While he was visiting her, Ian noticed a rather strange man at the end of the hallway. White-haired, he moved slowly as if with advancing years. Ian looked at him, and then looked at her. 'O, that's my man,' she explained, 'he got fed up with me so left for a flat in Glasgow. He seemed to be doing alright. Then he took TB and was wasting away. So I went to the city and brought him back to look after him.' You never know what is in people. Such was the notorious woman widely characterised as a disturber of Scottish society or at least of her neighbourhood in Stirling. Ian half recalled a play in which reference is made to flowers which can best grow on a dung heap. It surely had insight. Although with his customary candour he went on to say, 'When all is said and done, the same woman was a menace!' Love need not be blind to faults and failings.

In conversation Ian restates the high regard he has for community-life. How then, it might be asked, could he refuse to obey the law of the national community? 'Simply,' said Ian, 'it was bad law. It had to be resisted.' How then are we to understand what Jesus meant when he said, 'Render to Caesar the things that are Caesar's, and to God the things that are God's.' Ian is convinced that Jesus gave a wee chuckle as he wrong-footed his opponents and certainly rejects any suggestion that Jesus would favour the acceptance of bad law that discriminated against the poor. With this he adds an important rider. 'You have to test such matters out with others in community. Failure to do this can lead to a spiritual arrogance – I know it all – God has revealed this to me.' He sees this in the stance taken by some associated with the religious right in America.

Some have been charged with being unpatriotic while in fact they have being seeking to restore a true patriotism. If you say my country right or wrong or something near that, you produce a corrupt kind of patriotism. God is above all nations and the ways of God have to be established in every place. Nations need to be creative in their relationships with other nations; the trials for being un-American in the 1950s were not trials for unrighteousness. It is the duty of the citizen and the Christian to be questioning of what is done in their name. In all this it is possible to make a mistake. Ian is convinced that if we act in good faith God treats us with an inclusive forgiveness. He will limit the harm that might be caused. Where we get things spot-on we contribute to His plans for creative life for the whole of the cosmos. We do not need to be dithering all the time, though we should take time to reflect on proposed courses of action.

In Ian's submission to the court he made it clear that one of the reasons for pursuing the case against the council was his claim that there was no other road open to him. When challenged that the Poll

Tax had been introduced by a government through due political process surely it should be replaced using the same process, Ian restated the view as a Scot; for him the ultimate power lies not with the law but with the people. People should oppose a bad law wherever opportunity arises.

Petitions, protest and processions are valid means of expressing opinion. In the circumstances surrounding the Poll Tax Ian felt constrained to do what was open to him. There is no suggestion in any of the judgements given in response to him that he brought a frivolous case, with a view to simply wasting the time of the court.

Ian's reasoning may be instructive in other circumstances. A monopoly of power by one party in a democracy for a long period of time may weaken democratic institutions. Similarly where all the mainstream parties agree on a matter it may be that opposition is required outside parliament. Some would argue that this is or was the position that anti-nuclear supporters find themselves in from time to time.

Ian is quick to recognise the significant contribution made by Dietrich Bonhoeffer in his opposition to the Nazi regime in the 1930s and 1940s. He has encouraged other Christians to consider their situation and responsibility as part of what is required by anyone who opposes the authority of the day. While Ian was a student in Edinburgh, John Baillie asked the question, 'What do you do if you come to a crossroads where the three different ways forward all seem possible in the light of the gospel.' His students had no particular answers. He said, 'You toss a coin. You have to go somewhere. God will forgive you if you go the wrong way. As a human it is all that you can do.' Such was the surprising answer from a professor of divinity. When it came to the question of the Poll Tax for Ian there was no such ambiguity.

Ian recognises the value of community and at the same time the importance of personal responsibility. The powerful rule with the consent of the powerless in a democracy. While it seems clear that the Poll Tax was abandoned largely due to its significant rejection by the wider community, this in no way negates the value of actions taken by individuals. What Ian emphasises is the need even in this for such an individual to be rooted in community not least the faith community. This help to explain why Ian gave respect to individuals who stood for election as Independents but he maintained that larger social justice programmes need to be based in political parties. His own experience in Rosyth always reminded him of the constraints this placed on every individual.

Ian feels himself called to consider matters in detail. He values his genetic make-up. What seems to be original thinking may equally be seen to be qualities inherited from earlier generations. In a similar way we live on the basis of the contributions made by others; cotton sheets from Egypt, wool from Australia, wood from Scandinavia. We cannot get out the door in the morning without being dependent on so many others. 'Persons in community' is what matters. As John McQuarrie argued it is 'Persons in Relation' that counts.[61] It should be noted that it is not ever 'a person' who is required to live in community.

Others have asserted that the Poll Tax cannot be an unjust tax per se for the people of God were subject to just such a tax in the days of the temple. Jesus opposed (violently opposed) the tax collectors in the courts of the temple. He did this though surely not because the temple tax was a poll tax but because of the scandalous abuses that accompanied it as the haves exploited the have-nots. Ian remains convinced that the Poll Tax as introduced in Scotland was unjust. In this his daughter Anne supports him. She reminded her father that it had been abandoned in her adopted country where it had a history of being part of a concerted movement to disenfranchise the have-nots in American society.

There is an interesting historical take on all this. There seems to be general agreement that the assertion frequently made that Scotland was used by Margaret Thatcher as an experiment before bringing in the Poll Tax south of the Border, is just plain wrong. Had this in fact been the case she might have been expected to have taken note of the widespread opposition to the tax and had some formal review after a longer period of time to allow things to settle down. The truth is surely different. She was in fact wedded to the Poll Tax ideologically having decided that the rating system would have to go. But it seems much more likely that both George Younger and later Michael Forsyth who were her men in Scotland were anxious to lead the way in the implementation of this tax first north of the border. In time the latter was to suffer and perhaps justly at the hands of the electorate. Be that as it may it seems that if something is repeated often enough in a society such as ours it can become 'truth of a kind'.

There is still something deep in the Scottish psyche about the injustice of early implementation of the Poll Tax that might yet have undreamt of repercussions. Some would argue that it went at least some way to encouraging the double 'Yes' vote in the 1997 referendum on a Scottish Parliament. Ian has found it difficult to think well of Michael Forsyth but remembers that both George Younger and later his widow, who still lives in Gargunnock, took an interest in his writings not least in 'Wind and Fire' and 'The Way Ahead'. It is always possible to disagree without being disagreeable.

Given both the support Ian continued to enjoy and the results of his Biblical research it is no surprise that he made application to have his case heard by the European Commission for Human Rights. His application was acknowledged as having been received on 18 January 1991. In accordance with the Commission's rules of procedure, a single member of the Commission acting as rapporteur would carry out a preliminary examination for this application and report to the Commission on the question of its admissibility.

When John Major abandoned the Poll Tax within months of taking over from Margaret Thatcher as Prime Minister, Ian paid up his arrears of poll tax and abandoned his case at the 'European Court.' He had never raised his case against the Poll Tax because he could not afford to pay it – in fact he was better off under the new system than he had been with the rates. He spoke out because the poor were suffering.

Ian learned that he could not just inform the court that for him the matter was settled. Later that spring Ian received an acknowledgement of his letter of 10 May 1991 in which he had stated that he wished to withdraw his application to the Commission. It concluded thus: 'In this the Commission concurs.' At last Ian and a court were in agreement. He retains to this day the conviction that in fact the European legal authorities really had wanted to hear the case.

If any justification is required for this detailed consideration of Ian's actions in relation to the Poll Tax, it lies surely in the way they demonstrate that his theology is never just a matter of mere words.

Endnotes

[55] Quoted in The Poll Tax Rebellion – Danny Burns.

[56] Shop-floor proposals for alternatives to armament manufacture. See chapter 6.

[57] In his judgment Sheriff Henderson rejected Ian's contention that that the laws concerning public right in the Act of Union 'may be made the same throughout the whole United Kingdom' meant that 'they must be made the same.'

[58] See Chapter 10 of this publication, page 271.

[59] From a pamphlet 'City Cries'.

[60] The Raploch was an area of multiple deprivation in Stirling in earlier days.

[61] John McQuarrie: 'Persons in Relation' – the second of a series based on his Gifford lectures – the first being 'The Self as Agent' – which argued that it is by what a person does is he/she really known.

CHAPTER TEN

A READY WRITER

IN THE TWENTY-FIVE or so years since he reached the normal retirement age Ian has continued to live a very active and full life. One activity has given particular purpose to his life lived in the service of others. While the early years of retirement offered opportunities for further travel, the whole period has been marked by thoughtful reflection shared through his writing.

Of note among this are two books *Strange Fire (1994)* and *Salted with Fire (1999)* which provide folk with resources for their journeys. Their structure is easy to follow with stories from life linked to prayers and reflections organised thematically. Ian also produced two volumes *Wind and Fire (1986)*[62] and *Reinventing Church* describing the Spirit's reshaping of the church in Basic Christian Communities. 1995 saw the publication of *The Try-It-Out Hymnbook*, a collection of 60 hymns, the tunes written in collaboration with his good friend in the Iona Community, Donald Rennie - continuing his involvement with hymn-writing begun in the 1960s in Scottish Churches House.[63] In 2002 Ian was pressed by a number of individuals and groups in the locality to publish *R.B. Cunninghame Graham: Fighter for Justice* to mark the 150th anniversary of his birth.[64] Quite clearly some of what Ian has written and published in his 'retirement' had its roots in earlier years.[65] Just as clearly he writes creatively on new situations that interest him at this time.

In 1988 Ian was entrusted with the task of producing an Iona Community Jubilee broadsheet to celebrate the fiftieth anniversary of the Community. It says something both of the author and the Community that it was decided to ask the question 'How does Britain measure up in 1988?' rather than fall for the temptation of navel-gazing or self congratulation.[66] The analysis Ian produced considered some national trends over against the Biblical witness. The stated intention of the broadsheet was to provide a resource for Christians attempting to interpret current events. 'It is a study guide which is intended to lead to action'.

In the broadsheet, Ian contends that theology has as its central task the examination of situations we face as they are given to us as part of God's purpose. He identifies a creation part to attend to (life-as-is) and a redemption part to consider (life-as-promised). Christians must grasp the nettle to discover in practice what it means and what it costs to live the Christian life today. The discoveries they make together in faith must be brought to bear on actual government policies being advocated or pursued. The light that Jesus gives is to let us get on with life. It is that which frees us to journey together to a goal. In the Christian faith thought, word and deed are to form a seamless robe. Words are to be lived out. Truth is to be done. Faith resources should enable people to penetrate through smoke-screens of words to underlying realities.

Ian goes on to compare the Thatcher years to the reign of Solomon with its apparent successes. He characterises it as top-down rule of an authoritarian kind. Mrs. Thatcher made clear her intention when she announced in February 1979 that she was ready to run a conviction (as opposed to a consensus) government. The Genesis creation accounts agree on this at least that human beings are meant to act as trustees and stewards – they are not the proprietors but tenants under the power of Another.

Ian further distinguishes between the power of a government to act and its authority to do so. He was disturbed to find at that time much use of power but little sense of authority in government dealings with local authorities, specifically in relation to the poll tax and education. He notes that Mrs. Thatcher claims that the government has never flinched from telling the truth but he challenges this when he considers the suppression of inconvenient truths e.g. the Inland Revenue statistics in 1988 which showed a reversal of the trend to equality established since the 1960s. In 1988 the wealthiest one per cent owned twenty per cent of all marketable wealth while the poorest 50 per cent only seven per cent. Now Ian is never slow to call a spade a spade. Considering Scotland as one of the regions which suffers most from unequal distribution of national resources he notes, 'It was Scottish (sic) oil which fuelled the growth of the south-east (of England)'. It is men and women living together in community who are made in the image of God. According to the Bible we do not have to choose between collectivism and individualism. We are persons-in-community. Ian contrasts this with the Thatcher dogma – 'If you get on for yourself, there will be spin-offs for others and you will do all humanity good.' He recalled Mrs. Thatcher's assertion in an interview for Women's Own: 'There is no such thing as society. There are individual men and women and there are families.' Ian's assertion is equally clear: 'If in secular terms this is blindness to reality, in terms of Christian faith it is also heresy.' Ian would not use such a word carelessly. We are members of one another. The invitation to join in the enterprise for which life was created is expressed in the concept of covenant; and the substance of the enterprise is in the word, 'Kingdom'. He characterises good government as respecting the poor and rejecting idolatry which as we have seen underpinned his opposition to the poll tax. Here the comparison with Solomon remains relevant. The many wives in the harem were allowed to introduce idols; the people were subjected to forced labour and kept poor.

In his conclusion to the Jubilee broadsheet Ian strikes a hopeful note based both on signs of the marginalised countries in the poor world coming together to seek justice, and on particular situations he knows personally – e.g. 'Tullis Russell (where he worked as a labourer-pastor from 1942) is one of many examples of a work force having a share in the firm's progress.' For Ian a main sign of hope is the Iona Community itself. In its family groups . . . 'it helps members and associates to get to depth in personal sharing and in coming level with the implications of their commitments. It was an early child of promise which must now flex adult muscles.'

As early as 1986 Ian had produced as part of his Basic Christian Communities Project based in Scottish Churches House a 'D.I.Y. Theology on Mrs Thatcher's Britain'. He aligned himself with the Women's Institute who had denounced 'cover-up language' designed to conceal realities. He had concluded that the warning of Orwell's

'1984' was a present reality. As Jesus said, 'Ye shall know them by their fruits.' It is the fruits we must assess, not the propaganda.

Ian recognises some evidence that prosperity is seen as a mark of divine favour in the Old Testament. Equally the prophets were unsparing in judgment of the rich who had obtained their wealth through injustice at the expense of the poor. Jesus by his lifestyle and teaching makes it clear that the good news is to be particularly for the poor.

Ian further recognises that while poverty in poorer countries can be the result of failure of their own leaders, the responsibility of rich countries has to be spelled out. A similar understanding of deepening poverty in the UK is related to the handouts given to the already-rich. In words which seem even more prophetic twenty years later Ian is particularly critical of the way in which 'The City' is believed to be capable of self-regulation and challenges the arguments advanced to support widespread privatisation. He is sure that the main people to suffer are the public with lower standards of public services, and low wage earners who will be further squeezed by employers. He is in no way convinced that the income from privatisation has been invested for the public good. He asks, 'Is the government like a wage-earner who comes home on pay day and says, "I need more beer money. You'll have to do with less: but there's to be no drop in the housekeeping standards".'

'Features of the Thatcher Legacy: A Theological Critique' was produced by Ian in November 1992. It revisited much of the material included in his earlier writing with the benefit of time given to marshal his thinking. He concludes more in sadness than anger that

Margaret Thatcher's legacy is not as she proclaimed an enterprise culture but a culture of violence and deceit. He asserts that she used her parliamentary majorities to bulldoze through policies to get her own way. Specifically Mrs. Thatcher stands accused of doing violence to the unwritten British constitution. The evidence for this violence is clear – How can the massive impoverishment of so many people be other than an act of violence?

A second feature of the Thatcher era was the development of a culture of deceit and concealment. By the use of hype, appearance was made to substitute for reality. What passed for achievements were the bolstering effects of over £100bn bonus money from oil, billions from privatisation, and credit booms which encouraged people to sell future bread for jam today. Ian concludes with a symbol used previously. 'The churches cannot be even-handed in making their judgement. They have the resources to be prophetic. The only time Jesus was even-handed was when both hands were nailed.'

In a review of this later comment on the Thatcher legacy, Tim Duffy[67] writing in *Open House* suggests that 'The lady seems to have the same symbolic significance for Ian as does the redoubtable Babylonian lady to be found in the seventeenth chapter of the book of Revelation. Ian insists that it is the job of theology to find the truth behind the ideological masks, to exercise what liberation theologians call an epistemological vigilance'. He notes that 'the French poet Paul Valery suggested that a creator is one who makes others create and this is Ian Fraser's gift and work. Not for him the pat answers between book covers for armchair theologians to quibble over. He has the sense of theology as a basic tool for every Christian – the people's work; and his lifework has been in making many aware of the possibilities, and urging others to relate the stories of their faith journeys.'

The Handsel Press in 1989 published 'Scottish Self-Government: Some Christian Viewpoints'. It was edited by Jock Stein who for many years was the Warden of Carberry Tower, then a Church of Scotland Conference Centre.

Ian Fraser was invited to contribute to this publication. It is interesting to see the range of his fellow contributors.[68] In the introduction Kenyon Wright, the secretary of the Scottish Churches Council, presents 'A Claim of Right for Scotland.' This was the report of the Constitutional Steering Committee set up by the Campaign for a Scottish Assembly. He records an October 1988 meeting of a number of representatives of the Scottish Churches at Scottish Churches House.

Central to this 1989 publication is the record of the report on the governance of Scotland given that year to the Church of Scotland General Assembly by the Church and Nation Committee. The deliverance of the Assembly reaffirmed by a large majority the tradition of 'theological reflection on constitutional matters . . . (and the) view that the Scottish people should be accorded a greater say in the government of Scotland through a democratically elected Assembly within the United Kingdom . . .' The reactions to the Church and Nation report include a postscript by the convener of the authors of the report, Norman Shanks, who would later lead the Iona Community. He reminds readers of the long-established support for effective Scottish self-government within the United Kingdom by the

Church of Scotland, first expressed in 1948. A Roman Catholic perspective is offered by Tim Duffy a long-time friend of Ian Fraser who encouraged him to write for *Open House* – an independent Roman Catholic publication with a peace and justice emphasis. A number of contributors with more or less enthusiasm for a Scottish Assembly follow, the final contribution being by Ian Fraser who entitles his contribution, 'Probe: Biblical resources relevant to the Claim of Right'. While a case might have been made for the inclusion of his material as foreword rather than postscript what is offered follows his pattern of providing theological tools for the whole people of God to continue their process of 'doing theology' in relation to the world in which they find themselves.

Following a confirmation that the Biblical text makes explicit reference to nations and peoples in both the Old and New Testaments, Ian offers seven observations:

1. In the early chapters of Genesis place, speech, culture and community give nations their identity.
2. The Hebrews were chosen to be a people-under-God for the blessing of all. (Gen 12)
3. John, in the Revelation, notes that nations have not disappeared but rather are given a central place in the Last Things.
4. The church is likened to a body in the New Testament with many limbs and organs which both contribute to and receive from the whole. Scotland has her defined territory, language, laws, culture and flair. Her nationhood is not in question. When that nationhood is not respected or when it is turned in on itself, there is distortion.

5. Usurping power exercised by rulers who act as if they were God . . . expresses a rejection of God's way.

6. One of the aspects of the word 'sin' is the breaking of an agreement, the wilful rupture of a bond which should stay firm. As with the covenant with God, earthly covenants are to be respected – wilful rupture is sinful. It severely damages the communities involved.[69]

7. Is power being exercised in a way which usurps the rights of a nation? Jesus said with serious emphasis regarding the kings of the Gentiles' way of exercising power: 'It should not be so among you.' Their forms of power affront God's ordering of life, rupture agreements, destroy communities, deny true freedom. Is that what we have to counter in Scotland? Is the alternative continual consultation to provide protection against such usurping power?

During the last thirty years Ian has written frequently for the Iona Community journal *Coracle*. Following the form used in the Handsel Press publication on Scottish governance he describes many of his contributions as 'Probes'. The subjects covered are wide ranging including matters of interest and importance in national life, in the international sphere and in more specifically focused church matters. In each case Ian seeks to identify the core issues and to provide Biblical resources to deal theologically with the matters facing people, particularly faith people, in the modern world. Any consideration of these probes will of necessity require being selective in this context. A central feature of Ian's writing is its rootedness in the situation at the time of writing, but the significance of what he writes often seems to have a timeless nature and importance. Thinking he began years before finds fresh application in the contemporary situation and in time the prophetic nature of his contribution is seen to stand above and beyond the immediate circumstances.

While a personal bias is freely admitted in the selection from Ian's *Coracle* contributions, it was not difficult to find among heady stuff on great matters of state and significant economic questions the recurring theme of people and the value placed on them.

In the May 1996 *Coracle* Ian reflects on the March of that year. In a few lines he writes of the Dunblane gunman. Considering the Daily Mail's headline, 'Monster', Ian notes a recurrent theme of Thomas Hamilton being devalued as a human being. He can find no word of anyone trying to help him recognise his value in the sight of God. Ian is among the first to understand that Hamilton could have repudiated such an attempt; but concludes that 'it is of the gospel to help people appreciate their significance in the eyes of God'.

In that month of May Ian read a review of the American publication, 'The Real War on Crime'. The book provided a powerful critique of imprisonment policies in the USA and with insights of significance in the UK. It reported that 'Many offenders emerge from prison afraid to trust, fearful of the unknown . . . it appears that prison damages a person's mid-range response to their environment, leaving the choice of gritting one's teeth and enduring or full-fledged attack to protect oneself from perceived danger.'

The 1996 March 'Big Issue' gave qualified support to the new Scottish all-party initiative on drugs. There seems to be some evidence of a contrast between younger users and older people where their use had a lot to do with unemployment, lack of choice and despair. Ian reflects that he has seen human beings overcome conditions of poverty magnificently but saw others who were crushed, the quality of life drained out of them. Some start life shackled; some have starting blocks. The Bible is clear that poverty is *caused*; it is imposed by some on others, and diminishes them. Ian calls his readers to combat the devaluing of human beings – in personal relationships, in institutions, in systems. 'Does,' he asks, 'the gospel demand less?'

From later that year, 1999, under the title of 'Straight Talking' Ian comments on Jesus' encouragement to let our 'yes' be a plain 'yes' and our 'no' a plain 'no'. Ian suggests that it is the conduct of funerals which can reveal how well some of us respond to the test of plain speaking.

He relates two experiences for our learning. One of the two lassies who lived next door to Ian in Gargunnock died of cancer at an early age. Lesley had been a convinced atheist. Ian was on the point of leaving to lead a retreat in the south of England. He had tried unsuccessfully to finding any humanist 'church' within reach. He agreed should no alternative commend itself that he would be willing to lead an act of remembrance – without 'hymn, bible reading, prayer or testimony to a resurrection faith.'

On his return Ian was asked to officiate. What he did as they assembled was to provide a kind of 'basket' into which a gathering of friends could drop reflections on life with Lesley, meditations on life challenges and meaning, and any poems and prose quotations, hopes in going forward, memories that gladden. Then it was as if they handed the basket to Lesley as they might a birthday gift. She had abhorred the mere idea of a hearse; so they sent her off in her own camper van.

Those who spoke to Ian later made it clear that the respect shown to the belief of an atheist neighbour enhanced their own respect for the Christian faith and appreciation of its love-centred nature.

The other occasion was the funeral of one of the nastiest men Ian had ever come across. He found himself secretly hoping that he would not be the unfortunate asked to take his funeral. But that was the way it worked out. Ian faced the small congregation and began, 'You know, as I know, that the deceased man was a real bastard.' Those present reacted with a strange mixture of agreement and discomfort . . . 'it might be true, but we are in church . . .' Ian went on: 'He drove away his wife and, later, his daughter: they are not here even for his funeral.' That could not be denied. Then, 'I am not prepared to say over him such words as 'in sure and certain hope of the resurrection to eternal life through our Lord Jesus Christ' – words that he would have repudiated as having any relevance to his life had he still been alive.'

So what are we to do? – the question was on every face. Ian continued, 'Some of you may have known him pretty well. But none of us knows what caused the twist in his nature. Was he abused as a child? Was he let down in some heart-searing way which destroyed in him a capacity again to trust human beings and see some good in them. We cannot tell. But God knows him through and through. God sees the whole of his life and sees it from beginning to end. God can judge as we cannot; and in him is abundant mercy. So this is what we are going to do. We are going to entrust this life to the Creator who gave it, the Saviour who redeemed it, the Spirit who searches to the depths of everyone's being in confidence that there it will be truly judged and mercifully dealt with.' And that is what they proceeded to do.

In light of celebrations planned for 1997[70] Ian accepted the offer of a three-week scholarship at St. Deiniol's Library in Howarden, Wales. The fruit of this time was a pamphlet which examined the lives of Augustine, Columba and Ninian. He used the Venerable Bede as his primary source but considered other ancient records. The ambivalent picture presented of Augustine is contrasted with the remarkable life of Columba. Ian identified five marks of the life of Celtic saints which Columba amply demonstrates.

a) parting – the willingness to give up all for Christ.
b) pilgrimage – one walks with others in a shared life
c) a balanced lifestyle which placed prayer in the lonely place alongside involvement in the world's affairs
d) an ascetic lifestyle which Ian with tongue in cheek contrasted with the Margaret Thatcher tendency 'The voice of one crying in the wilderness: 'Prepare ye the way of the self' '.
e) a commitment to martyrdom be it red with the loss of life or white – a long life of service in submission to God's will.

Ian accepted that less is known of Ninian – he takes comfort in this for many of the disciples of Christ lead less celebrated lives; but he also fastens on the lay training of which he finds some suggestion in the record of Whithorn.

Ian saw particular relevance from the times of his chosen subjects in the church and the world today. He sees a clear line between the

Celtic monasteries and the basic Christian communities of our time. He rejects Augustine's either-or approach, sure that the new forms of church can live alongside more traditional forms for their mutual benefit. Ian rejoiced in the recognition in the Celtic tradition given to the created order of the world and in contemporary calls for moderation in lifestyle to conserve our planet's scarce resources. When he turns to the question of the primacy of Rome Ian rejects some simplistic understanding of the Celtic Church as having independence over against the Roman see. In commenting on Pope John Paul VI's (sic)[71] 1995 encyclical *'Ut Unum Sint'* [72] Ian called on the see of Rome to rediscover primacy through service and with a commitment to preserving Christian orthodoxy. He sees this call standing in the tradition of a letter sent by Columbanus, a contemporary of Columba, to Pope Boniface IV around the end of the sixth century.

In a final footnote Ian reminds his readers of the Jubilee provision in Scripture which calls for a focus on the poor and debtors and in this he heralds Jubilee 2000.

The very human face of Ian is revealed in an anecdote he has sometimes shared from his time in Wales. Needing to clear his head before continuing with the reading and writing Ian chanced on a charity shop in a neighbouring town. On the wall of the shop he noticed a suit that seemed to be roughly his size. It turned out that it was a Saville Row suit which fitted him perfectly. He paid £5 for the smart grey suit. Cut from the finest cloth Ian took great pleasure in wearing it on special occasions for years. This is the same Ian who lived a life of risk-taking – on more than one occasion he purchased clothes in her absence for Margaret and believed that she would wear them!

In 2000, responding to an editorial article in *Open House*[73] – 'Reversing the Decline: Some Practical Suggestions', Ian wrote a series of significant articles. He is identified as a 'Member of the Church of Scotland and pioneer of inter-church relations.' Ian acknowledges that the church in Britain is reckoned to be in decline but notes there is 'no temple in heaven', and that in his earthly life Jesus Christ proclaimed Kingdom not church. He asks the question as to whether the church is acting as the servant of the Kingdom. Is it commending it, promoting it at whatever cost to its own reputation and power-base in society?'

Ian recalls a visit to the Fuller Theological Seminary in the United States and seeing tee-shirts which proclaimed on the front 'Don't go to church' and on the back, 'Be the Church'. He contrasts churchgoing in an 'age of certainty' and in an 'age of faith'. He describes life in Forres in his childhood as an age of certainty when churchgoing was a badge. Churches were full. Churchgoing . . . gave respectability. Sunday was the dreariest day, devoted to church meetings and reading 'improving' books.

Ian contends that 'Vatican II made an important change of emphasis. In place of Vatican I with its focus on the hierarchy with a tail-end of laity, it characterised the church as the 'People of God'.

He concludes with a further illustration. 'A pastor in the Outer Hebrides was worried about a woman in his congregation who lived a very poor marginal existence. He knew she had a son abroad. He gently enquired as to whether he ever sent her anything. 'He never sends money,' she said. The pastor felt he had to press the point . 'He never sends anything?' 'Weel, at times I find wee bits papery inside his letters.' She showed him money orders, never cashed. The gifts of the Spirit, distributed among the people, the wealth of the church for the work of proclaiming the Kingdom, have so often likewise been tucked away without being cashed. Their release would provide a missing dimension.

In the second article in the series Ian examines some pointers from the New Testament Church. He is clear that 'we are not required to become clones of that church, not least because it is very varied in its shape and because the context of our life is different.' But he is convinced that the way in which the church took shape in its early days is vitally instructive. Ian affirms that 'Worship is the most revolutionary action open to humanity . . . It empowers people to do and be what otherwise would be beyond them.'

As in worship, so in life, every member of the church has an active part to play as happens in a body. Jesus Christ is the Head but there is no 'neck' of clergy between the head and the rest of the body. Ian questions how we have reached a one-man-band/one-woman-band direction of church worship with laity dumbed down in the pews. The missing dimension (as Ian sees it) is the release of the Spirit in gifted people to build up the church from below.

Ian goes on in his next article in the series to ask, 'What hinders church renewal?' He quotes Jesus, 'If you know these things, happy are you if you do them.' He is of the opinion that what hinders church renewal in the official churches in Britain can be put down in part to 'culpable lack of knowledge; but more to culpable lack of will.'[74] He reaches the conclusion that there is a culpable lack of knowledge because information is available about new ways of being church which are not being appropriated. Such sources of knowledge include the pioneering work of the Iona Community and the growth of small Christian communities on every continent. He recognises the enterprising work of the Craighead Institute and the growth of church house groups across Scotland. Such new ways of being church have been written up in for instance Fr. Jim O'Halloran's 'Small Christian Communities' and his own 'Living a Countersign: from Iona to Basic Christian Communities'.[75]

Key to the way the church needs to be patterned is the dynamic development of relationships between different levels which he identifies as 'oikos, paroikia and oikoumene' being respectively, 'the small group normally house-based in the first century, the larger group – the parish, and life in the whole household of humankind'. The church's life is to be spent for the sake of the whole world which God so loved that he sent his Son that it might find true life.

The lack of will to take risks is a more stubborn problem to overcome. Dr. Archie Craig spoke of clergy retreats which he conducted where participants would envisage more effective forms of service – but in the end retreat into their shells saying of their present practice, 'It'll see me out.' Such an attitude contradicts the prayer, 'your kingdom come, your will be done on earth as in heaven.' Ian makes it clear that in matters concerning a renewal of the church he is not speaking theoretically. He gives examples from his experience of his 12 years as parish minister in Rosyth.

Ian then turned in his next article to the nature of ordination appropriate to the church in the modern world. He is firmly of the opinion that the church needs to be both movement and institution; without the latter it would lack the means of sharing its discoveries, without the former it would develop a hardening of the arteries which would resist the flow of its life blood. Too often the ongoing management of the church is in the hands of the clergy.

Mainstream churches including the Catholic Church now affirm that the ministry of the church is that of the whole church. But practice has not caught up with belief. Ordination should be taken to be a primary resource '. . . to equip the saints for the work of ministry, for building up the body of Christ.'[76]

Jesus had a gift for separating off particular followers for particular purposes, without disrupting the solidarity of the community. He chose twelve. At other times he chose three to go with him. Ian questions the concept of apostolic succession where it is limited to an ordained 'thin red line'. He questions a view which while it affirms Peter's confession of faith at the same time marginalises a similar confession by Martha.[77] Ian stands with the Dominican theologian Schillebeeckx in contending that the main resource will be laity – 'catechists, delegates of the word, pastoral animators'. Ian affirms that there will still be a need for a due proportion of scholars and specialists but the main resourcing will be more widely dispersed and will not be clergy-dependent: rather 'From Christ the whole body, joined and held together by every supporting ligament, grows and builds itself up in love, as each part does its work.'[78]

Building on his contention that the church has failed to recognise the importance of the laity – the whole people of God – in the August 2000 edition of *Open House* Ian maintains that women particularly have suffered through the sidelining of the laity. He recognises the particular contribution being made in the new millennium by women such as Ofelia Ortega in Cuba and Elsa Tamez in Costa Rica. Ian tells of an earlier encounter with Prof. Katarina Halkes who spoke of the way women's contribution to the faith journey has been ignored or devalued – she concluded with what has become a watchword. 'They have stolen our names!'

In the December 2000 *Open House* Ian gives an account of a visit to Nicaragua in the autumn of that year.[79] There he had witnessed not just the renewal of a church but of a nation. He had previously visited the country in 1980 on the first anniversary of the overthrow of the Somoza dictatorship; his second visit was in 1986. In the intervening period the Sandanistas had done much to advance the cause of the poor. Ronald Reagan could not leave well alone and through the CIA he promoted and funded the raising of an illegal army of Contras to destroy the symbols of the new order. With the aid of a trade embargo Nicaragua was brought to its knees. When, in 1986, the World Court investigated the American actions and found against the USA, they simply ignored the judgement. In the 1990 elections, massively interfered with by the USA, the Sandanistas were narrowly defeated. They stepped down and poverty returned to haunt two thirds of the population. Life had sadly been normalised!

It was with this background that Ian went back to Nicaragua in October 2000 as part of a group of seven representing the Nicaraguan Solidarity Campaign. Ian found that he had to change gear. His preoccupation with past wrongs needed to be replaced by learning how the second poorest country in the region[80] was responding to the terms dictated by the IMF and the World Bank. Ian was there when Xavier Gorostiaga shared with journalists the priorities of the new Nicaragua. Besides the redistribution of land seized by Somoza's extended family, the main focus was on education and medical care. The first targets of the Contras were schools and medical clinics – 'the hated signs of better priorities than the USA adopted'. In addition to visits to many small Christian communities Ian focused on three main areas:

- International Debt and national policies – Ian noted the double standards of the money men.
- Institutions on the ground. Ian developed a new perspective on the benefits of the collaboration of agencies such as Oxfam and those promoting Fair Trade: he found them to be literally life-giving instruments.
- Women breaking free. Ian found that women were being given a new status in a traditionally macho society.

Ian concluded that bodies such as the Nicaraguan Solidarity Campaign are of crucial importance to encourage the mutual enlightenment of rich and poor countries. He was impressed particularly by Fair Trade policies which give people hope who might otherwise have thrown in the towel. Cooperative success reminded him that 'People are made for community'.

In this series of articles in *Open House* at the beginning of the new millennium Ian clearly set out to grasp the nettles of controversial aspects of church life particularly but not exclusively in the Roman Catholic Church. He sets these matters in the context not only of the church but the 'oikoumene' – the whole inhabited world, with particular reference to the poor world made poor by the injustice of the rich. Ian's article in *Open House* on Nicaragua was carried without alteration by *Coracle* in its February 2001 edition.

In 2000 Saint Andrew Press in association with the Board of Communication of the Church of Scotland published a book of 25 stories for young people *'Caring for Planet Earth'*. In the introduction Ian makes clear his purpose: 'The stories, prayers and questions in this small book are designed to encourage children from an early age to care for our planet and its inhabitants.'

It is surely no surprise that Ian should make such provision for young people. In a number of places he delighted to discover children involved in the life of the church not least in small Christian communities. He particularly notes occasions when young people were leading adults in all-age-worship. With his concern that those often marginalised should be brought to the centre he carefully crafts stories which are graded to suit children and young people by age and stage. He blends very familiar situations that children will be able to relate to with other more exotic scenarios which appeal to that sense of adventure which will both educate and entertain. From the first story which teaches very young children the importance of the Incarnation to the concluding parable, 'The Shield People', which raises the significance of the ozone layer and which acts as a suitable conclusion for the whole collection, Ian draws his readers and their listeners with him. He is happy to develop stories set in the background of countries around the world of which he has firsthand experience and on one occasion retells an experience which he has previously shared with adults almost unaltered.

With the riches on offer selection again is invidious but few of the collection are so immediately appealing and yet work at so many different levels as the 'Arun' tale.

'In a distant country lived Arun, a bamboo tree. He was proud of himself, with justice! He grew taller than all the trees around. Up and up he went till he reached about 35 metres high! The secret of his height was this. The area around him was cut in two by a stone ridge. Where Arun stood there was a strong spring of water which ran down the slope to feed rivers further down. Arun had as much water as he needed. So there was no hindrance to his growth.

'On the other side of the ridge were fields which had no such water source but needed good rain to thrive. People depended on the crops for their livelihood.

'One year the rains failed. Week after week people looked up at the skies longing for a change in the weather. But it appeared as if all the crops would die.

'Some of the people who lived on the produce of the fields crossed over the dividing ridge to where Arun stood. They studied other bamboo trees around and shook their heads. 'Too small,' they said. Then they looked at Arun. 'That's the only one big enough,' they decided. 'We'll have to cut him down.'

'Arun was horrified. But then it looked as if he might be saved after all.

'We think of this tree, Arun, as our friend,' said one woman. 'We are very fond of him – he somehow seems part of the family. It would be a sad day if we were to lose him.'

'He gives direction to travellers,' said another. 'He stands so high that they know where they are when they see him and can plan their journey exactly and safely.'

'But what alternative is there?' asked a third voice. Reluctantly they agreed that there was no other option open to them. No other tree would do.

So Arun was cut down.

'What do you think the fields-people did? How would what they had done help them?

'First they made sure that the hollow middle was completely clear of pith which might block the passage of water. Then they put one end into the spring of water and the other end over the ridge to the lower fields on the other side. The water flowed into the fields! The crops revived and went on to produce a good harvest of grain and vegetables.

Arun said to himself: 'I thought I had lost my life, my tall beauty, the sign I was for travellers. Now I have found another kind of life. I provide means for life-giving water to reach places which need it.'

The prayer which follows is surely accessible to a wide age range without patronising any. It balances thankfulness with the responsibility to live respecting the lives of others.

Prayer:

'Lord God,
We thank you for water to drink, to bathe in, to play with. We remember countries where water is scarce and people suffer.
Make our lives like a bamboo pipe so that all people may be able to have enough water which they can drink safely and wash in, and have enough water to make the crops grow.
We ask it in Jesus' name.
Amen'

The questions which follow[81] are real questions. They give expectation that thoughtful answers are required. The first puts the ball in the court of the young person him/herself while the second encourages a belief in the self-worth of the young that is often neglected by a busy adult world.

The story is accompanied by a simple professionally produced illustration. It goes a long way to fixing the story in the minds of young and old alike.

When Ian speaks of this book he hardly ever fails to mention three matters which have brought him delight. Without any initiative on his part, Stirling Council[82] contacted him and offered some finance so that in their words, 'illustrations that would enhance his writing could be professionally commissioned.' Ian was delighted at their commitment to his work and the more so when he saw the illustrations produced by Miles Forde. Ian was further delighted when the opportunity was granted to have the *Caring for Planet Earth* launched in the local primary school in Gargunnock. The book is dedicated to Laura Henderson, an eight-year old when the book was published. The Hendersons were neighbours of the Frasers and Laura's mum used to read some of the stories to her daughter when they were still in typewritten form. We just know that had Margaret been there in more than spirit she too would have voiced her own delight, teacher that she was. The icing on this particular cake was provided in two complementary layers. On two occasions headteachers on establishing that the Ian they were talking with was in fact the Ian M Fraser who had produced this volume of stories commended his work as 'just what we had been waiting for to use with our pupils'. All surely that Ian could have hoped for as he made these stories available.

Certainly he had avoided some tempting pitfalls. He makes no attempt to turn these pithy parables into allegories and so lose the elements of timelessness and freedom to think. Equally he refuses to heavy-handedly link the stories to theological straitjackets for all that theology is never far from the surface. But he wants more. We should allow him the last word on this occasion. He concluded his introduction thus: 'Finally it is hoped that the stories and their dramatic potential, the prayers and the questions may encourage parents and teachers to try to make up other stories, prayers and questions of their own (whatever their faith).'

In the last twenty-five years or so Ian has done much more than write. He has taken particular delight in visiting his extended family and more often recently of hosting get-togethers at Ferndale. To this he has added many other commitments among which are:

- 1992 Ian chaired the Scottish Churches World Exchange Conference in St. Andrews. His 'The Fire Runs' (1975) was used as the basis for the conference. A delegate from the Scottish Borders wrote to Ian; 'I cannot think when I came away from any Church conference or meeting feeling so encouraged and exhilarated.'
- 1993 Ian was the keynote speaker at the Justice and Peace Scotland annual conference in Clydebank. The subject given was 'Discovering the good news of the gospel in our times.' One quote was highlighted in a report of the conference: Paul VI, 'Justice is love's absolute minimum.'
- 1995 Ian shared in the dedication of Kob Cottage, Kalk Bay, South Africa. The cottage was the property of Margaret and Colin Legum and was set aside as a Columban House – a place of hospitality and study.
  In the same year Ian worked with local people in the Gargunnock Village Group on the Central Regional Council Action Plan to determine priorities towards year 2000. The study Ian devised included considerations of a) Education b) Sustainable life-styles and c) Stewardship of the Environment.
- 1997 Ian attended a conference in Graz, Austria and presented the Iona Community thinking on 'Sharing Holy Communion', followed shortly afterwards by visits to communities in Ireland in the company of Jim O'Halloran

- 1998 At the Hymns Society Conference Ian gave report of the Dunblane enterprise in the 1960s writing new hymns. He identified Erik Routley as the 'dynamic of the whole development' and accepted Erik's description of himself as 'gauleiter'. 'I was to breathe down necks and twist arms to ensure that work promised for gatherings ahead was in fact done and made available in time.' Ian identified three theological perceptions:
  a) Our time and place in history is a gift of God.
  b) Worship is directed to God and has to be worthy
  c) The significance of the participation of children
- 1999 Ian was part of a group who visited Cuba in the name of the Department of World Mission of the Church of Scotland. He led sessions based on 'Reinventing Theology as the People's Work' which had been translated into Spanish. Ian was recently heartened by a 2008 visit by Iona Community Members and Associates to Cuba and the *Coracle* published at the end of 2008 which combined news of the 2008 visit with earlier writing of Ian's featuring previous visits to Cuba.
- 2000 As part of the Nicaraguan Solidarity Campaign Ian revisited Managua as one of seven from England, Ireland and Scotland. They investigated the effect of heavy debt burdens and considered what was being done in the local macho culture with regard to violence against women.
- 2001 Ian visited China in a group of ten; the others were catholic and Roman, he catholic and Reformed. This was the 95th country Ian had visited in his work on and for the world church. On this visit he had firsthand experience of the official churches in China and collected reports of basic Christian communities in that vast land. It was suggested to

Ian that 10% of the Chinese population is Christian with the numbers equally divided between the official churches and the bccs.

- 2003 Ian stood (unsuccessfully) for a district council seat as the Scottish Labour Party candidate, fifty years after serving as a Dunfermline town councillor. Four other ministers stood in the locality in these elections including his good friends Canon Kenyon Wright and Maxwell Craig until recently a member with Ian of the Iona Community.

In the autumn of 2006 Ian's book *The Way Ahead* was launched in the Stirling Smith Art Gallery and Museum. The director, Dr Elspeth King has long been a supporter of local writers and of Ian in particular. Those who were only half listening thought they heard that it was to be the last of his books. More careful attention would have confirmed that this was in fact the last of a series of books Ian was committed to in his own mind to complete what had been begun with Margaret some years before. A good company of those who know and have benefited from his craft, including his daughter, Anne, on a visit from the States, gathered. The session was introduced by Elizabeth Templeton, a Scottish theologian who clearly values what Ian has done in her field of expertise. *The Way Ahead* was introduced by Tom Fleming, the well-known radio and television broadcaster who in recent years has endeared himself to many within and beyond the Iona Community with his 'Every Blessed Thing' – in which he presents an evening in the company of George MacLeod. His words on the day of the book launch in Stirling are summarised in his commendation by way of introduction to *The Way Ahead.*

'Dr Ian Fraser is a treasure trove of biblical scholarship, wisdom and common sense. *The Way Ahead* draws on a lifelong and worldwide experience of Christian communities 'on the edge'. With inspirational hope, Ian Fraser points to a bright and valid future for the church, shorn of ecclesiastical irrelevances. It is a prophetic vision that cheers the heart. It will not meet with universal approval – but then you know what they say about prophets in their own country (and in their own time).'

Tom Fleming[83] is an interesting churchman having been involved in what was formerly Canonmills Baptist Church which is ever more inclusive as a post-denominational worshipping community, to which he has regularly encouraged Ian to contribute in public worship and teaching.

The Way Ahead (with its subtitle – 'Grown Up Christians') takes most of its readers by surprise from the outset by identifying the present as a time of God's favour for the church in the West. Ian reaches this conclusion on the basis that the church no longer exercises dominating power in our world as once it did and therefore is better placed to serve her Master. Ian draws on his experience over many years and from many places and reminds followers of Christ that they are called to live a holy life – a life of separation not *from* the world but *for* God *in* the world.

For Ian dogma can be belief-become-constipated. It invites conformity. Orthodoxy invites a journey. It takes seriously and together past tradition and present perceptions afforded by the Holy Spirit. Ian calls for enlightened use of scripture which he is convinced will lead us to an inclusive faith community. He recalls the African woman who expressed the particular nature of the Bible thus: 'Other books I read – this book reads me.' Ian celebrates all that is best in life and sees the dance of the Spirit in life at its best.

Ian remains committed to a larger vision of ecumenism than has sometimes been promoted in Scotland. He sees the continuing relevance of Scottish Churches House with its threefold purpose made plain at its beginning:

a) to serve the world with integrity, especially using lay resources

b) to let the churches meet honestly and humbly about what separates them

c) to make fresh discoveries in the life of faith and devotion.

In the face of some official pronouncements from leaders in the traditional churches, Ian is delighted to find so many marks of life in a 'church-in-the-becoming' state. Using the analogy of tides it suggests to him that, contrary to popular opinion, the tide is not just on the turn but coming in.

Ian hardly sets out to endear himself to some present church leadership when he describes hierarchy (as) a 'late and dodgy invention.' Yet he recognises that, with imagination, forms such as these can be made to serve gospel purposes. He recalls visits to the diocese of Bishop Mendez Arceo in Cuernavaca, Mexico and bishop Escaler in Ipil in the Philippines, where he saw effective use of hierarchical structures. In such cases a common factor prevails. Grassroots Christians and their insights have substantive participation up to the highest levels of decision-making. They are not dropped on the way. Ian displays scholarship and a familiarity with the early church fathers in his consideration of developments in the early patterns of church leadership. In contrast he gives voice to a way of being church as he discovered it around the globe where the whole people of God are valued. At a time when the perceived wisdom notes a shortage of clergy, Ian contends that where those who are ordained are not committed to the equipping of the whole church 'there may still be too many of us!'

Ian goes to the heart of the matter of oversight in the church by focusing on the 'epi' in 'episcopos' – the Greek word for bishop. 'Epi' is traditionally understood as 'over' as in oversight and overseer. He is convinced that the essence of 'epi' is in fact 'giving concentrated caring attention'. This is simply illustrated by his consideration of the experience of the Czech Church in the days of Communist control and a re-visiting of days in Rosyth in earlier years.

Jan Kofron, a recognised leader of the persecuted church in Czechoslovakia is Ian's main source of knowledge and understanding of the Prague underground Christian community. This group developed following the occupation of Czechoslovakia by Soviet troops after the 'Prague Spring'. Many of the previously ordained theological teachers found themselves in prison. To a large extent they continued their ministry among the prison community. In their absence other members of the Prague Community took on responsibilities. Pruning through persecution led to new growth. The result was a church with members contributing according to their gifts and experience.

Marks of this 'new' church included
a)   clergy did not wear special clothes
b)   clergy worked for their living to earn their keep
c)   they were free to marry
d)   they preferred to celebrate Mass in homes rather than cathedrals
e)   they believed that ordination services for priests and consecration services for bishops were better held in workplaces than cathedrals; they made more impact.

Ian recalls the last Mass he attended in Prague when the hidden church was able to enjoy the new freedom of 1989 and the years which followed the collapse of Communism in Eastern Europe.

'The last Mass I attended went thus: Bishop Fridolin presided, Bishop Jan at his side. The adolescents formed a band to lead hymn singing. A time of confession was announced and about half the people present offered prayers (out of around 40 participants). About the same number were later to contribute to the intercessions. There was a responsive psalm. Bible readings came from members of the congregation. The New Testament reading was the responsibility of an 18-year-old girl who proceeded to give the sermon. The children, who had gone out for their own sermon-equivalent, rejoined the company for the communion. They brought the elements to the table and removed them at the end. The bishops together gave the blessing. They had presided over participant worship very like that which Paul describes as being characteristic of New Testament times.'

In his final chapter Ian sets out the challenge to the church of our day, 'either to affirm the Kingdom of God or affirm itself.' For as Ian concludes: 'The great promise of these times is where the church becomes a Kingdom sign of a new world order in justice and peace.'

Had this publication been the last will and testament on the threshold of his 90th year it would have been remarkable enough. In fact it served not only as a launch pad for new ways of being church for us all, but also energised Ian himself to be ever more active with his pen in the months and years that have followed.

He concludes *The Way Ahead* with a rallying cry:

'We are called and empowered to live the resurrection . . . We can live in the confidence that Easter brought and brings.

'To believe in God the Father is to believe that someone is in charge who sees the whole game. This should provide enough confidence to allow us church people to be prepared to see developments go out of our hands – without that meaning they become unfruitful or bring chaos. The insistence on having a controlling agent, like a Communist Party or a Curia or a bureaucracy is a sign of unfaith (in process of history, or in a Father of all). Episcope, the need at many levels to keep an eye on developments, test and relate them, is a different matter. Means to exercise it must never degenerate into instruments of control.

'To believe in Jesus Christ is to be confident that, from a position stripped of power and privilege, we can successfully (though it may be, in the end, over our dead bodies) confront the massive and commanding powers of the world and help to make them serve the purposes for which God brought them into being.

'To believe in the Holy Spirit is to believe that people can find resources in themselves beyond all expectation, sprout capacities to handle life, surprise themselves and others by what they can accomplish, and thus 'bring the house down', gaining the applause of the universe.[84]

Endnotes

[62] Written jointly with his wife, Margaret.

[63] While most of the music was composed by Donald Rennie a few melodies were provided by others e.g. John Bell.

[64] based on his PhD thesis.

[65] Many of the writings from this period have served as source material for this biography.

[66] Is it noteworthy that although Ian gives a significant place to the Iona Community as a sign of hope he makes no mention of the opening of the MacLeod Centre on Iona which gave a focus to the Jubilee Celebrations of the Community on the island?

[67] Of whom more later.

[68] As an aside we note that the cover design for the book was by Graham Maule another member of the Iona Community.

[69] It is perhaps surprising that Ian does not refer to the 'old' and 'new' covenants made much of by the writer to the Hebrews. This lack perhaps

makes clear that the points made are representative rather than exhaustive as biblical insights into the place of nation states.

[70] 397 AD saw the death of Martin of Tours, the father of western monasticism and by tradition the founding of Ninian's Candida Casa in Whithorn. 597 AD, the year of Columba's death coincided with the arrival of Augustine in Canterbury.

[71] Ian can surely be forgiven this Freudian slip given the esteem in which he holds the previous Popes John XXIII and Paul VI – though on balance this may simply be a printer's error!

[72] 'That they may be one'.

[73] *Open House* describes itself as 'A Scottish religious magazine of comment, opinion and reflection from within the Catholic tradition.' The editor in 2000 was Ian D. Willock. Ian Fraser acted at that time as one of the Advisory Group which included his close friend, Tim Duffy.

[74] John 13.17.

[75] Still available through the Iona Community.

[76] Ephesians 4.12.

[77] It can be noted that Martha was the sister in Bethany marked by her practical service rather than having a penchant for contemplation. Luke 10:38ff.

[78] Ephesians 4.18.

[79] Ian's penchant for a disciplined approach to writing often means that he produces material that is fresh and relevant. Writing is not to be done in haste, nor is it to be delayed through lack of effort over long hours.

[80] after Haiti.

[81] What do you want your life to be like? How can it be best made a blessing to others?

[82] The Council Ian took to court in his Poll Tax action. Some evidence if evidence is needed that his legal foray was courteous perhaps even welcome.

[83] 29 June 1927 – 18 April 2010.

[84] Romans 8.21–end.

CHAPTER ELEVEN

POSTSCRIPT

WHILE IAN WAS unstinting in his sharing of his life story he insisted that I was responsible at all times for what was included and what was not. Following Ian's own method of interview we recorded our conversations. They were then produced as transcripts. The text of 'I've Seen Worse' was based largely on these transcripts. As we proceeded to meet it seemed sensible to let Ian read what had been written. He confined himself to correcting matters of fact – and even in such matters he left final decisions with me. I am therefore without excuse!

By way of drawing Ian's story to a close I was keen to revisit some parts of Ian's life. This postscript combines some of the journey I have been privileged to share with him and some material from his long life that has come to me in recent days. The hope is that where readers have shared some of Ian's journey, they will be stimulated to enjoy roads travelled with him in life and word.[85]

$$- \text{o} - \text{o} - \text{o} - \text{o} -$$

An opportunity arose to see Ian's home town of Forres. As we visited Nelson's Tower, Grant Park, Leys Cottage and the area around Findhorn, it was obvious that it all remained very familiar to Ian.

While it is more than seventy years since he lived in Forres he has hardly been a long-term absentee over these years. It has never been a chore for him to visit his roots. There was real warmth in the welcomes received from those of the family still living there. This was balanced by the pleasure Ian showed as he discovered again the esteem the older townsfolk still have for the memory of his elder brother Alex, who never left the town but served a lifetime in the family business.[86]

On other occasions I had the pleasure with Ian of visiting his sister Margaret in her latter years, living in care in Annan at the opposite end of the country. Ian had a continuing commitment to visit her when he could – normally travelling from Gargunnock to Annan by bus and spending an overnight there. It was a pleasure there to meet George Lind, a local minister, who continued to visit Margaret even after she moved beyond his particular parish responsibility. George spoke well of input that Ian had as a visiting lecturer during his training for the ministry in Glasgow.

To return to Forres days – among some papers from long ago a few lines penned by Ian in his middle teenage years came to light. They need no further comment.

After the End

One star in an empty vacuum of space.
One tear shed by a child for another.
One candle burning for the lost.
And the blood of one man on the hands of another.

One rose to purify any innocence left.
One ocean to play its music.
One song to listen in the dark.
And one spark of hate for an inferno of evil.

One pearl left to wonder about.
One diamond left to sparkle.
One life left to cherish
And the tears that fall like rain.

One castle left to burn.
One sky slowly falling.
One glimmer of love shining through the smoke.
And no one left to care.

One world imprisoned in eternal slumber.
One race no one has won.
One child left alone forever.
After the war is done.

$$- o - o - o - o -$$

The war was not yet done when Ian and Margaret were married in 1943.[87] Some words from the wedding service have been recorded from that day in 1943. In his word to the happy couple Dr. Black said, 'Ian, you are not to stand here and insist "I'm on my rights". And Margaret, you are not to stay over against him insisting, "I'm on my rights." The only right you have from now on is to love and serve one another'.

Ian recalls that it was indeed wartime. He had agreed with Margaret that if they had but a year of marriage before bombs got them it would be worth it. Margaret had borrowed her sister-in-law's wedding dress. They were unable to get the Edinburgh photographer they would have preferred. The wedding cake was about the size of a medium-sized Christmas pudding. It was covered with white cardboard to simulate icing. But for them none of that really mattered. They were two become one. Little wonder that what was thus begun lasted long into the setting sun.[88]

Ian and I were fortunate to be able to visit the Tullis Russell Paper Mill where he worked as labourer-chaplain in the 1940s. We met Pam McNamee who had worked there since the 1980s.[89] She was Secretary to the Chairman David Erdal, grandson to Sir David Russell, who took over the Mill from the younger David Russell in 1985. Erdal was a prime mover in the 1990s converting the company to being completely employee-owned. He writes, 'The key to making a success of that is precisely the kind of practices that it sounds as if Ian Fraser advocated – informing and consulting and involving ALL the workers. I believe that it is impossible to stop the kind of power-orientated behaviour that ended (your) experiment and to protect the interests of all employees, unless the power is distributed in a democratic manner . . .'

In conversation Ian and I heard of two incidents from the forties that gave a flavour of the division between workers and management at that time.

One of the workers from the mill on his way to work parked his car outside a newsagent and went in for his newspaper. He waited to be served. While he was still waiting a manager from the mill entered. 'Is that your car parked outside,' he asked aggressively. 'Yes,' replied the labourer. 'Well,' said the manager, 'It should not have been there. I have just run into it.'

On another notable occasion one of the workers had parked his car in a parking space in the mill car park. One of the management arrived and ran into the parked car. The shouting match could be heard across the whole site. 'I always park in that space,' he thundered. 'You will have to pay for the damage.' And that was what happened. We can only speculate that the worker was so afraid for his job that he went ahead and had the car repaired although the blame was clearly not his. Changed days indeed and a reminder that the world of work was a very different place when Ian went to labour and act as chaplain in the Rothes and Auchmuty mills.

$$- o - o - o - o -$$

Two themes tend to mark large parts of Ian's life, travelling and writing. On many occasions the visits he made became the raw material for writing that would follow. At the end of the war the World Student Christian Federation took over Alpenblick Chalet in Grindelwald, Switzerland. It was to provide a break for students who had been malnourished during the hostilities and under real strain. The chalet was under the leadership of Dale Brown. In 1946 it was decided that two of the British SCM staff should visit them by way of support. All the names were put in a hat. Ian was fortunate to be drawn as one of the two chosen.

Ian noted that the English have an awkward habit of arranging bank holidays on different days from the Scots. He arrived in London on one such holiday and was unable to get Swiss francs. But he had his train ticket. In those days trains to Switzerland were incredibly crowded. He had a booked seat; but he could not move his feet because a man facing him had placed his feet between his and there was just no space to move. He had no way of reaching his food which was on the rack above. When the train stopped at a junction a tap was spotted. Hot thirsty passengers left the train en masse with any container they could find. The driver just had to wait till his passengers decided to get back on board.

When Ian reached Thun and handed over his ticket, the ticket collector said that he could not board the train to Grindelwald because his ticket ended at that point. So Ian waited till the train started moving and hopped on to the last carriage. He still had no Swiss money. He decided the worst they could do was throw him off. In fact he got as far as Grindelwald where the return half of his ticket was impounded till he returned with money to pay for the last leg of the journey. It was a weary, hungry traveller that trudged to the chalet in a baking hot sun. Some leftovers from the previous meal was all he was offered. But he was there; and Miss Jackson loaned him enough money to retrieve the return half of his ticket.

Ian's abiding memory of his visit is of being in a party going up the Wetterhorn – all but the final cliff at the top. Ian maintained that he had climbed more than its height for on the way up he found that he had left his camera lower down and had to climb down 1,500 feet to get it. He decided the Swiss behind his group were either incredibly honest or thought such a cheap machine not worth acquiring. The ascent passed largely without further incident. The descent was different. Two students lost their nerve when they saw the narrow path stretch away beneath their feet. Ian was volunteered to chaperone them down slowly while the rest of the party went ahead to make sure they got down in daylight. Every time the path changed direction Ian was required by his charges to stand on the outside of the corner with his arms spread out to form a human fence. They got back safely two hours behind the rest of the group and just before darkness fell.

$$- \text{o} - \text{o} - \text{o} - \text{o} -$$

In the 1949 Scottish Journal of Theology Ian published an article on 'Theology and Action'. It represented his thinking as he arrived in Rosyth. The next twelve years would hone his understanding of the faith in the life of a parish.

The article made clear a number of principles and guidelines that he held as important:

- 'It is of urgent importance that sound theology and right action should have a church wedding.
- 'We need to hold the biblical record and the particular needs of our time in a fruitful tension.
- 'The gospel is redemptive of our times.
- 'There is a temptation to substitute for action itself the carefully worded definition of right action. People may feel righteous when their blood boils at wrongs they see, and consider that reaction as sufficient.
- 'The early disciples were sent out into the world bearing the Announcement of the Kingdom. This involved preaching and

healing; the Announcement comprised both word and act of compassion.

- 'When we respond to Christ we must always walk by faith – never by sight.
- 'Sound theological thinking is a necessity of the life of discipleship . . . when it is mature it helps to authenticate and make rich the obedient life.'

A recurring theme that became apparent as I spent time in conversation with Ian was the way in which lessons learned in one context or time of life were relevant in other areas and at other times.

Ian compares writing a thesis to the skills of 'drystane dyking'. Rosyth days were informed by earlier life experience. His uncle John introduced him to this form of wall-building on his small farm, Branchill, near Dallas. If a wall was needed there was never enough money spare to call in a specialist. The work was done by family and friends.

The method followed a tried and tested pattern. Stones would be spread over quite a large area. There was no good picking out stones of the same category or shape. It was impossible to identify beforehand which of the stones would be needed. The skill was to produce strength by fitting the awkward shapes together. Of course, strong stones were needed to make a foundation. Similar shaped stones could be useful to top off the work. For the rest the wall was built a stone at a time. There had to be a memory for shapes, where a jutting out bit in one would find a groove in another and so on. In the end maybe less than one in ten of the stones would prove to be 'fit for purpose'.

If at too early a stage in writing a thesis, things, which do not seem to apply to the subject in hand, are combed out, much which might seem awkward and ill-fitting might be lost. Some of what is rejected might in time have firmed up significant parts of the work. In the end perhaps only one tenth of the material available may be gathered into the final framework. That, Ian concludes, is fair enough.

In Rosyth and beyond, nothing seems to have given Ian more pleasure than to recall red letter days in Margaret's life and service. There was particular pleasure if he could put himself down at the same time. During her time in Rosyth Margaret led the Women's Guild. Her commitment and expertise brought her national recognition. She became national vice president towards the end of her time there. In 1968 she was asked to speak to a gathering of 3000 women in Edinburgh's Usher Hall. She had clearly given some thought to what she might say. 'Ian,' she asked eventually, 'if you were in my shoes how would you tackle these women.' Ian somewhat surprised gave a thoughtful answer. Margaret thanked him and departed to continue her preparation. 'Now at least I know how not to do it!' A partnership made in heaven!

It is equally true that Ian valued the day to day contributions that Margaret made to family life and life in the wider community. He held on to her lesson planning when she was working with the youngsters marking time before going on to secondary education. A selection of topics from the first half of 1956 gives a flavour of class work undertaken.

Date	Work in class
17.2.56	The Joy of snow and frost
9.3.56	How I'd spend £5
30.3.56	An amusing incident or story
20.4.56	Corporal Punishment
27.4.56	Capital Punishment
1.6.56	How to use private and public telephones (with or without dials)

Alastair Stewart acted as church treasurer for the whole 12 years the Frasers were in Rosyth. The Stewart's daughter Wilma was just a lassie when Ian and Margaret moved to Dunblane. Later, on a visit to Rosyth, Ian met Mrs. Stewart and knowing that Wilma was now grown up and married, Ian expressed a hope that the marriage was turning out well. Mrs. Stewart's reply was clear. 'We all noticed that when Margaret and you came within reach of one another, your faces lit up – even if it was quite a short time since you had parted. Well, it is just the same with Wilma and her husband.'

It does not seem to have taken long to recognise the special bond that Ian and Margaret shared. During their visit to the USA in 1955 when Ian did his research on Cunninghame Graham they spent time at a holiday town of about 5000 people. It was built around a lake shaped like a kidney bean.[90] Some people were resident the year round; some came for holiday. It was set out for leisure activities – opera, the theatre, pavilions for orchestras, athletic facilities and so on. Ian took a morning service each day in an amphitheatre – some three to five hundred people would turn up at 7.30 a.m. Later in the day he gave a lecture. In exchange Ian and Margaret were able to stay as guests of the town.

The young people had their own organisations with a coordinating group. The day came when they told the Frasers that each summer their group nominated a couple as their favourite. They announced that Ian and Margaret had been chosen. They just wanted them to know – there was no reward or prize as such attached. Ian concluded, 'This had nothing to do with my lectures or the conduct of the services but with the way we wandered around in our leisure time, hand in hand utterly content to be with one another.' In this we can be sure that Ian speaks the truth. When I tell folks this I remember that I never met Margaret. I always feel that this is a lesser truth. To have known Ian in some measure is to have known Margaret too.

There was considerable interest in the Fraser children while they were in Rosyth. The Boys' Brigade Company prided themselves as the oldest youth organisation in Rosyth Parish; the Scout troop was the largest youth organisation in the parish in the fifties. Some pressure was brought to bear on the minister to guide his sons aright in their choice of youth group. Father was having none of it. He remembered his lack of space back in Forres. He made it clear that if the boys wanted to join an organisation, they would do so without any interference from him.

Not that the boys were short of entertainment of their own making. The hose from the twin-tub washing machine improvised as an 'alpenhorn'. Hidden behind a hedge they would let out a blast that had passers-by all shook up. Together the boys perfected their own version of the Rosyth rope-trick. A fine nylon rope was stretched across a road to capture any unsuspecting vehicle passing by. The day came when our intrepid twosome had the rope in place, only to discover that the first car down the road that day was the local police car. Imagine their panic when later that day one of them answered a knock at their door only to find Sergeant Cowie, the local bobby, standing on the doorstep. The boys imagined the worst. In fact the constable was visiting their father about some matter related to parish-police cooperation. The boys could breath more easily and probably found some alternative form of mischief-making. We may well wonder if the role model of Dennis the Menace featuring in The Beano[91] had particular attraction in the lives of these two boys in Fife.

In reflecting on his years in Rosyth as the Parish Minister Ian acknowledges the great debt he owed to the Iona Community with its encouragement to experiment – to share experience and develop fellowship. Ian understands worship as that activity whereby folk are given new eyes with which to look out on the world, and learn how to live a new and common life in it. To really live today in the world, we must first appear together before God. The key word in worship is participation. Too often folk are expected merely to spectate.

After the Frasers' time in Rosyth, Moira Brown, the daughter of the local fishmonger asked Ian if he would sit for a portrait. It was agreed that some ten sittings would take place. During 1968 after more than half the sittings Moira turned up one day only to be completely frustrated. On the day in question, she threw her brushes on the floor and asked Ian accusingly, 'What has changed? You are not the man you were when last we met?' In time they came to the conclusion that Ian's distress at the Soviet invasion of Czechoslovakia, ending the 'Prague Spring' had so affected him, that he was visibly changed in the eyes of this perceptive artist. In the remaining few sittings Moira started afresh. She was far from impressed by the outcome. The family tended to agree that the second attempt was lacking something. That said the portrait was hung in the National Portrait Gallery in Edinburgh before being displayed in a gallery in London. While there, the painting was slashed by someone who also found it unacceptable! Moira did what she could to restore the work. Rumour has it that it now lies, discarded in the attic of one of Ian's sons, gathering dust. Of the first painting nothing survives. Perhaps it was painted over. Fortunately Moira was an artist who refused to be easily deterred. When Ian and Margaret left Rosyth in 1960 Moira produced a painting as a parting gift showing a floral still life. It hangs still in Ian's lounge in Gargunnock. The quality of that work was commended by no less an authority than Ricky Dimarco.[92] When asked if Moira's dad was an elder in Rosyth Church, Ian seemed wrong-footed by such a sectarian enquiry. 'No he wasn't – they were a Roman Catholic family' to which Ian added the telling, 'I think.'

During one of our visits in recent years to Annan to spend time with Ian's sister Margaret we arranged to have lunch with Ruth Harvey who had often worked with Ian as she served the Iona Community as the editor of *Coracle*. She was then working with a group of churches in the South of Scotland. Ian was remembering his time in Rosyth fifty years earlier. Ruth listened with interest but concluded that we live in a very different world these days with very different churches. Something jarred with me but I could not put my finger immediately on it. I later remembered that Ian was adamant that his time in Rosyth and the report of that time[93] was not offered as a model for others to copy or follow. Yet surely we are all agreed that if we do not learn from the past we are condemned to make the same mistakes again and again. Could it be that the Rosyth experience does provide principles and guidelines that can be applied in very different times and places? But they will need to be worked out afresh to give new life.

$$- \mathrm{o} - \mathrm{o} - \mathrm{o} - \mathrm{o} -$$

In the month leading up to Ian's 90th birthday he invited me to spend an evening in Scottish Churches House where a report was to be given on the future of the House. Concerned by what he believed was planned Ian had written an open letter to the ACTS trustees demanding the continuation of the place if it was clear that it could serve the churches in the future not just stand as a monument to a significant past. The ACTS Forum met in late November 2007. They decided to support the continuation of Scottish Churches House if £500,000 could be raised through an Appeal timed to last to their next meeting in May 2008.

At the beginning of December[94] Ron Ferguson had entitled his regular column in the (Glasgow) Herald 'The perfect birthday gift for a great man of vision.' Writing from personal experience Ron noted that under the first warden, Ian Fraser, Scottish Churches House was 'an ecumenical venture which concentrated much more on the needs of the world than on the internal problems of the churches.' He focused on the appeal to allow the house to be transformed into a 21st century conference and hospitality centre at the forefront of ecumenical work over the next 50 years.

Ron continued his reflection, 'In the dining room of Scottish Churches House stands a clock made by the inmates at Aberdeen Craiginches Prison as a token of their solidarity with the parents of the children massacred at Dunblane Primary School in 1996 . . . Can this old and rather beautiful house and chapel with its tradition of radical thinking and encounter designed to resolve conflict be a basis from which new and imaginative plans for cooperation between Scotland's churches will be developed?' He concluded, 'The announcement of this renewed commitment (to the house) could not be a finer 90th birthday present for the grand and vigorous old man of radical ecumenical thinking in Scotland.'

The launch of the Jubilee Appeal for the refurbishment and development of Scottish Churches House was held in January 2008 at a civic reception hosted by Stirling Council. One of the keynote speakers on that occasion, Dr. Elspeth King[95] gave voice to her support of Scottish Churches House: 'You can no more contemplate Dunblane without Scottish Churches House than you could Iona without its Abbey.' In conversation Ian gave me permission to make some contribution of time to service the Jubilee Appeal at the expense of immediate work on 'I've Seen Worse.'[96] The four months set aside for work on the appeal ran on till the beginning of 2009. The appeal was deemed to have been a success. Sadly although much refurbishment has taken place other factors have militated against the use of the centre and in early 2011 ACTS decided to close the house and seek a different use or form of management if such can be discovered.

Those who have used the house since its opening in 1960 have often found one part of the property of particular significance. The Chapel at Scottish Churches House is, according to Ian, in the nature of a mystery gift, an unexplained addition to the largesse of God in providing Scotland with a House of the Churches Together. To those who set in hand the restoration of the 18th century building alongside the Cathedral in 1960, one part was an obstacle course which was tackled by a World Council of Churches work camp. It lay hidden behind a thick screen of ivy in wild ground.

The original purpose of the structure has been suggested by among others, Elizabeth Barty, as a wine cellar (unlikely as it had a window), or the house of the Archdeacon of the Cathedral clergy (again unlikely as no record of a dwelling exists in such a position). The 1960 work-campers were faced with a pile of rubbish which had accumulated inside and around what was otherwise known as the 'Old Chapel'.

Whatever the truth of its original use at least one matter is plain – Eric Stevenson produced a brilliant architectural design for the development/restoration of the chapel. The skill of the plan is shown in this: if two or three are gathered together they do not feel there are large empty spaces around them, yet 40 persons can comfortably be accommodated[97]. We need to be relaxed about the past but can be committed to continuing prayer in these days for it remains a possibility that the chapel comes down to us as a gift of the undivided Christian church.

$$- o - o - o - o -$$

In more than a decade between 1969 and 1982 while Ian was based in Geneva and Selly Oak, he travelled the globe. Some of his visits were to significant places; on other occasions it was his visit that was particularly significant.

His travels began long before Geneva. Among the significant places he visited he remembers well going to Taize in 1962. The occasion was the opening of The Church of Reconciliation. Ian had been offered a place to stay in the brothers' quarters and a lift to Taize from Paris. It was on this journey that he met Bob Dodds, who hailed from the USA. He confessed to Ian that he had made no arrangements for his stay and could not speak a word of French. So Ian gave up his place at the heart of the Taize community and found billets in a nearby village for the two of them.

There was no cause for annoyance in this. Ian was more than willing to change his plans to help out a brother. But he could not get Bob moving the next morning. They missed the bus that would have got them to Taize in time. By the time they did get there, the place was filled to overflowing. People were spilling out the door of the church.

Shortly afterwards the person appointed to lead the service appeared, followed by a Taize brother carrying a Bible. In that moment Ian felt he had done enough for Bob. He fell in behind the Taize brother and processed into the church as if that was what had been planned. Ian peeled off as they reached the font. He found a place. When the service finished Ian rejoined the procession as it left. What a cheek? Ian confessed to an element in his make-up, as he never tired of reminding folk, 'God is the God of Abraham of Isaac and of Jacob, the godly twister'.

Now we might ask whether Ian's visit to Taize mattered. Ian would have been in his mid-forties when he went to Taize. On the eve of his 90th birthday a note was received from Taize from a Brother Thomas. He wrote to Ian:

'It has been good to have news of you. I send my greetings and best wishes for your 90th birthday. You will certainly not remember me, but I did in fact meet you many years ago, before I came to Taize in 1965. I get news of Iona through my good friend Jack Laidlaw, and I had the joy of visiting Iona again with Jack and his wife in 2005. He also took me to visit Uist and Pat MacDonald in their home in Perth.'

Once again the significance of people and places is seen in the unexpected.

$$- o - o - o - o -$$

While serving the WCC in Geneva, Ian attempted to interview Ian Paisley, the Ulsterman. The first response was that Dr. Paisley had no use for the WCC – as the front for the ecumenical movement which he characterised as 'the slippery slope to Rome.' Then out of the blue came an offer to meet, if Ian Fraser agreed to report exactly what was said to him. He readily agreed that he would do this if the Northern Irishman would answer all the questions put to him. The meeting took place in the Palace of Westminster. Ian tape recorded the conversation anxious to keep his side of the bargain.

Looking back at the interview with Ian Paisley reminded the other Ian of a frosty Murrayfield rugby pitch of an earlier era. Protected by a straw blanket the pitch gave the crowd the impression of a perfect playing surface. The players knew better. Beneath the frost free surface was earth as hard as iron that jarred every bone in your body when you were brought down by a crunching tackle. Certainly others can confirm that in the right circumstances a genial impression could be left by Ian Paisley; no one could doubt the hard man behind this exterior.

When Ian returned to Geneva he gave the tape to the Publishing Department and asked them to transcribe some excerpts for an in-house publication. He was dismayed to discover that this done, the tape had been destroyed. You cannot always guarantee that others will have a sense of value equal to your own. In defence of the publishing department we need to note that all this took place some twenty years before Ulster's loudest son discovered words beyond the slogan, 'No surrender.'

In 1980 Ian visited Mexico, Guatemala, El Salvador, Panama and Venezuela. He spent time with basic Christian communities, carrying news of the work of the Spirit manifest in many places. Margaret was normally very supportive of the visits Ian took alone but this was the exception. The problem was that Guatemala and El Salvador were killing fields at that time.

Margaret began by arguing that there was already enough information to make Ian's visit unnecessary. Some days later she noted that people were leaving these dangerous places and this meant that Ian need not take risks of visiting these countries. He remained committed to collecting information from people where they were. Margaret reluctantly gave her blessing.

The visit to Mexico to meet Bishop Mendez Arceo was straightforward. Four hours before Ian was due to fly to Guatemala he was advised that all his contacts there and in El Salvador had been killed, fled their country or gone underground. There would be no one to meet Ian. Ian took time to think things through – and became convinced that he should 'lippen on the Holy Spirit'.[98]

When Ian landed in Guatemala he asked around after his expected contact Sister Angela. In time some nuns offered to transport Ian in to the city. He mentioned 'Iglesia la Merced'. When the car arrived at the church house a priest was on the point of putting his car away. Five minutes earlier he would not have been there; five minutes later and no one would have answered the door – too often a gun had been fired through the metal grille and the person answering the door shot. This encounter gave Ian a base for his visit to Guatemala.

When Ian arrived in El Salvador he adopted a different tactic. He made for Bishop Romero's headquarters and asked around, seeking some guidance. None was offered. On leaving, Ian approached two men in the vicinity. One turned out to be Romero's link to the basic Christian communities, the other was in charge of the Roman Catholic radio station which gave voice to the truth in spite of considerable opposition.

Ian was invited to see round the radio station. His rucksack was placed in a room for safe-keeping. As the visit ended it became clear that his bag was now locked up – it would be the next day before he could retrieve it. So there he was with no baggage, passport or money. He considered sleeping rough but this seemed problematic. Death squads roamed the streets.

Ian put his hand in his pocket and discovered a card with a phone number and some local coins. He had no idea where they had come from. He called the number and was given directions to a house in the locality, abandoned because of pressure from an anti-Romero military neighbour. There was still a caretaker who provided a bed for the night. As George MacLeod was often heard to say, 'If you think that is a coincidence, I wish you a dull life!' The next morning Ian retrieved his rucksack.

In time Ian moved on and stayed with Xavier Gorostiaga, the 'Gordon Brown' of the new Nicaragua. When Ian had to travel on the basis of 'go-and-I'll-show-you-on-the-road-what to do-basis' Ian had a prayer; 'Look God, I may have misread the signs – or maybe you want me out of the way to act through other people. You know the total scene. But if you want me bear fruit, please, put the people I need to work with in touch with me.'

The time came for Ian to fly to Panama. Ian arrived with a single name and no address. He could easily have spent three days looking for his contact. Ian still recalls what did happen. 'When I was flying to Panama my contact was driving away from the airport on some assignment. He experienced a very strong sensation that he was required to turn back on his tracks . . . The pressure to turn round became so strong that he yielded. He drove up to the airport just as Ian was leaving (the terminal building). They did not know each other but somehow recognised one another immediately. Ian found that he had arrived at a rare time for the Panamanian communities. They were having three days of interchange – not meeting in a block but visiting one another as part of a process of mutual learning and supporting one another. Ian was able to share in this process.

Ian recalls another similar incident (it may have been on an earlier visit). He was flying to Caracas, Venezuela attempting to make contact with the shanty-town dwellers around the city. On the way to the plane he committed the journey and the purpose of his visit to God.

Ian remembers the incident. 'The pilot was a show-off! Never in my life have I been on a plane which took off at such a steep angle. When he levelled off, a lass came forward from further down the plane with my plastic file in her hand. It had slipped through the back of the seat and slid back to land at her feet. I thanked her. Then she said, 'I wanted an excuse to see you in any case. I think you work for the World Council of Churches.' Ian wondered what committee or commission they might have worked on together. It was not that. 'It is just that some time ago I went on the tour of the World Council Headquarters (in Geneva) and I think I saw you there. When you came on board I recognised you. The arrival of your file at my feet gave me the excuse to come and talk to you.'

'It turned out that she was on the social services staff of Caracas City Council and her main job was to act as liaison between the council and the slum-dwellers around the capital. Ian concluded 'There is a mystery in all this. Did I prove to be inadequate martyr material? I was not killed even once by death squads or by other means! Margaret never complained that I returned safely from each visit. Sure the Holy Spirit was guide, comforter and friend. But that does not guarantee survival in this life. However, I shared Margaret's relief!'

Ian was aware that his brief visits to folk in countries around the world could always be written off by others as just too short to be of significance. Brian Crosby, a member of the Iona Community has an interesting memory of a short visit in 1973 Ian made to Likhubula House on the slopes of Mulanje Mountain in Malawi. Likhubula House was a youth centre belonging to the Church of Central Africa Presbyterian. Brian had been its warden since 1969. Ian was working for the WCC in the field of lay training and was, as Brian remembers it, touring the world in search of innovative programmes. His visit was brief and after Brian and his colleague had shown him the centre and described the work they were doing, they were soon back at the Christian Service Committee vehicle which was waiting to take Ian on his way. Ian stopped at the Land Rover's door, turned back to Brian and asked, 'But are you doing anything innovative?' Grasping at straws Brian said, 'Well er . . . we take them up the mountain!' Apparently unimpressed, Ian turned and with a wave, leapt into the vehicle and shot off down the hill.

A few years later Brian was asked to give a report about his work to members at an Iona Community Week. As Ian was present Brian decided to relate this little story by way of illustration of how unexceptional his work was and how ordinary blokes like him can feel pretty insignificant compared with the array of brilliant talent in the Community. Afterwards, Ian approached Brian and hotly denied that he could ever have behaved in such a way! Brian felt that he had touched a nerve for on the next few times they encountered one another the matter was raised. Time and more frequent encounters now that they are both 'retired' in Scotland has allowed the matter to rest! It seemed opportune to relate these varied memories of this incident to underline the truth that Ian is the primary source of much of his biography. For all that he remains his own severest critic. And to accept that his way is not the only way to visit the people of God.

$$- o - o - o - o -$$

Given the pressure that was brought to bear on Ian to follow a life in academia when he completed his theological degree in Edinburgh it is interesting that thirty years later he responded positively to the call to Selly Oak Colleges. A record exists of one of the early teaching assignments which he undertook soon after his arrival. He was working with about eighty people who were in the George Cadbury Hall.

Ian discovered among them there was a group of students who had very local languages back home in Kenya. There were ten of them. They became the focus of small groups. The others in the groups were invited to try and find the picture that the word for salvation in the area language generated. Once a group believed that they had got as much of a picture as possible and a feel for the word and the way it lit their imagination, then they had to share what 'salvation' meant for them in their own traditions. In this way different nuances and emphases could be considered.

After some time Ian took a microphone round and encouraged sharing both of the original understanding of 'salvation' and of other sharing that had taken place. Ian then tackled the Old and New Testament words for 'salvation'. He set them in their cultural and historical background and got the whole company working on an understanding of these words. From this people realised how many-faceted the idea of salvation is; how different cultures contributed to the richness of such an understanding. Ian suggested that there are at times challenges and maybe even contradictions; and at other times confirmation and enlargement that follow from different understanding of the work of salvation.

The most illuminating exposition for that company came from an Indian woman who spoke of the impact the word had made on her when she first heard it as a child. She said it was as if she had been close-confined in a cupboard (but her hands described something more like a coffin standing on its end). Salvation for her was like the door (lid) bursting open and her running out into the free air with the sunlight and the song of the birds. She had then to learn that the word 'soteria'[99] is the making of and taking of space – in contradiction to the work of would-be evangelists who want to drive the sheep into their own favoured enclosure.

Not that Selly Oak was all work. On one occasion a toddler accompanied parents to a social evening. Ian had always encouraged parents to bring children with them even to lectures as circumstances demanded. The child's attention was taken by a glass-topped coffee table that Ian had purchased in Geneva; he thought of it as Clyde-built, the frame being made of metal and its design reminded him of the shape of a ship's propeller. A heavy Caithness glass paper-weight sat on the glass top. The young visitor proceeded to hammer the glass top with the paperweight. The parents were clearly amused by their young percussionist. Ian was less impressed and firmly without fuss separated child and table. The next day Ian got round to examining the table and paper-weight. He was pleased to discover there was not a scratch on either. He concluded that the glass was not just bullet-proof . . . but child-proof!

$$- \text{o} - \text{o} - \text{o} - \text{o} -$$

The village of Gargunnock which lies a few miles west of Stirling has a population of about 800 and is growing with new houses being built in the locality. It has an ageing population with increasing numbers of retired folk and a decline in children less than 4 years of age. About a fifth of the villagers are incomers from England; three-quarters of the folk own their own home. Gargunnock is marked by a high percentage of inhabitants with academic qualifications and car ownership is also high. This is the place that was home to Ian and Margaret for the five years they had together and it continues to be the community which he finds mutually supportive.

From time to time during her ministry in Gargunnock Catherine Hepburn would ask Ian to stand in for her when she had to be elsewhere on a Sunday. On one occasion the service was to focus on the problem of bringing up very young children so that they developed their understanding of the Christian faith while at the same time learning to think for themselves. Ian's own experience of rearing the very young was not even in the middle distance – he was about eighty years of age at the time! He asked four parents whose children were at that stage if they would take the prayers that Sunday. 'Certainly not! They would not think of speaking in church!' 'Then would they meet with him for an hour during the week.' That posed no problem.

When they met, Ian asked them how they dealt with their children – what attitudes, prayers, actions and words were relevant to them. The discussion was animated; experiences were shared. Ian then asked them what other influences they might hope to be beneficial. They looked in turn at peer groups, teachers, neighbours, books, TV and radio. Every now and again Ian would stop a parent and say,

'Such and such is your point, not mine, and it is in your own words. Please take a note of it.' Within the hour, with very little tidying up, the points were fashioned into prayers. The only weakness, when the service took place, Ian said, was his fault. He should have provided each of the contributors access to a microphone! The hour spent with the parents ensured that contributions were not superficial as can be the case when they are off-the-top-of-the-head.[100]

Ian's elder over many years in Gargunnock, Eric Abell, speaks well of Ian as a parishioner who welcomes a visit. Clearly what Ian expected of others in his Rosyth days was the standard he set for himself. Eric recalled that there was no point in knocking on the door of Ferndale and expecting that a pastoral visit would be the work of a few minutes. Nor should we assume that the ensuing conversations were cases of one-way traffic. Eric had cause to remember with pleasure, when his own family was under stress and strain, Ian, without making a fuss, took on the role of carer. His letter-writing habit honed over a lifetime so often was a source of blessing to those who received his notes or longer epistles. Ian is also known as always willing to act as host to those who call and took considerable pleasure in providing a meal for many in the village as well as members of the local church.

Life at home and life away. In the autumn of 1982 Ian and Margaret stopped off in Israel-Palestine en route for the Philippines, Australia and New Zealand. The pilgrims were looking for the house of Simon the tanner[101] a candidate surely for the position of patron saint of ecumeniacs. They were observed by a man leaning over the wall of his property. In the ensuing conversation he remembered, 'As kids, Jews and Arabs, we played together.' He then groaned as he considered the circumstances of the day. Well might we ask, 'Thirty years or so later has anything really changed?

Margaret as a matter of course left Ian to write up their travels while they were based in Gargunnock. Fortunately we have one article that she wrote for the SCAWD[102] newsletter in the summer of 1984. Given that so little of what Margaret wrote exists, it seems prudent to quote this article in full. It clearly has a number of insights that Ian shares.

'Basic Christian Communities Resource Centre at Dunblane

'At the recent assembly of the Church of Scotland much concern was expressed about the image of the Church and ways and means suggested for its up-dating and the renewal of its life. In the past two years, visiting basic Christian communities in eastern as well as western Europe, we have discovered very different ways to celebrate and be challenged by the Christian faith. These ways are less formal, more intimate; getting away from 'the anonymity of the few', away from relationships that are superficial to ones which are more meaningful, more demanding therefore. Denominational barriers are proving irrelevant. What matters most is the mutual depth of caring, witness to the community served and practical involvement in the struggles for peace and justice at home and in the wider world. The Bible is central and its interpretation crucial to understanding life-situations and for guidance in action. There's a sense of liberation, a creative new vision releasing new energies to help build a better world.

'The Resources Centre, now housed in the Robert Mackie Memorial Room at the top of the main building of Scottish Churches House, Dunblane, has been established to help people with a concern for the Christian faith, whether church members or not, to grapple more adequately with the problems and opportunities of their own particular situations in search for renewal in church and community. To assist them they will find there a unique collection of material comprising mainly interviews with members of basic Christian communities in the Philippines and Europe (gathered in 1982-84) but also in many other countries and continents (1970-81) available both in typescript and on tape. Supplementary documents on basic Christian communities' own self understanding, structure and priorities are included; as is background reading to provide contexts for different developments.

'A memorial fund has been established in memory of Dr Robert Mackie – a Scottish pioneer in the ecumenical movement who was Associate General Secretary of the World Council of Churches in its early years. This fund allows free accommodation for a week or ten days to be applied for by people outside Britain. They will be mandated by basic Christian communities in their own countries to examine evidence of the ways other communities live their lives and on their return will contribute some of the fruits of their research to those who gave them the assignments. Two members of the Lutheran Church of Sweden have recently done precisely that.

'The main aim of the Centre is NOT to provide material for academic research. We should like to see the resources used by small groups of people concerned for local mission ecumenically, to enable them first to stand back and consider what faith requires of them and then to use the stories and insights collected there to provide fresh perspectives and perceptions for that up-dating and renewal many of us long for.'

It is hard to miss the teacher in Margaret as she wrote that article. Her summary of the purpose of the Resources Centre which belonged so clearly to the ethos of Scottish Churches House as a whole could surely not be bettered even by Margaret's man.

When Margaret died Ian was overwhelmed by the sense that she had done him proud in life. He knew that she had loved him deeply. But he wondered if she felt much the same about him. Then he got her last message.

About nine years before she died, Margaret had been at a loss one Christmas or birthday to find a gift for Ian. He had suggested a zipped Bible in a modern translation for use when he was away from home on a variety of tasks. He got the Bible, but observed, 'You haven't inscribed it.' The reply came 'O, I didn't know what to say.' Every few years Ian drew Margaret's attention to the lack of inscription. In return she said, 'Can't you see that I am busy at the moment?' He concluded that she really could not decide what to say.

Then when they were in Bossey for the last visit, when she was fighting the cancer which carried her off so swiftly, Margaret said quietly, 'I have inscribed the Bible.' To get her back home for treatment Ian was busy rearranging the conference programme. He had to bring forward a contribution planned for a later time. His mind was on these tasks. He responded to Margaret with an 'O, good!' and got on with matters in hand.

About three months after Margaret died Ian was at a conference in Woudschoten near Utrecht, in the Netherlands. He opened the Bible. There was Margaret's last message to him.

To Dearest Ian

My gratitude for love and companionship over so many happy years,

Margaret

'No words more marvellous,' Ian concluded, 'in all that I have ever written.' He took great strength from the fact that Margaret had added to 'love', 'companionship'! He read it as an affirmation that they had journeyed through life side by side.

Ian recalls an occasion when Margaret had got grubby with some cleaning work. She took a shower. When she came out she announced, 'I feel like a new woman!' Ian said, 'I hope the new woman is very, very like the woman I knew previously.' She was delighted.

On another occasion a woman asked Ian for a short description of marriage. He said he could give her a one-word answer – 'fun'. His questioner was not only taken aback. She seemed rather appalled. In time perhaps she discovered that Ian meant exactly what he said.

− o − o − o − o −

One of the joys of visiting Ian Fraser in his home is the people you meet. This goes beyond the people who are also visiting. On one occasion we were talking about his friend from Dublin, Fr. James O'Halloran who has done such illuminating work on small Christian communities in many parts of the world. The phone rang. It was Fr. James on the other end of the phone. After a few minutes Ian passed the phone to me. I recalled with gratitude reading some of the caller's writing almost twenty years previously as I explored what it meant to live as a member of a Christian community.

Jim was pleased to hear that what he had written was useful, but he was even more interested in commending to me his recent article in 'The Furrow' − a journal for the contemporary church. In it he considered 'Rural and Urban Isolation.' Jim wrote, 'Rural isolation has been worsened by the decrease in the number of pubs and post offices, where they were focal points of social interaction.' (I had cause on that same visit to Gargunnock to be reminded that it lost its post office a short time before).

James O'Halloran is fascinated by what he likes to describe as a growing world phenomenon that could be the antidote to this problem of isolation, namely the small community. He highlights what he found on a recent visit to India. He went to Vasai in the province of Maharashtra. In a little fishing town he found small Christian communities in all the neighbourhoods. 'It was wonderful to experience people gathered in homes to share the word of God, pray together and plan for active outreach. The spirit of community in the place was palpable; the residents kept on inviting you in for tea and giving you presents of the most tempting fresh fish. Apart from the meetings in the neighbourhoods, the communities flowed together for the Sunday eucharist. And they all gathered in a large public meeting place on Wednesday evenings for an hour's prayer together – men, women and children. I was present for one such session and the fervour was truly moving. There were a thousand people in attendance. If the men hadn't been at sea fishing, there would have been two thousand present. Out on the sea, the men conduct prayer sessions over the radio.'

Jim reminds his readers that Vatican II gave a vision of Church as community in the 'image of the Trinity'. One way of this vision being realised in the world is through small Christian communities that are open to one another and combine to help their parishes become communities of communities.

Some of Jim's new thinking had been shared in his 90th birthday greetings and a Christmas letter to Ian. In it he commented on a further dimension to his recent Indian experience. This was the growth of small human communities made up of people of all faiths. In these small communities people came together to see how they can improve their lives. As well as being in their own small Christian communities, the bishops encourage Christians to participate in small human communities as well.

In such a small human community in India you may find a couple of Christians urging the members to gradually save rupees that will enable them to build a village toilet. In this way Christians reach beyond the confines of their own church to build a better world, if you like, to build a wider kingdom. Now the building of a toilet can be a matter of life or death. The alternative is to go to the forest. When Jim was visiting a village, a young girl, was attacked by a leopard. Her mother ran screaming at the animal and amazingly it withdrew. The child was mauled but survived.

The April 2008 edition of 'The Furrow' has much else of interest. Given the Irish Roman Catholic context it includes articles of an astonishing breadth of interest and perception. It deserves to be better known not least beyond its denominational roots.[103]

On the occasion of Ian's 90th birthday celebration the local Iona family group gathered with Ian. A variety of thoughts had been collected to share with him including many from friends round the world who had forwarded memories to him.

The evening was concluded by a song from Maxwell and Janet Craig entitled 'A Song for Ian'. It went a long way to summing up his life.

He is a splendid Forres man,
A butcher's boy to boot,
But when he came to Edinburgh
He donned a cleric's suit.

Rosyth was full of shipping
And Ian worked there too;
He practised what he preached there
Thought the Cooncil something new.

A PhD was on the stocks
Cunninghame Graham was the thesis,
A man who knew the only way
Was left of the main stream.

Margaret and Ian made Churches' House
A place of welcome braw;
Prophets, painters, men o' pairts
Came to their open door.

But foreign fields called this fine pair,
Geneva, Cuba, world:
So many people glad to see
Them both to God's grace thirled.

Then back it was to Birmingham,
Where Selly Oak had called
Ian and Margaret all inspired
And students were enthralled.

And so to sweet Gargunnock
Where Margaret said Goodnight,
And Ian travelled far and wide
Then set his brain to write.

Wi' books and pamphlets by the score
Composing hymns forby
No wonder we're amazed and say
His limit is the sky!

And still our man grows veg, brews soup
And warms our tums just fine.
At ninety we salute oor Ian
And wish him ninety-nine.

Those of us, who have been privileged to know Ian as a friend, be it long or short, have benefited from meeting and making new friends through him. If there is a real sense in which we reveal something of our true selves by the people we spend time with it is interesting to consider some of those Ian numbers amongst his friends.

Reference was made earlier to the dedication of a coastal cottage in South Africa as a Columban house, a place of hospitality which Ian formally opened with an act of worship.[104] The notes of that day indicate that a number of people joined with him in the prayers on that occasion. Significantly only one of these prayers is recorded in his notes of the occasion; Rosie Dalcarme, the housekeeper prayed as follows:

> *'We thank God for all fishermen who go out into the deep sea to supply us with fish; and for their wives praying and waiting at home for their safe return. May all people in this community stand together so that this remains a fishing village whose members are one and are friends; and that people from other places will feel welcome here. Amen'*

I was pleased to have many words of congratulation around the time of Ian's 90th birthday to pass on to him. Among unsolicited greetings came a personal word from Tim Duffy, who has worked with Ian in respect of *Open House*. He said:

'I probably first became aware of Ian Fraser through his writing on basic communities. His direct transcripts from the various third world communities seemed at first more disjointed than the more theoretical work coming from third world theologians like Leonardo Boff. Later I came to appreciate their immediate nature and the absence of ideological commentary . . .

'I got to know Ian personally (in the 1980s). He exemplified for me the best of the Reformed tradition: biblically rooted; the product of a long and deep Christian formation; an awareness of the great Catholic oikoumene from which we all derive our tradition. I had taught ecclesiastical history at a Catholic seminary, discovering the distinctive culture of all Scottish traditions. I found in Ian a fine example of the Scottish reformed tradition, individual and pawky, humane and socially concerned and spiritually grounded . . . I consider him the most significant theologian Scotland has produced in the second half of the twentieth century.

'We are regularly in contact these days and I'm proud to consider him a friend. He sends me some of his occasional pieces (handwritten of course) to see what I think of them . . . There's more than a touch of the Socratic gadfly in Ian and while he is happy to stir up controversy, he never does it for its own sake. Rather he is constantly asking folk to be aware of their situation in the world, of what their faith tells them and to be a critical part of a believing community that tries to put the social vision into effect.'

And then there is Blackwell's 'Radical Christian Writing' edited by Christopher Rowland and Andrew Brickstock which contains a selection of 63 contributions, the first half of which include Justin (Martyr), Jan Hus, William Tyndale and John Bunyan. The second half includes writing by Oscar Romero, Kenneth Leech, Daniel Berrigan and Gustavo Gutierrez. Between these two groups is one Ian M Fraser. Significant company indeed.

$$- \, o - o - o - o -$$

In recent years, not least since Ian decided to travel the world less, he has enjoyed the company and support of his extended family as well as friends old and new. There appear to be times in families when the circumstances of life dictate that those we are closest to are not always those we spend most time with. Happily Ian has been able to enjoy in the years since Margaret's death the company of his children, grandchildren and great grandchildren. In February 2009 he was rejoicing in the fact that he still has his three children, nine grandchildren and 4.9 great-grandchildren.[105]

At the time of writing Anne and Gene have now retired from the medical practice that they shared in North Carolina. Keith and Hazel were shortly to join them in retirement; the former took early retirement recently on health grounds from his post in management in a local secondary school, the latter was to retire shortly from a senior position in social services – they live in Tillicoultry, in Scotland's smallest county and within easy reach of Gargunnock. Ian and Kathy live near Penicuik, south east of Edinburgh. Ian, the other doctor in the family, had plans for semi-retirement in 2009; Kathy continued in further education.

It goes without saying that an extended family, such as Ian enjoys, has over the years, experienced illness and other testing times. Those who know them can only speculate at the cost borne by each member of the family not least in earlier days as Ian with Margaret gave themselves to the service of local, national and global communities.

It was surely significant that at the time of the much celebrated 90th birthday Ian selected, from the hundreds of valued good wishes sent, the card that a son and daughter-in-law gave him. It read:

'Dad, Congratulations! – not just for reaching the age of 90, but for doing so while keeping your sense of world justice, your ability to be patient and non-judgmental and your determination to use your knowledge and linguistic abilities to fight for the cause you believe in . . . You continue to be an example for us all to follow. May you continue to thrive as you do now . . .[106]'

Endnote

[85] Where Ian is mentioned by name in the Postscript it is invariably to be understood as Ian M Fraser.

[86] In a report of Ian living in retirement in Gargunnock printed in the Forbes Gazette he is described as a 'FORRES churchman whose brother Alex was a master butcher in Forres and who still lives in the burgh.' Ian liked that.

[87] The ultra observant reader will note the absence of any additional observation from Ian's university days in Edinburgh. You should not attribute this to my West of Scotland background or my attendance at academic institutions in Glasgow. Rather it reflects the wise words shared with me on Iona, perhaps even by Ian himself – 'Remember it is not

necessary for you to have an opinion on every subject under the sun and certainly it is not necessary to always share them with others!' Then again among Ian's verses you can find some words first heard in the capital city – see Appendix C.

[88] In recent months this story was told as a blessing was sought on a marriage in the brave new world of this millennium. It seemed worth repeating.

[89] In recent days Pam has acted as the archivist for Tullis Russell and was able to introduce us to written records of the company and to an employee who also worked in the mill in the 1940s.

[90] The Native American name was Chautauqua, New York State – meaning 'the bag nipped in the middle'.

[91] A DC Thompson publication which had its origins in Dundee.

[92] He who appeared in the Scottish Churches House chapter.

[93] See Chapter 4.

[94] Monday 3 December 2007.

[95] Director of the Smith Library and Art Gallery in Stirling.

[96] Ian's commitment to the Appeal was underlined by his public five-figure donation to the Appeal to as he said 'prime the pump'.

[97] Allowing guests and residents to worship together when discussions were in session.

[98] 'lippen' Scots word – 'rely on or trust'.

[99] 'soteria' the common NT Greek word for 'salvation'.

[100] Following Paul's approach in 1 Corinthians 14 where worship contributions are prepared beforehand.

[101] Acts 9.43.

[102] SCAWD : Scottish Churches Action for World Development.

[103] 'The Furrow': A journal for the contemporary church published monthly – details available at www.thefurrow.ie; the title comes from Jeremiah 4.3 'You are to drive a new furrow.'

[104] See Chapter 10.

[105] The decimal point was explained by the fact as Ian said that great-grandchild number 5 was due within the month.

[106] The card is signed 'H & K'.

CHILDREN'S TALK – IAN M FRASER

THERE WAS GREAT excitement in the toy cupboard. It was Belinda the wooden doll's birthday. There was going to be a party and a birthday cake and all kinds of good things to eat. A special guest had been invited from the Outside Place, Froggie. He was a great favourite, always jumping around, full of fun, making every party he attended go with a zip.

Excitement grew as time to start the party grew near. But there was still no sign of Froggie. Teddy's tummy began to rumble at the thought of the food. 'I'm hungry,' he growled softly to himself. Squeaker the mouse could not contain himself. He could not think of anything to say, so he just danced around squealing, 'Whee, whee, whee!' Sailor Boy felt he had to be more on his dignity; but you could see, if you looked carefully, that he was getting impatient and longing for things to start. Belinda went around seeing to last minute touches, making sure that everything was ready. The time to start the party came and went. There was still no Froggie. The clock ticked on. They became very disturbed and anxious. 'What can have happened to Froggie?' they asked one another. Sailor Boy was all for starting the party without waiting any longer for him.

Suddenly a snowbird appeared at the window of the toy cupboard and tapped on the pane. They opened the window and found that he was a messenger from Froggie. He told them that he had been flying in their direction on that winter's day and had seen Froggie stuck in a snowdrift. He had fallen in and could not get out. He shouted to the snowbird to tell the others what had happened to him. The snowbird then flew off, and they closed the window against the cold.

'This is terrible, terrible,' squeaked Squeaker. 'Froggie might die of cold.' 'Somebody may come that way and pull him out,' said Sailor Boy. Teddy said nothing. His stomach had been expecting the food and was telling him so very loudly. At the same time, Froggie was a special friend and he was very sad to think of the accident that had befallen him. He was torn between the two feelings, and sat gloomily saying nothing.

Belinda was more business-like. 'It is no good just sitting around,' she said. 'What we must do is this. We must all pray as hard as we can that Froggie will get out of the snowdrift and find his way safely here. Come on, now. Let us all pray hard.'

So they prayed, and prayed and prayed. After a bit they heard some bumps and the squeak of the door beside which Teddy was sitting. They prayed on for a bit more. Then Belinda looked up and saw Teddy's seat was empty. 'Oh, that Teddy!' she said 'He's just not willing to take his part with the rest of us. It isn't fair of him. The rest of us will have to pray all the harder to make up.' So they prayed more. Then they opened their eyes and sat gloomily looking at one another.

But before too long there were bumpy and scrambling sounds outside the toy cupboard. The door burst open. Froggie appeared, danced round the room and hugged all of them.

A little behind him came Teddy. 'Oh, Froggie,' said Belinda, 'We are so glad to see you. We were all praying hard that you would get out of the snowdrift safely and our prayers have been answered – that is all of us prayed except Teddy who went away leaving the rest of us to do it all. Why did you not stay with us, Teddy?' she said, turning to him and giving him an accusing look.

'Well, it was like this,' said Teddy. 'I said to God "God, you've got to get Froggie out of the snowdrift in which he is stuck." God said to me, "Teddy, there is a shovel in the cellar." So I went and dug him free.'

Froggie listened to him, nodded his head vigorously in agreement, and then capered around the room with his arms high in the air. As he went he shouted with glee, 'Teddy's the one who knows how to pray! Teddy's the one who knows how to pray!'

SERMON BY IAN M FRASER
AT WEOLEY HILL CHURCH
ON 7 DECEMBER 1975
BROADCAST BY B.B.C. RADIO

SEE A HEAD of one kind and a body of another and you'll exclaim 'That's an oddity.' That's what the church must often look like – an oddity. The body so often does not seem to belong to Jesus Christ, the Head.

Last week the theme was the persecuted church. There you could see the Church at one with its head in suffering. Today we turn to the church as persecutor. How can that kind of church be at one with its Head? Look at the situation as it has been in history.

- When, in the 4th century, Roman emperors adopted the Christian faith (with the usual privileges accorded to clergy) state and church entered into an unholy alliance to persecute nonconformists; and that lasted for centuries.
- The Crusades stain the record. What things were done in the name of Christ! When Christians captured Jerusalem in 1099, every man, woman and child in the city was slaughtered. One historian writes of 'heaps of heads and hands and feet to be seen throughout the

streets and squares' and another 'The town presented the spectacle of such carnage, such rivers of blood, that the victors themselves must have recoiled in horror and disgust.' When the Muslims recaptured Jerusalem, they spared lives.

- The horror of the Inquisition, of people being racked and tortured to get them to confess a certain faith, lasted for centuries.
- Jews, Baptists, Quakers hounded, imprisoned, killed for falling out of step or for not fitting in.
- In the religious wars of the 16th and 17th centuries Christian sought to eliminate Christian to the greater glory of God.

And these are but samples.

'Unbelievable' you say. No, understandable. You see

- If it is crucial for humanity's destiny that people hold the right kind of belief then it's up to you to see that as many as possible think that way. You're doing man a service. You're giving God glory. In St. Augustine's 100th letter he pleads with an official not to kill the Donatist heretics (Donatus had asked the disturbing question 'What has the emperor to do with the church?') and goes on 'It is not their death but their deliverance from error that we seek to accomplish by the help of the terror of judges and laws, whereby they may be preserved from falling under the penalty of eternal judgment.'

- The Good Book can be used to back it all up. 'The one who does not acknowledge the truth is an enemy of the cross of Christ.'[107] Those who 'have exchanged the truth of God for a lie' are under judgment.[108] The sinister phrase was used devastatingly 'Compel them to come in.'[109] Separate soul and body (which a biblical faith will not allow you to do) and you can do havoc to the body for the sake of the soul.

A persecuting church is quite understandable given this assumption: if you are concerned for your fellow-men you will make sure they find the straight and narrow and stick to it.

- Then again the church came into a power position in society. It is almost impossible to hold power and not to use it. Power is simply the means to get things done.

For God's sake, the church needs to get things done.

- So Churchmen became princes with retinues and muscle-men to back them up.
- Concordats were worked out between church and state with privileges bestowed both ways. The theory was that concordats allowed the church quietly to influence government policy. More often than not, it meant that the church was nationalised.
- There was a tie-up between Christian missions and colonialism. Sometimes brute force was blatantly used. Early this century R.B. Cunninghame Graham wrote of Arabs and Berbers, thinking of their resistance to Christian missions; 'A day will come no doubt when their hearts will prove more malleable; but I fear before that time their bodies will have to be much wrought upon by rifles revolvers and other civilizing agents which commonly precede the introduction of our faith.' Said a Chinese student to me a month ago, "Never forget that Christianity came to China in the barrel of a gun." "Who would not feels as if a slug were crawling on his soul," as Cunninghame Graham said.'

All right, we say, but we're different. We're more tolerant. We wouldn't act as our fathers did. In any case, as a church we no longer have power. I wonder.

- **We are more tolerant,** I believe. That's not something to be despised as if tolerance were wishy-washiness. The fact is this – we have broken through ages of certainty into an Age of Faith, in which all must venture for truth. That is great gain – to be alongside others, venturing for Truth.

- **We are not like our fathers?** Jesus would surely say to us, as he said to the religious in his own day – we are the sons of our fathers. Our fathers developed racialist policies towards many people of the earth. That work has to be undone by something like a programme to combat racism. But when about 250 churches asked the World Council of Churches to launch such a programme, a howl went up in Britain – not about the whole spread of the programme, but about areas where white domination was threatened. Well, are we to put right the wrongs of our history or not?

Take this. Hundreds of slayings have taken place in Northern Ireland. But when English lives are destroyed by bullets or bombs the cry goes up 'Bring back the rope.' What happens in London brings it all home to an innocent population. Innocent? What produced the deep trauma in Irish society but invading Englishmen taking over land, spreading oppression, humiliating a whole people and their culture – with Scots as accomplices? We can't dismiss our history. We have to live with it till, through our penitence and amendment of life, the poison burns itself out.

African, Asian and Latin American Christians are now rejecting in anger our style of thinking and living in this part of the world. For, going to them in the name of Christ, we have robbed them of their lands, their freedom, their identity, their very mission. We have to live with that history – it belongs to the hearing of faith in our time.

The Archbishop of Canterbury might have thought better than to have made his defensive statement about British colonialism, reported yesterday from Nairobi – if he had been listening seriously and sensitively to the voices of the world church.[110]

Of course all this is not the whole story. But it is a serious, a crucial part of that story. We must not avoid it. We have not to ignore our history or try to forget it. We have to set ourselves to redeem it.

But then, at least, we are no longer in a power position.

The church still has a power of wealth, and that gives it a wealth of power. It encourages it to fit in with the system. It provides a disincentive to act prophetically and righteously when the real crunch arrives. A test is coming our way. When the World Council of Churches establishes a Bank for the poor (one thing decided in Nairobi!) will churches in this country put their money there?

Another consideration. Protestant churches in Britain are largely middle class. When the pressures of inflation grew, we gained percentage differential wage and salary increases. Percentage differentials widen the gap between the well off and the badly off. Yet everything comes out of one kitty. So the worst off are made worse off still. How come that Christians were indistinguishable at that time from other middle-class people who were securing their position at the expense of others, silent, unprotesting? You see, it is what we do which indicates what we really believe, not just what we say. We still relate to other people in power and in judgment instead of in grace and truth: so one who came to us in grace and truth will come to the religious world in judgment. It will be as in the time of the prophet Malachi, from whose book we now read in chapter 2 verses 4-9 and in chapter 3 verses 1-5.

(Second part)[111]

The niggling thing is the contrast. The riddle and the mystery is that the church is the bearer of a great hope for mankind. Yet it is so unlike its Lord and head. It craves a secure position for its God. It craves a secure position for itself. But Jesus Christ laid all that aside – every possibility of convincing others by making them dependent on his handouts, or dazzling them into following him, or coercing them by armies. The church craves a place of strength in society: but the word used for Jesus Christ is 'doulos', a slave – you could describe him as a nothing. Hear how the epistle to the Philippians describes his coming, and what it should mean for our style of living. We listen to it in chapter 2 verses 1-11.

So he came in weakness, without privilege and protection. What does it mean to the church today which has so signally failed to relate truly to power? Does the great graph of descent in Philippians which equates him with the lowest and the least among humanity warn us that power bedevils life, that all who care for his kingdom should keep their hands off it?

I believe at least two things are said to us (that we might have the mind in us which was also in Christ Jesus):

- He showed by word and life that everyone can have a share in bringing God's new world into being, however powerless they might seem. He was a nothing. Yet, as such, with no hands on the levers of power, he produced the profoundest change ever wrought in human history. Now, in his name, people who are nothings can change the world. Good news!

  – You're only a housewife and mother. Only? You are a leader, a shaper of the future. What we become as a people is as much in your hands as in the hands of any of the power boys. I know you'll have your suffering – Jesus Christ had, too.

  – You're a basic worker, last in the queue for benefits and opportunities, first on the dole? Jesus Christ chose to be last in the queue. You're in good company. From where you are, you who help sustain the world can change the world, though there will be a price.

  – You're handicapped or otherwise set aside from life. Jesus Christ came as a slave, like you tied into his situation, denied freedom of manoeuvre. He looks to you for an ally in transforming human life.

- I believe he showed one other essential thing – that people have to wield power also, and that they must learn to wield it creatively and responsibly. He reaffirmed essentially what is said in the first two chapters of Genesis – in those marvellous stories in which the essential relationship of human beings to God, to their fellow human beings and to the earth is set out. Men and women are together given charge of the earth and have a mandate to fulfil 'replenish the earth and subdue it; have dominion.' That means 'take power.' So much of what follows illustrates how power must be used to enrich life and bless the earth or it leads to self-destruction. When Jesus faced Pilate he did not challenge the power over life and death which government wielded. What he made clear was that the power Pilate wielded was developing power, to be used for legitimate ends, to see things done right in God's world. And Pilate's condemnation is not that he exercised power, but that he failed to do so as a trustee in fulfilment of God's purposes.

Let me tell you one thing – if you are called to power positions and you refuse to take them because you're scared about landing in 'Pilate' situations, you may be refusing the claims of a particular kind of compassion which can only find expression in the imaginative and loving, responsible use of power.

– You're a politician in local or national government. You get plenty of kicks and few bouquets. It is scandalous the way we depend on you and yet dismiss you. There's good news for you in the coming of Jesus Christ. Power can be put at God's service. It will be hard, you'll have to swim against the stream as well as with it, and you may go under. But this 'nothing' man had his Cross.

– You work in a multinational corporation? There's good news for you. An imaginative use of power is in enterprises which draw people of many nations of the world together to work for the good of mankind. Is yours an exercise in cooperation between nations – or a means whereby some powerful nations strip others of their resources? Is power in your company answerable and responsible – is it operating for the good of mankind or a moneyed few? Live seriously with these questions. You may be denied promotion. You may be dismissed. But from where you are, you can take your share in changing the world.

– You are in the police or army. There's good news for you in Jesus Christ: Legitimate power, legitimately operated is a great gift to mankind. You must ask, when God presses us to worthier relationships of justice and brotherhood for all mankind, whether power which simply underwrites and sustains the status quo is legitimate. It'll be uncomfortable to work that one out in living – but it's part of a great calling.

So it's good news for everyone that Jesus Christ came as he did. Whoever you are, whatever your calling, the kingdom's for you. If we are willing to have the mind in us which was in Christ Jesus there will be the joy of helping to shape life in a way to bless humanity and a cross to bear as there was for him.

But what of the church, which has as often looked unlike its Lord and has let mankind down. If you and I throw our lives on the scales for a new world, will the church sustain us?

Take heart – new things are happening in the church. It is no longer the soft mark it was, easily misled by the powers-that-be.

In Korea, the churches are dangerously involved in protest against injustice and deprivation of liberties. The Presbyterian Church in Taiwan has just issued a statement which shows it has gained new courage to stand up to authority and press for self-determination in that land. The Archbishop of Manila in the Philippines is now adding an official Church protest against martial law and all its dehumanising consequences, to that of Christians who have joined the underground to oppose the Marcos regime. The White Fathers **did** withdraw from Mozambique because of the oppressive tie up of church and state, and this **did** have some effect in undermining Portuguese colonialism. In many countries of Latin America the church is entering into a new solidarity with the poor and the oppressed. Last Sunday, in Monsenat, in Spain, two women and two priests started a hunger strike to press for more liberal policies towards the thousands of Spaniards who are in prison or exile, than the new king has shown signs of granting. Just before that,

Monsignor Bruce Kent challenged the chairman of Consolidated Gold, the largest employer of British labour in South Africa on the migrant labour system which separates husbands from families, the low wages of Africans, and the firm's attitudes to black trade unions. There can hardly have been a time in history when so many laity, pastors, priests and nuns have been bloodily eliminated or jailed. At least there are signs that some part of the world church is no longer a trial to mankind, but again under trial, bearing a cross of suffering in fierce joy.

We in Britain seem so preoccupied with ourselves, so small-minded about God's large purpose for the world. We must rejoin this world church, live in its life, nourish ourselves at its sources. For the one who has come is coming. He has a marvellous capacity to jerk people out of self-concern into playing their part in making this world the world of God's promise.

We can yet be saved – yet so by fire.

He who all power and might commands
Of time and space the king
Is in a mother's hands
Is made a little thing.

Lord, make our calling high and sure
Bend us beneath your grace
That in our lives, like his made poor,
men see the Father's face.

Prayer: Even so, come Lord Jesus. Amen

Endnotes

---

[107] Philippians 3.18.

[108] Romans 1.25.

[109] Luke 14.23.

[110] During the WCC Conference in Nairobi which Ian might reasonably have expected to attend.

[111] Due to time considerations Ian was required to slightly shorten the second part for purposes of the broadcast.

POETRY

Ephesians 5.25–28

Christ and his church
like you and me
down here among the hay?
body to body
breath and flesh pulsating
ecstasy?

Christ and his church
like you and me
here
down among the hay!

Fighting Partner

When (sometimes) I'm creative
and (sometimes) chance my arm
you scorn a spirit caitiff,[112]
deploy your fighting charms
all lingering doubts disarm.

O God-sent wife
to nerve me for faith's gambling life!

Margaret, my treasure

The want of her
the want of her
the empty space, the haunt of her:
I did not grieve
I do believe
just deeply felt the want of her.
Margaret, my treasure o
Source of my pleasure o
The sweetest hours that e'er I spent
She blessed with love past measure o.

The joy of her
the joy of her
the pleasure of each ploy with her
It left me rich
in mem'ries which
refreshed my springs of joy in her.
Margaret, my treasure o . . .

The grace of her
the grace of her
the lovely laughing face of her:
The way she walked
and gently talked
enhanced the native grace in her.
Margaret, my treasure o . . .

The charm of her
the charm of her
the talent to disarm in her:
With tensions eased
and hurts appeased
folk loved the love so warm in her.
Margaret, my treasure o . . .

The steel in her
the steel in her
life's testing would reveal in her:
Her fearless stance
defying chance
disclosed resilient steel in her
Margaret, my treasure o . . .

The soul of her
the soul of her
encompassing the whole of her
My dearest wife
now crowned with life
I long to join my soul with her.
Margaret, my treasure o . . .

The Valentine[113]

Said, somewhat piqued, my special quine
'You've never sent a Valentine!'
– as if I'd bother with such tosh
so full of sentimental slosh
when each day lived's designed to show
in myriad ways the love we know.

Yet lest I miss some trick of fate
and just to set the record straight
here's one to show how weak words prove
compared with daily living love.

Dancing in the streets

When my time comes
please, please, please
no penguin parades,
no solemn posturing:
but folk in jeans,
children playing,
babies crying
and dancing in the streets.

NEW COLLEGE STAFF

At the end of each academic year a member of New College staff was asked to be guest of the class at a social evening where he (it was an all male show in those days) was given the privilege of some scurrilous verse about himself and his colleagues. On one occasion the work of supplying material was allocated to Ian Fraser. Samples of this comic verse are offered largely to remind readers of his wit and humour that makes him such good company.

Prof Rankin, Old Testament

It's Rankin's delight to reveal Moses' plight
for he'd no copyright for his stories he thinks:
It really was shabby – he cribbed Hammurabi
and borrowed from old Babylonian ginks.

Prof Curtis, New Testament

Curtis, dear Curtis, with scholarship girt is
and under his shirt is a heart of pure gold:
whatever the weather he'll blether and blether
till everyone's poor nether regions are cold.

Prof Manson, New Testament

Prof Manson is shyer than you or than I are
He'll join the bright choir with no hint of disgrace:

So spotless his way that there's nothing to say
If he'd been a bit gayer we'd give him more space.

Prof Baillie, Theology

From Baillie we hear that there's nothing to fear-
His Calvinist rearing has gone by the board:
To minds in a fog he recounts dialogue
With his son or his dog – peace of mind is restored.

Prof Burleigh, History

The trouble with Burleigh is not that he's surly,
It's just that he's thoroughly lazy at heart:
He doles out rehashes and chews his moustaches
And understands 'Nash's' much better than Barth.[114]

Endnotes

---

[112] *caitiff – captive, cowardly.*

[113] This is the only Valentine Ian ever sent Margaret.

[114] He unwarily confessed that he could not make much of Karl Barth. 'Nash' was a popular periodical of the day.

A summary of the educational background, career and publications of Ian M Fraser, M.A., B.D., PhD. (Edinburgh University), Ordained minister of the Church of Scotland.

Date	Career	Publications
1936–42	M.A., B.D. with distinction in Systematic Theology *New College Awards:* Cobb Fellowship, Gunning Prize, Cunningham Fellowship.	
1942–44	Labourer and worker/pastor in industrial works in Fife, Scotland.	*My Faith and My Job Epworth Press (1944) (chapter on labourer/pastor)*
1944–45	Interim appointment to Hopemount Church, Arbroath, Scotland.	
1945–48	Scottish Secretary of the Student Christian Movement.	

Date	Career	Publications
1948–1960	Parish minister in Rosyth, Fife, Scotland, the dockyard town. During this period served on Dunfermline Town Council, for 5 years convenor of Streets and Lighting.	*Theology and Action in Scottish Journal of Theology (1949)* *PhD The Social and Religious Outlook of R.B. Cunninghame Graham (1955)* *Bible, Congregation and Community SCM Press (1959)* *Faith Comes Alive Saint Andrew Press (1960)*
1960–69	Warden of Scottish Churches House, Dunblane, Scotland. Secretary of the revived Scottish Churches' Council from 1964. Committee member of World Council of Churches, Department of Laity.	*Sex as Gift SCM Press (1967)* *Let's Get Moving Scottish Churches Council (1968)* *Live with Style Scottish Churches Council (1969)* *People Journeying Scottish Churches Council (1969)*
1969–73	Executive Secretary in the World Council of Churches; (Education and Renewal) Responsible for 'Laity and Studies' [with Ralph Young] and Leisure Tourism; Coordinator of WCC Programme 'Participation in Change' based in Geneva, Switzerland.	*Leisure Tourism: Threat and Promise World Council of Churches* *Women and Ordination WCC (1970)*

Date	Career	Publications
1973–75	Consultant and continuing coordinator of WCC programme until the Nairobi Assembly, December 1975.	*The Fire Runs SCM Press (1975)*
1973–82	Dean and Head of the Department of Mission, Selly Oak Colleges, Birmingham, England.	*Re-inventing Theology as the People's Work WCC (1980)* *Living a Countersign Wild Goose Publications (1980)* *A Theology of Britain in the 80s' Co-ed (1981)*
1982–90	Voluntary Research Consultant to the Scottish Churches' Council.	Contribution to *Duty and Delight Festschrift for Dr Erik Routley Canterbury Press (1985)*
1982–87	With wife Margaret on assignment by the British Missionary Societies and Boards.	*Wind and Fire with Margaret Fraser (1986)*

Date	Career	Publications
1990–Present	Voluntary Research Consultant to the Action of Churches Together in Scotland (ACTS).	*Sharing Holy Communion Wild Goose Publications (1994)* *Strange Fire Wild Goose Publications (1994)* *The Try-It-Out Hymnbook (1995)* *A Celebration of Saints Wild Goose Publications (1997)* *Signs of Fire Wild Goose Publications – audio cassette (1998)* *Salted with Fire Saint Andrew Press (1999)* *Caring for Planet Earth Saint Andrew Press (2000)* *R.B. Cunninghame Graham Fighter for Justice (2001)* *Reinventing Church Private publication (2001)* *Ecumenical Adventure Saint Andrew Press (2002)* *Many Cells: One Body WCC Risk Series (2003)* *The Way Ahead Wild Goose Publications (2006)* *A Storehouse of Kingdom Things Wild Goose Publications (2010)*

. . . and finally

Thank you God for
ninety plus years of Ian Fraser
traveller
theologian
lover
community member and builder
parent and grandparent
tutor
writer
boundary pusher
friend

Ian
May God continue
to bless you and keep you
in love and in wonder
all the moments of your nights and
days.

Ruth Burgess
Iona Community Member